THE NEW DEAL'S SEC

The Formative Years

SEC'S FIRST MEETING, JULY 2, 1934

Left to right: seated—Ferdinand Pecora, Joseph P. Kennedy, James M. Landis; *standing*—George M. Mathews, Robert E. Healy

THE
NEW DEAL'S
SEC

The Formative Years

RALPH F. DE BEDTS

COLUMBIA UNIVERSITY PRESS
NEW YORK AND LONDON, 1964

Ralph F. de Bedts, Associate Professor of History at Old Dominion College, Norfolk, Virginia, is on leave during 1964 under a Fulbright grant to teach in the Department of History at the University of Hong Kong.

To Ruth

without whom there could never have been

a beginning

PREFACE

In the growing accumulation of writings on the New Deal, frequent references are made to the various agencies that the Roosevelt administration brought to the national scene temporarily or permanently. Works of the period, however, are rarely able to examine the historical origins and legislative growth of such agencies. They cannot pause to examine at length the relationship between an agency incorporating enduring reforms, such as the Securities and Exchange Commission, and the men and the political climate that called it into existence.

This study attempts to consider not only the historical origins and antecedents of the SEC but also its growth and formative years in the light of the financial and political happenings of the times and in relationship to the many individuals involved. Chronologically, these formative years are regarded chiefly as the period 1933–38, when the New Deal itself, by historical consensus, came virtually to an end. Politically, the establishment and expansion of the SEC had the aid of staunch partisan leaders in both House and Senate. Additionally, much Congressional agrarian support of "anti-Wall Street" measures had Bryanesque overtones of earlier years, and a strong group of Western Senators carried on the aims and moral values of the Progressives.

Administratively, the enduring reforms of the SEC were introduced and pragmatically implemented by some of the most phenomenal talent that the New Deal ever crowded into any regulatory agency. The Commission was able to establish itself in the hostile territory of the financial community with the aid of that canny and persuasive former Wall Streeter, Joseph P. Kennedy, as its first chairman. A large part of the violent opposition of the investment and securities world was gradually converted to at least grudging respect even while the SEC expanded its regulatory powers under the intellectual stimulation and administrative ability of subsequent chairmen James M. Landis, William O. Douglas, and Jerome N. Frank.

Much of the executive strength, and a continuity of Progressive values, was furnished by President Roosevelt himself, aided by New Deal devotees and legislative draftsmen. Roosevelt's participation, with his background of concern for utilities investor and utilities ratepayer alike, was most active in the Public Utility Holding Company Act of 1935. But his devotion to the Brandeisian principles of "other people's money" prompted him to describe securities legislation collectively as one of the major efforts of his administration.

In the course of treating these considerations the SEC emerged as a vital part of the New Deal's pragmatic experimental evolution, with its Progressivism more antifraud and anticorruption than antibigness. The conclusion was reached that the SEC furnished an outstanding demonstration of the New Deal's intent to revitalize American capitalism rather than seek its destruction. This successfully consolidated agency brought about both acceptance and expansion of some of the New Deal's most enduring reforms, replacing improper financial practices with standards of ethical conduct. Not only did this regulatory agency furnish the answer to the protection of the investor, but through the SEC the New Deal accomplished the necessary democratization and social control of the world of finance.

I am deeply grateful for the critical acumen and the support and encouragement I have unfailingly received from Arthur W. Thompson of the University of Florida, and for the careful reading and the valuable comments and suggestions of Arthur M. Schlesinger, Jr., Special Assistant to the President of the United States. C. K. Yearley and Franklin A. Doty of the University of Florida have contributed unstintingly of their time and valued advice, and I am indebted to William J. Schellings of Old Dominion College (formerly Norfolk College of William and Mary) for his careful reading of the manuscript.

I wish to acknowledge my gratitude to Chester Dunton, SEC librarian, and to his assistant, Annette Peabody. Sincere thanks are due Elizabeth Drury, director of the Franklin Roosevelt Library at Hyde Park, New York, and to the library staff for their very efficient and courteous aid.

Finally, neither the first nor the last word of this work could have been possible without the unflagging devotion and enthusiasm of my late wife, Ruth Brandes de Bedts.

RALPH F. DE BEDTS

July, 1963
Old Dominion College
(formerly Norfolk College
of William and Mary)
Norfolk, Virginia

CONTENTS

THE NEW DEAL'S SEC

The Formative Years

Above all things, good policy is to be used that the treasuries and monies in a state shall not be gathered together in a few hands, for otherwise a state may have a great stock and yet starve. Money is like muck, not good except it be spread.

FRANCIS BACON

YEARS OF FALSE SECURITIES

IN THE history of man's attempts to preserve integrity in the realm of financial transactions, some continuity in the insurance of such honesty can be seen from century to century. The passage of laws and the accretion of custom have aided; occasionally government itself operated a medieval bank of exchange. However, in that area of financial honesty concerned with protecting the unwary investor from the fraudulent activities of the dishonest stockbroker or issuer of securities, no faintest semblance of orderly progression can be found. The actions and the experience of one century seemingly have no connection with the legislative flurries in a subsequent period, and the observer is acutely aware of an utter lack of continuity. Only one thing remains in common in several centuries of legislative efforts to regulate the exploiter of the investor. Inevitably such attempts come about only when the disastrous results are seen in retrospect. Calamity must befall those who have ventured their funds before protective measures may be launched.

The earliest measures in English legislation were of guild origin in their professional restrictions. Statutes of the thirteenth century required licensing of brokers, and evidence exists that during the century there were numerous prosecutions of brokers engaging in unlicensed activity.[1] Several hun-

---

[1] Loss, p. 3.

dred years later the heavy losses suffered through the fraudulent manipulation of prices by brokers provoked a special commission's complaint, "The Pernicious Art of Stock-Jobbing." Parliament's tardy answer in 1697 to the tolls that stockbrokers had exacted was "An act to restrain the number and ill practice of brokers and stock jobbers." [2] Under the terms of this legislation brokers were required to take a fiduciary oath. Their number was not to exceed one hundred in England, their fee was limited to a modest 10 percent, and each was required to keep on his person a metal token properly stamped to establish his identity.

Fraudulent practice originating in abuse of corporate privileges, rather than through the activities of brokers, required no such restrictive legislation prior to the seventeenth century in England. Before the issuance of shares was common, large commercial undertakings were generally carried out by guilds, rich merchants, or through partnerships. With the development of joint-stock companies to finance expanding privateering and colonizing activities, their capital wealth grew amazingly from less than £10,000 in 1560 to approximately £50 million, or about 13 percent of the estimated national wealth, in 1720.[3] With the dispersion of ownership into numerous hands, the joint-stock company revealed itself as not only a valuable instrument for financing new industries and colonization but as an ingeniously irresponsible device for defrauding that portion of the public eager to invest its surplus wealth.

The Chartering of the Bank of England in 1694 and the forming of the London Stock Exchange two years later inaugurated a period of financial experimentation and credit expansion. The wars of the Spanish Succession aided in a general development of trade and industry, marked by a number of increasingly hazardous trading ventures in the opening decades of the eighteenth century. These wildly speculative promotions had their apex in the meteoric career of the South Sea Company, chartered in 1711 for ventures that included

[2] Frankfurter, "The Federal Securities Act," p. 53.
[3] Scott, pp. 439, 461.

everything from lending funds to the government to the pursuit of whale fishing and the slave trade. Its scheme to assume the national debt in return for unlimited trade privileges in the seas south of America resulted in an immediate subscription of £10 million. With George I installed as one of its governors, the company directors manipulated its share prices from about £100 in January, 1720, to over £1,000 in August. The directors, and a few wise speculators like Robert Walpole, made fortunes before the stock was permitted to slip back to its former price. Other "bubbles," as similar projects were called, took ready advantage of the mania exhibited by those who could not accommodate themselves to the price of South Sea shares. A thousand persons flocked in one summer's morning of 1720 "to pay two guineas each as an instalment for shares in a company 'for carrying on an undertaking of great importance, but nobody to know what it is.' " [4]

The "Bubble Act" of 1720, passed by a Parliament exceedingly aware of the contemporary wave of suicides, ruination, and imprisonment of high officials, caused a setback in corporate development overcome only by the industrial growth of the following century. Additional protection for the investor through the principle of disclosure and the imposition of penalties against violators was included in the Companies Act of 1844. Various amendments to the Companies Act, which became the English corporation code as well, continually expanded the prospectus requirements and liability provisions into the twentieth-century version of the act.

Some regulation of securities issuance was enacted in the United States on a restricted basis as early as 1852, such as that directed solely at common carriers in Massachusetts. An early recognition of the perils of buying stock on margin was found in a prohibitory clause of California's constitution of 1879.[5] The first Federal regulation was also of the limited variety that the Interstate Commerce Commission exercised over

[4] Melville, pp. viii, 97.
[5] Loss and Cowett, pp. 3–4.

the issuance of securities by the common carriers under its jurisdiction. Legislation primarily for the protection of investors was, like railroad regulatory laws, first enacted by the various states.[6]

Widespread losses through the activities of fraudulent stock salesmen and promoters first received legislative recognition in the Midwest, at the end of the twentieth century's first decade. Swarms of stock sharpsters had descended on Kansas as one of the most prosperous areas, and were greedily foraging their way through the accumulative greenbacks of the Kansas farm population. A legislator at the state capitol in 1911 informed his fellows with angry, fist-shaking incredulity that stock swindlers would sell shares in the blue sky above if action was not immediately forthcoming. The Kansas statute of 1911 that emerged was the predecessor of many similar state laws and reputedly the source of a name—"blue-sky" law—applied generally to securities legislation for the protection of the investor. Most states followed with legislation similar in intent, though varying widely in approach. Lower Federal courts uniformly held these state laws unconstitutional, and six such decisions were appealed to the United States Supreme Court in 1917. Considering these cases together, the Supreme Court reversed the lower courts and upheld the constitutional right of the state to regulate sales of securities.[7]

At the Federal level, attention in the early twentieth century was centered more on national banking activities and the dangers of concentrated financial control. A House of Representatives committee, headed by Chairman A. P. Pujo of Louisiana, compiled a report after investigations in 1912 and 1913 that centered largely on commercial banking practices and on the corporate control exercised through investment banking. The Pujo report did, however, enumerate improper stock market activities, putting the emphasis on those of a speculative nature.

[6] The first five SEC acts specifically avoided any preemption of existing state laws by Federal legislation, considering the latter to be used in conjunction with the state regulatory acts rather than as replacing them.

[7] Dept. of Commerce, *A Study of the Economic and Legal Aspects of the Proposed Federal Securities Act,* p. 94.

The committee used a convenient statistical yardstick to distinguish between speculation and investment. The number of shares sold on the New York Stock Exchange served to illustrate the former, and those shares shown as actual transferals of ownership on the company's books were accepted as a fair test of investment intent. Using the stock of the Reading Company as an example, the committee found that the company's entire common-stock issue, listed and subject to sale, was actually sold at least twenty times and even forty-three times over in every year since 1906. The number of shares transferred to new owners on the books of the company, however, was only 8.6 percent of those sold. Such activity was equated with race track gambling. A vast waste of capital resulted, the committee stated, when quantities of investment funds found their way into the pockets of a privileged few instead of going into productive industry.[8]

The Pujo Committee's recommendations, which included outlawing stock manipulation, separating the banking and investment functions, and preventing officers from borrowing their own bank's funds, found little response in Congress. The emergency efforts of the Federal Trade Commission during World War I in the securities field proved entirely ineffective but furnished the basis for some legislation that attempted correction of fraudulent security issuance. Introduced by Congressman Edward T. Taylor of Colorado in 1919, H.R. 188 was based on the disclosure principle, and made corporate officers liable for losses suffered by virtue of material misrepresentation in the securities offered. The bill was referred to committee but never appeared on the House floor.

A bill introduced in the same year by Republican Andrew J. Volstead of Minnesota would have given the Attorney General the power to determine whether securities might be fraudulent. This was likened to the Food and Drug Act by its sponsor. In this comparison, Volstead pointed out, "there are requirements with regard to the purity of the ingredients. The

---

[8] House, *Report of the Committee Appointed Pursuant to House Resolutions 429 and 504,* esp. pp. 44, 45.

conception is similar." [9] This bill suffered the same fate as its predecessor.

In 1922 a different approach was attempted by Republican Congressman Edward E. Denison of Illinois. His bill was aimed at those who used the mails or interstate agencies to circumvent the state blue-sky laws, and was to be enforced by the Department of Justice. Fines and imprisonment were imposed on violators, and provision was made for recovery of damages suffered by the security purchaser. The National Association of Home Loan Institutions announced full approval of the intent to curb fraud but insisted such legislation was not the answer. Rather, this organization felt, relief should be sought through existing fraud laws. The New York Curb Exchange's representative scoffed at the necessity for any legislation. The Exchange was seeking business, William A. Lockwood told a House committee. If they were foolish enough "to list securities which would be fraudulent and worthless, the market would pass out of existence shortly." [10] Although successful in passing the House, the Denison Bill died in Senate committee.

The years immediately following the failure to pass securities legislation also marked the era of the widest participation, up to that time, of the small purchaser in the American securities market. In the opinion of many this amazing plunge of financial small fry into the stock market was largely traceable to the new and widespread acquaintance of the American public with World War I Liberty bonds as a means of investment.[11] Evidence existed in the doubling of branch offices by the larger brokerage firms. In the period 1925–29, brokerage branches appeared in such unlikely metropolitan centers as Steubenville, Ohio; Shabona, Illinois; Gastonia, North Carolina; and Chickasha, Oklahoma. The "odd-lot" houses—those brokers who deal solely in stock purchases of less than one hundred

---

[9] House, *Proposed Federal "Blue-Sky" Law*, p. 23.
[10] Senate, *Regulation of the Sale of Securities*, p. 33.
[11] Ripley, p. vi. See also Weissman, p. 24.

shares—reported a phenomenal increase for this period. Loans of brokers for the purchase of stock on margin advanced from $3 million in February, 1927, to nearly $7 million in February, 1929.[12]

An additional source of funds that aided yet more purchasers to take part in the pursuit of easy riches appeared in the form of corporate surplus. Surging into the market place in the late 1920's, these funds frequently represented proceeds of security issues diverted from their original or ostensible purpose of production expansion. Instead, they were channeled into broker's loans in order to profit from rates ranging up to 15 percent. Funds were pumped into the call-money market by corporations such as Cities Service Company largely in answer to brokers' demands for margin-purchase financing. In 1929 this firm made 912 such loans to brokers in the cumulative amount of $285 million.[13] The Electric Bond and Share Company contributed some $867 million during this period. Granddaddy of them all, however, was Standard Oil Company, which made over 20,000 loans to brokers in 1929 in the cumulative amount of more than $17 billion.[14] Peak amount for one day was reached on September 9, 1929, with some $97 million in brokers' loans outstanding from this one corporation.[15]

Able to finance stock buying as never before, the small purchaser had no reason to doubt his wisdom in venturing into corporate ownership, even if only for short-term speculation. There were virtually no voices raised until after the debacle of 1929 to contest the virtues of participation in this best of all possible markets. As one writer pointed out, big business was not an object of distrust when the purchaser held its soaring stock. The corporation, even though its ownership by the small shareholder was virtually nonexistent, became for the holder of its stock a "benevolent philanthropic institution"; it readily

---

[12] Merz, pp. 642, 643.
[13] Senate, *Stock Exchange Practices*, p. 16.
[14] The cumulative amount of such loans was computed by multiplying the daily average of the loans by the number of days on the loans outstanding.
[15] *Ibid.*

assumed the image of "a jolly partner in an admitted hold-up." [16]

In such an atmosphere of financial euphoria, issues as value-less as the bonds of the Republic of Peru were snapped up without question when they bore the imprimatur of such in-vestment banking affiliates as that of the National City Bank of New York. Offered to the general public in 1927 by the bank's securities affiliate, the National City Company, they appeared despite the warnings of the bank's Peruvian representative that Peruvian governmental finances were "positively distressing." Several years previously the organization's foreign securities adviser had recommended declining the Peruvian government's business as a "moral risk." Despite reaffirmations of this view in 1925 and 1927, coupled with alarming evidence, National's president, Hugh B. Baker, pressed through an additional $50 million issue of Peruvian bonds in December, 1927. The pro-spectus accompanying the issue told nothing about matters Peruvian except the country's geographic location and popu-lation. Six years later President Baker admitted that the public would not have purchased the bonds if faced with the truth. By that time they were down from their issued price of 96½ to between 7 and 8, or just slightly more than the bank's origi-nal five-point commission.[17]

On the stock exchanges, investors were frequently the un-witting participants in manipulated pools, a form of stock activity that someone has aptly described as simply a "violent marking up and down of other people's possessions." In an operation such as Harry F. Sinclair, head of Sinclair Consoli-dated Oil, managed with the use of his own company's stock, a trading syndicate was formed in 1928. Composed of corpo-rate officers and market operators, the pool syndicate, through a succession of almost equally matched buying and selling orders, created an atmosphere of feverish activity in the Sinclair stock. Aided by judiciously placed rumors and the public wish to cash in on a good thing, the price was driven up to several

[16] Merz, p. 645.
[17] Senate, Stock Exchange Practices, pp. 126, 128–29.

times its original value between October, 1928 and April, 1929. The pool syndicate was able to sell its share of the stock at the height of its artificial activity and realize a profit of nearly $13 million. With its false props withdrawn, Sinclair Consolidated stock promptly sank to its prepool level.[18]

Evidence of such abuses was neither clearly seen nor publicly admitted as such in the atmosphere of 1929. Even the voice of caution was rarely raised, although in the summer of 1929 the New York *Times* and the *Commercial and Financial Chronicle* warned of delusions in the inflated common-stock values of the day. Such minor notes of disagreement as were sounded usually limited themselves to the more clearly seen speculative nature of stock activity. The governor of the state in which this activity was principally centered interjected one of few such warnings. Speaking at Poughkeepsie, Governor Franklin D. Roosevelt of New York criticized the "fever of speculation." [19] Secretary of the Treasury Andrew W. Mellon had also hinted at the danger inherent in stock prices spiraling steadily upward. The market "offers an opportunity for the prudent investor to buy bonds," was the Secretary's unheeded advice. "Bonds are low in price compared to stocks." [20]

The prevailing tone of public utterance, however, was one of calm assurance. Even the preliminary tremors of September, 1929, portended no financial earthquake, it was thought. Rather, these were the expected shakes that dislodged merely those small-scale speculators with the least tenacious grips— actually a fortuitous happening, Wall Streeters told each other, since it left the market in even stronger hands than before.

As the market statistics of Black Thursday, October 25, moved downward to the even more funereal shades of another "black" day, Tuesday the 29th, the reassurances became more nervously insistent. A Boston investment trust called on the public through a *Wall Street Journal* advertisement to "heed the words of America's greatest bankers." [21] Stock Exchange

[18] *Ibid.*, pp. 63–66.
[19] Galbraith, p. 112.
[20] Myers and Newton, p. 14.
[21] Galbraith, p. 111.

jargon repeatedly fell back on the phrase "technical readjust-
ment." In what Frederick Lewis Allen has described as one
of the most remarkable understatements of all time, Thomas
Lamont, spokesman for the organized support that was des-
perately trying to halt the panic, referred to the events as "a
little distress selling on the Stock Exchange." [22] President
Hoover, at press insistence, issued a statement to the effect that
"the fundamental business of the country . . . is on a sound
and prosperous basis." [23] This was the sentiment that Hoover
uttered always with stubborn conviction but one that became
more mournfully inappropriate as the next four years turned
up increasing evidence of financial mishap and misdeed.

But fraudulence alone was scarcely responsible for the speculative debacle of October, 1929. While it was agreed that the
stock market collapse added immeasurably to the depression,
there were few attempts to assign, even approximately, its
quantitative contribution. An outstanding economist and a
student of the Great Crash considered the stock market as
properly being a part—and a vitally important part—of the
entire unsound corporate and banking structure. In an edifice
already weakened by a maldistribution of wealth and an over-
production of capital goods, such a collapse of security values
then assumed a "role of respectable importance." [24] International assessments preferred to deal with the depression in
terms of weaknesses in the entire postwar economic structure.
Both schools were able to agree that evidences of the depression
were clearly discernible in 1928 and in the summer before the
Great Crash.[25]

While dramatic events of note may precipitate a cataclysmic
period, the event can trigger such a reaction only when the
proper ingredients are there to react. But from the viewpoint
of the American public, investor or noninvestor, the sudden
stock market collapse was a veritable financial and even social
earthquake. Its shock waves were transmitted around the

[22] Allen, *Only Yesterday*, p. 330.
[23] Myers and Newton, p. 23.
[24] Galbraith, p. 191.
[25] Robbins, p. 10; Galbraith, pp. 179–80.

country through a succession of great black headlines, followed by persistent ripples of lurid detail concerning the relative or friend or the fellow down the street "caught in the market." The Great Crash, therefore, was the highly visible and dramatic episode from which most depression troubles were to be dated, and in computing its effects this must be borne in mind.

/ One of the outstanding factors that enabled the stock market to reach such dizzying heights was the tremendous excess of corporate surplus funds poured into the call-money market to finance speculative margin buying. In both 1928 and 1929 it was estimated that the excess of corporate net income over cash dividends paid out left balances of $11 billion for investment purposes. Yet of the more than $9 billion of securities issued by domestic corporations in 1929, less than $2 billion provided genuine "productive" capital.[26] The balance went to finance the speculative fever that must also bear a large share of the responsibility for disaster. As Walter Bagehot demonstrated regarding the South Sea Bubble, a period of prosperity resulting in a swollen accumulation of investment funds readily induces a high degree of faith in even the most fantastic of investment opportunities.[27]

While the feverish activity of speculation was partly responsible for the creation of false values, many unsound and fraudulent securities were part of the vast flood issued. As in most major booms of history, the rising market was attended by large-scale fraud. Later computations estimated that in the ten years before 1933, total investor losses through worthless securities were approximately $25 billion, or half of all those issued. The financial experts of the Senate Committee on Banking and Currency concluded that the losses of investors even before the depression reached a staggering annual total of $1.7 billion of which $500 million alone was accounted for within the state of New York.[28]

[26] Schumpeter, II, 822, 861, 879.
[27] Galbraith, p. 175.
[28] Senate, *Regulation of Securities*, p. 20.

The echoes of the crash itself produced considerable outcry against the evils of speculation, but little at first directed specifically toward regulation of the security markets or concerned with the fraudulence in the stock issues themselves. Public reaction in the light of the morning after tended to lump together indiscriminately bankers, promoters, and the professional market operator under the disrepute of the label "speculator."

Hoover's remonstrances to the stock exchanges and the echoed complaints of press and periodicals were limited to the evils of short selling and excessive speculation on margin. Nothing was said of the public losses resulting from market pools rigged by exchange insiders. No mention was made of protecting the public from securities fraudulently issued, other than periodic pleas for better business ethics.

As the institution that handled 80 percent of all stock transactions in the country and 90 percent of all such business on a dollar basis, the New York Stock Exchange was the logical focal point for an administration concerned with the evils of speculation.[29] In 1930, however, President Hoover began to take more cognizance of the fact that operations within the Stock Exchange itself might mark the source of the trouble. In October, President Hoover sent for Richard Whitney, the new head of the Exchange, and strongly urged that the Exchange itself take action to curb the manipulations of stocks by insiders. Hoover informed Whitney that regulatory powers rested with the governor of New York State, and that there was no desire to stretch the powers of the Federal government. In his memoirs Hoover says:

I stated that I preferred to let American institutions and the states govern themselves, and that the Exchange had full power under its charter to control its own members, and to prevent it from being used for manipulation against the public interest. Mr. Whitney made profuse promises but did nothing.[30]

President Hoover closed the interview by warning that unless self-curative measures were practiced, some attempts to

[29] SEC, *Second Annual Report*, 1936, p. 116.
[30] Hoover, *Memoirs*, III, 17.

force Federal regulation would be inevitable. In order that an opportunity for internal regulation be insured, no public statement would be made at that time.[31] The President's party leaders were also concerned with Exchange activities in relation to their partisan effects. They, as did Hoover, seriously considered that the pool manipulations, and particularly the large-scale bear raids in the stock market, were part of a conspiracy by the Democrats to discredit the administration. The name of John J. Raskob, financial leader and heavy Democratic contributor, was commonly mentioned in this role.[32]

The Exchange had been more severely shaken by the traumatic experience of October, 1929, than at any other time of panic since its founding in 1792 under the now traditional buttonwood tree on lower Wall Street. The venerable institution had seen the price for a membership in its ranks plummet from an all-time high of $625,000 in 1929 to a 1931 low of $186,000.[33] The call money that flooded its facilities for stock purchases even at the Federal Reserve Board imposed rate of 20 percent [34] was available in 1931 at the unpressured rate of 1½ percent.[35]

Even in the prosperous flush of the latter 1920's, however, the Exchange had consistently worked to strengthen the regulations it imposed on its members and on the corporations that listed their securities on the "Big Board." It had required corporations to furnish a clear-cut statement of depreciation policy as a prerequisite to listing their industrial securities. The Exchange had early recorded its opposition to the issuance of nonvoting common stocks, and urged its listed companies to publish their quarterly earnings. In 1929 a special report was prepared outlining the future Exchange requirements in regard to stock dividends. As severe a critic as Adolf A. Berle, Jr., co-author of *The Modern Corporation and Private Property*, could

[31] Myers and Newton, p. 52.
[32] Alsop and Kintner, "The Battle of the Market-Place," p. 8.
[33] *New York Stock Exchange Yearbook 1930–1931*, p. 37.
[34] Although, as Herbert Hoover properly pointed out, "people who dreamed of one hundred per cent profit in a week were not deterred by an interest rate of twenty per cent a year" (*Memoirs*, III, 18).
[35] *Ibid.*, p. 99.

say of those years that "the listing committee of that Exchange made more forward steps during that period than any other body in the United States." [36] None of these or other efforts, however praiseworthy, were aimed at curbing the two practices the administration and, increasingly, the public considered most destructive. The pools formed by professional exchange operators to create, through inside information, violent fluctuations in a particular stock, which they were then able to exploit for considerable personal gain, continued operating unhindered. The so-called bear raiders, who specialized in driving stock market prices downward so that they might profitably engage in the practice of selling short, pursued their activities unmolested by Exchange officials.[37]

Both of these practices were vigorously defended by Richard Whitney, Exchange president and its tireless spokesman, as legitimate market functions. In his presidential report covering 1931 and 1932, Whitney reasserted that short selling was not the cause for the whole downward price movement in securities. He also pointed to the fact that complete statistics on the total short interest in all stocks were now being compiled and made public on a monthly basis. This was an indication of the New York Stock Exchange's concern over the subject, and Whitney hailed this compilation as "unique in the annals of this or any other stock exchange in the world." [38]

In the years following the Great Crash, both administration leaders and the heads of industry tirelessly echoed the theme that the "fundamental business of the country is on a sound basis." The Stock Exchange corollary to this was sounded with similar insistency by its own leaders. As President Whitney stated it, "one great duty" of the New York Stock Exchange

---

[36] Weissman, pp. 109, 111.

[37] According to the SEC, "short sale" is defined as "any sale of a security which the seller does not own or any sale which is consummated by the delivery of a security borrowed by, or for the account of, the seller." From the individual's point of view, the purpose of selling short is to take advantage of an anticipated decline in the market price of the security sold short. See *General Rules and Regulations* (Washington, D.C.: Securities and Exchange Commission, 1954), Rule x-3 B-3.

[38] New York Stock Exchange, *Report of the President 1931–1932*, p. 92.

"was to maintain a market place." [39] Out of this continued emphasis on the alleged free-market functioning of all Exchange activities gradually emerged the concepts that were to remain in common use for the next few years. The Stock Exchange, as reflected in Whitney's addresses, statements, and Congressional testimony, was a completely laissez-faire institution, the impersonal operations of which were aseptically referred to as a barometer that simply recorded national business and industrial pressures. Any reference to activities of its members in pursuit of personal gain at the violent expense of the public economic good was effectively forestalled. This was accomplished by a refusal to consider that the mechanics of Exchange operations or the practitioners thereof were of public interest or subject to public criticism. As SEC commissioner William O. Douglas described it several years later, the image presented was one of a private club in which the members could do no wrong, so long as their behavior toward each other was governed by club rules.[40]

The administration had given no sign of harsh handling of exchange transgressors. President Hoover's outburst of July, 1931, following the widespread short selling of wheat futures on the nation's commodity exchange, was couched in terms of moral indignation. "If these gentlemen have that sense of patriotism which outruns immediate profit," Hoover pleaded, "they will close up these transactions and desist from their manipulations." The President's reaction to these activities was one of unmistakable petulance; such action "tends to destroy returning public confidence." [41]

The presidential election year of 1932 brought with it more such operations rather than less, and the administration tone sharpened in reaction. Further bear raids (that is, short-selling assaults on the market), this time in anticipation of gold difficulties, brought a warning from the President in February that

[39] *Ibid.*, p. 9.
[40] Rodell, pp. 119 ff.
[41] Myers, *State Papers of Herbert Hoover*, I, 596.

stronger measures must be used to curtail such practices or the government would ultimately have to regulate the Stock Exchange.[42]

The resulting amendments to the Exchange rules were evidence of the lack of seriousness with which such a threat was regarded. After April 1, the Stock Exchange resolved, brokerage firms must get express permission from the holders of stock if they planned to use that stock in any short-sale transaction on the market. As the financial periodicals pointed out, this was an almost meaningless gesture. It merely meant filling out a separate blank, the editors of *Business Week* reported, since brokerage clients already gave written permission for such stock usage.[43]

In a press conference of February 19, President Hoover expressed his dissatisfaction with the Exchange measures and with continuing short-selling waves that "unquestionably affected the price of securities and brought discouragement to the country as a whole." The President and other administration officials had "again expressed [their] views to the managers of the Exchange that they should take adequate measures to protect investors from artificial depression of the price of securities for speculative profit." The conference concluded on the reiterated and dominant note of damaged public confidence. "Individuals who use the facilities of the Exchange for such purposes are not contributing to recovery of the United States." [44]

One week later, no further Exchange action having been announced, Hoover requested Republican Senators Peter Norbeck of South Dakota and Frederick C. Walcott of Connecticut of the Senate Banking and Currency Committee to initiate a Senate investigation into those practices of a minority group in the New York Stock Exchange that was acting contrary to the national interest.[45] This served to widen the scope of an earlier investigation authorized under Senate Resolution No. 84, introduced December 14, 1931, by Republican Senator John G.

[42] Myers and Newton, p. 175.
[43] *Business Week,* March 2, 1932, p. 7.
[44] Myers, *State Papers of Herbert Hoover,* II, 118.
[45] Myers and Newton, p. 178.

Townsend, Jr., of Delaware. On its initial appearance Resolution No. 84 mentioned only the investigation of short-selling practices, and it had been adopted and referred to the Senate Committee on Banking and Currency for implementation.[46]

After these words of encouragement from President Hoover a considerably amended resolution was reported back to the Senate on March 4 by Senator Townsend. Instead of investigating short selling a Senate subcommittee was directed to investigate all "practices with respect to buying and selling and borrowing and lending of listed securities." In place of specifically "the New York Stock Exchange" appeared a more inclusive version, "the various stock exchanges." The subcommittee was additionally directed to inquire not only into the practices of exchanges but also into their effect on the value of securities, and consequently "upon interstate and foreign commerce, the operation of the national banking system and Federal reserve system, and upon the market for securities for the United States Government." Instead of posing the question of "prohibiting" short-selling practices, the subcommittee was to consider whether the much wider field to be investigated should be "regulated." The most telling point in the new tone and direction of committee activity was the changed financial status accorded the investigation. In this amendment, funds for committee investigation expense were jumped from $3,000 to $50,000, and the committee's probing took on the qualifications of a major activity.[47]

Journalistic comment still confined itself to the short-selling theme. *Business Week* "frankly admitted" the allegation that short sellers circulated false rumors. However, the writer pointed out, this profited a bullish market equally well, since manipulators hoping for a rise were just as glib with their own false rumors.[48] Presumably this was an example of the untrammeled workings of a free market place.

Commenting in the *Magazine of Wall Street*, Charles Bene-

[46] *Congressional Record*, 72 Cong., 1 Sess., LXXV, Part I, 447.
[47] *Ibid.*, Part V, p. 5241.
[48] *Business Week*, March 2, 1932, p. 7.

dict recalled that similar Congressional flurries "toward the close of the other great depressions" had produced no important or enduring legislation. Nor would this one, he prophesied. In fact, "legislative bedeviling might conceivably drive the principle security market of the country to a more hospitable clime—possibly Montreal." Short selling as a legitimate market function was treated expansively without reference to the common pool practice of jiggling market prices, except to say that the "spotlight of publicity may prove painful to some operators; unless it is shaded by political considerations. . . ." [49]

In the first ten days of April, 1932, an alarming wave of liquidation swept over the stock market. President Hoover hastily conferred with his principal financial adviser in the Senate, Frederick C. Walcott, Republican, of Connecticut. The Senate Committee on Banking and Currency, of which Senator Walcott was a member, was called into session. Information, based in part on rumor and on a telegram never subsequently verified, was turned over to President Hoover. This purported to be a plan for a general stock market decline, culminating in a gigantic bear raid on Saturday, April 9, or Monday, April 11. [50] A committee witness subpoena was rushed to Richard Whitney's home, and in an attempt to forestall the alleged raiders, a subcommittee of the Senate Banking and Currency Committee began on April 11 the investigation and hearings it had been discussing for months. Expanded under the stimulus of its revelations with two subsequent resolutions of ever-widening powers, this became the prime source for the ultimate creation under the Roosevelt administration of "Truth-in-Securities" legislation, the Securities Act of 1933.

The first witness to appear was the star witness, whom the subcommittee had hastily summoned to open the proceedings. Richard Whitney, the president of the New York Stock Exchange, looked, according to the *Herald Tribune*'s Mark Sullivan, "like a football player who has kept in perfect condi-

[49] *Magazine of Wall Street,* March 19, 1932, p. 647.
[50] *Literary Digest,* April 23, 1932, p. 42. See also *Saturday Evening Post,* June 11, 1938, p. 8, and *Nation,* May 11, 1952, p. 528.

tion." [51] Whitney was a smooth-shaven, ruddy-faced man of middle age, with an urbane and confident manner that impressed members of the subcommittee and representatives of the press alike, and his defense of short-selling tactics in the market was reported with admiration by financial journals.

Whitney's insistence that the American public was to blame for the speculative mania and his offhand estimate of the numerical strength of this public appeared on the nation's front pages seemingly without editorial challenge. Americans "interested" in the stock market either through speculation or stock ownership were 20–25 million in number.[52] After all, Whitney said, American Telegraph and Telephone alone accounted for 640,000 shareholders. Subsequent statistics compiled by Senate investigators, however, set the figure for 1929 at one and one-half million instead.[53] Using the accounts of all member firms of the nation's twenty-nine exchanges, the million and a half total was then broken down into about 950,000 cash accounts and 600,000 on margin. Allowing for some duplication, "speculators" (or margin accounts) still numbered less than one million.[54] However, to this should have been added an indeterminate number who owned stock outright and no longer maintained accounts with any broker. These would have appreciably raised the number of shareholders, but they were not reflected in the official estimate.

Although Whitney's view was gravely echoed throughout the press, Walter Lippmann's comment in the New York *Herald Tribune* dissented in part. Whitney might be right about the American people in general being responsible for the wave of crazy speculation, Lippmann commented soberly. "But what sticks in their minds," he went on, "is that they were encouraged, often by the methods of high-powered salesmanship, to give themselves up to this folly." The New York *Evening Post* had no such misgivings. "If half the short sellers called

[51] New York *Herald Tribune*, April 12, 1932.

[52] Florida *Times Union* (Jacksonville, Fla.), April 13, 1932.

[53] Out of a population of 120 millions, or approximately $1\frac{1}{4}$ percent, instead of Whitney's more lavish 16–20 percent.

[54] Senate, *Stock Exchange Practices*, pp. 9–10.

before the committee can make as truthful and well-poised witnesses as President Richard Whitney," the *Post* confidently predicted, "the Stock Exchange need have no fear of the investigation's outcome." [55]

The "Senate Bear Hunt," as it popularly appeared in the headlines, found plentiful evidence of skulduggery in its May and June hearings. The role of the publicity agent, whose services were usually paid for by the stock he touted, came under the committee's scrutiny. A financial column called "The Trader," which appeared in the New York *Daily News,* was largely responsible for his ten-month profit of $1,138,322, a free-lance trader, John J. Levenson, testified. The writer of the column, Raleigh T. Curtis, received $19,000 in the stocks that he "tipped" to his eager readers.

Representative Fiorello La Guardia of New York appeared before the subcommittee with documentary evidence of the huge sums spent by pool operators for publicity favorable to their stocks. The sum of $286,279 was paid by one pool organization to a publicity man, A. Newton Plummer, to have its propaganda published in the daily and periodical press in the guise of straight financial news.[56]

Revelations in the first month of committee operation failed to impress journalists who moved in the shadow of Wall Street. *Business Week* commented, "The investigations have uncovered practices which do not look good in brutal daylight, but the excitement was dulled by a pretty general knowledge that such things went on." "More sensational sins must be displayed," was the consensus, "before the Wall Street disclosures produce the political dividends that were hoped for it." In spite of the pool disclosures and the bribed financial writers, *Business Week* added sourly, the administration "is tryng to restore confidence in securities," and thus it was a poor time to heave bricks at Wall Street.[57]

In late May the "political dividends" referred to proved to

[55] *Literary Digest,* April 23, 1932, p. 42; May 7, p. 9.
[56] *Ibid.,* May 7, 1932, pp. 9, 45.
[57] *Business Week,* May 4, 1932, p. 5.

be of an embarrassingly bipartisan nature. Boring into pool manipulations by market specialists led the committee's investigators to the brokerage firm of M. J. Meehan and Company, which largely conducted the activities of a syndicate organized in March, 1929, to trade in the common stock of Radio Corporation of America.[58] The stock had been pumped up from 79 to 109, and in the seven days of operation from March 12 to March 19 the pool managed a net profit of $4,924,079. Participants included Mrs. M. J. Meehan, wife of the broker, and Mrs. David Sarnoff, wife of the president of Radio Corporation of America.[59] Particularly damaging, however, was an account of the participation of bigwigs from both major parties, a list that included John J. Raskob, conservative chairman of the Democratic National Committee, and W. F. Kenny, an Al Smith supporter, on the Democratic side, with Charles M. Schwab of Bethlehem Steel and Percy A. Rockefeller and Walter P. Chrysler, heavy contributors to the Republican party. In detailing the seven-day operations that brought, for example, Raskob and Kenny $291,770 each, the *Nation* commented that "never had there been a clearer-cut example of the way prices are rigged on the Stock Exchange." [60]

On May 26 the New York Stock Exchange, acting under Sections 4 and 7, Article XVII, of the Stock Exchange constitution, suspended David Manning McKeon for selling securities with the "purpose of upsetting the equilibrium of the market." McKeon, the New York *Times* reported in matter-of-fact fashion, was "not known in the financial district as a large short seller," nor had his name ever appeared in the lists of transgressors issued by the Senate bear-hunt committee. Under the columnar title "Topics in Wall Street" appeared the comment that despite the many prominent men mentioned in the course of the investigation, one of exceedingly minor stature had obviously been made "Official Bear" of the Street.[61]

[58] M. J. Meehan was the first major broker indicted by the SEC three years later for similar manipulative activities, this time in Bellanca Aircraft stock.
[59] Senate, *Stock Exchange Practices*, p. 47.
[60] *Nation*, June 1, 1932, p. 609.
[61] New York *Times*, May 27, 1932.

During the months leading up to the selection of a new national administration the average newspaper reader was thus subjected to a continual front-page drumfire of financial corruption and downfall. The abdication of Samuel Insull from his utilities empire, and the subsequent realization that literally no one was able to put this financial Humpty Dumpty together again, was but one of the many shocks. Bankruptcy proceedings against Kreuger and Toll, the huge holding company for the Ivar Kreuger interests, revealed that Kreuger's recent suicide had left personal debts and liabilities totaling an unprecedented $168 million. After eight years of fraudulent bookkeeping, a committee reported from London, this left "little, if anything, for distribution to unsecured creditors." [62]

On the same front page the newspaper public could also read the testimony of Walter E. Sachs, president of Goldman-Sachs Trading Company. Closely questioned by Counsel William A. Gray and Senator James Couzens of the Committee on Banking and Currency, Sachs unfolded a tale of devious maneuvering that had left investors holding $90 million in worthless stock. Over a period of four years the company's officers had amassed personal fortunes while the value of their stock fell from 104 to 1¾ and the status of a current musical comedy joke.[63]

The nation's press, however, largely refrained from commenting on the staggering implications of its front-page headlines. In Florida, home state of the committee's ranking Democrat, Senator Duncan U. Fletcher, metropolitan area newspapers revealed a uniform unwillingness to comment on the Goldman-Sachs revelations or the disclosures of the RCA pool manipulations. The Tampa *Tribune* in the same week reported Charles M. Schwab's participation in the latter activity, yet reprinted with favorable editorial comment his remedy for the national ills. Schwab called for a restoration of confidence, which must be effected through balancing the budget, in order to "protect our national credit," and his detailing of the tax-

---

[62] *Ibid.*, May 21, 1932.
[63] *Ibid.* See also *Nation*, June 1, 1932, p. 609.

payer's groaning burden was approvingly echoed by the *Trib-bune*.[64]

The only adverse Florida comment on the Senate committee disclosures came from a small, predominantly rural county of the state. The Tallahassee *Democrat,* unlike all the urban area journals, chose to relate the fiscal experience of the past to present economic difficulties. "The times when the clever market manipulator and trader could clean up a million without investing a cent of his own were directly responsible for the times of 8 million unemployed," the *Democrat* stated. As the Senate investigation wore on, this journal endorsed the suggestion advanced by William Z. Ripley of Harvard University that corporation books be open to public inspection. This seemed radical, the *Democrat* admitted, but reminded the public that the corporate privilege of secrecy frequently meant the use of such inside information to fleece the investor.[65]

Editorial agreement on the Ripley proposals for Federal regulation of corporate accounting also came from the *Rocky Mountain News* of Denver, while the Senate disclosures forced even the revelations in the Lindbergh case to a less prominent spot in the St. Louis *Post-Dispatch.* After the RCA pool and the Goldman-Sachs losses there was "no need for further wonder," the *Post-Dispatch* said, regarding the people's loss of confidence in "captains of industry and masters of finance." That journal's harsh and direct language left no doubt of its judgments of the Senate committee's disclosures, during the course of which headlines carried the story of a naturalized Czech sheet-metal worker who had accumulated "nearly $50,000," but having lost $30,000 in the stock market, had committed suicide.[66]

Newspapers such as the Detroit *News,* the New York *World Telegram,* the Houston *Post,* and the Milwaukee *Journal* tied in the disclosure of prominent personages and their stock market rigging with criticism of the Senate's failure to tax the

[64] Tampa *Tribune,* May 25, 1932.
[65] Tallahassee *Democrat,* May 25, 1932; June 20, 1932.
[66] Denver *Rocky Mountain News,* May 20, 1932; St. Louis *Post-Dispatch,* May 19–21, 1932.

upper-income brackets. "Gambling with stacked cards," was the *World Telegram's* characterization of the market disclosures. The Houston *Post* compared it with the fake oil stocks of Texas oil boom days, while the Milwaukee *Journal* likened the manipulations to the "old shell and pea game." "If they knew how to do it," reported the *Journal* grimly, "an overwhelming number of citizens would rise up and smash it [pools] to smithereens." [67]

Editorial pages of conservative bent, however, commented cautiously or remained discreetly silent. The New York *Times* confined itself to saying that if the activities "were really, as they appear to have been, in violation of the regulations, somebody ought to be brought to book for the offense." On the Pacific Coast the San Francisco *Chronicle* directed stern words about "the rule of honor" to Mayor Jimmy Walker during the concurrent Seabury investigations but did not comment on the Senate exposures. Pilfering by public officials was cause for rebuke, but pilfering of the public by stock exchange members was evidently beyond that journal's purview. The New York *Herald Tribune* and the Louisville *Courier-Journal* refrained from any editorial comment whatever. In Chicago the *Tribune* felt that David Sarnoff was "duty bound to explain the transaction (his wife's 'purchase,' with no deposit, of 10,000 shares of RCA) or resign." However, the *Tribune* pessimistically editorialized, "it is doubtful if any law can put an end to such abuses," and suggested instead that self-denying restrictions for corporate officials be made a part of the incorporation process.[68]

A month later the Senate committee recessed to devote its energies to the presidential conventions. Recognition of those frauds and abuses just emerging from the Senate investigation formed an important plank in the Democratic party platform. Of modest length and subdued rhetoric, the platform adopted by the Democratic convention in July, 1932, stated in unequivocal terms:

[67] Detroit *News*, New York *World Telegram*, Houston *Post*, Milwaukee *Journal*, May 26, 1932.
[68] New York *Times*, San Francisco *Chronicle*, New York *Herald Tribune*, Louisville *Courier-Journal*, Chicago *Tribune*, May 20–27, 1932.

We advocate protection of the investing public by requiring to be filed with the government and carried in advertisements of all offerings of foreign and domestic stocks and bonds true information as to bonuses, commissions, principal invested, and the interests of the sellers.

Regulation to the full extent of federal power, of

(a) Holding companies which sell securities in interstate commerce;

(b) Rates of utility companies operating across State lines;

(c) Exchanges in securities and commodities.

Elsewhere the platform attacked the "indefensible expansion and contraction of credit for private profit at the expense of the public," and it called for banking reforms that would protect depositors from the "use of their moneys in speculation to the detriment of local credits." [69]

In contrast, the Republican equivalent stated the party's concern with several needed banking reforms but failed to mention securities or exchanges. It said nothing regarding protection of the investing public, and refrained from mention of regulation other than of charges for electricity transmitted across state lines. [70]

The two major opponents who clashed beneath these standards had publicly treated the issue with varying emphasis during the previous two years. Both had denounced excessive speculation and its attendant evils, President Hoover in the national press, and Governor Roosevelt in his annual message to the New York State legislature on January 7, 1931. [71] Both had become more specific and denunciatory in early 1932. The President had taken bitter exception to the activities of pool operators and bear raids on the Stock Exchange. Hoover, additionally, had conferred with Stock Exchange President Whitney and threatened governmental regulation if the proper controls were not forthcoming internally. He had inaugurated a Senate investigation that had already turned up a politically embarrassing spate of ethically dubious stock market antics.

Governor Roosevelt had specifically stated his position in

[69] Commager, *Documents of American History*, p. 418.
[70] Porter and Johnson, p. 347.
[71] F.D.R., *Public Papers and Addresses*, I, 107.

his last annual message to the New York State legislature on January 6, 1932. He insisted that there must be "revision of the laws relating to the sale of securities to the public." The idea of publicity and of truthfulness should be combined, Roosevelt said, "to tell an unskilled public . . . about the contents of what in the past has been a package too often sold only because of the bright colors on its wrapper." The larger problems of the national financial system, he was aware, "were to a greater degree Federal rather than State," but New York State "ought to start to apply the lessons learned during 1930 and 1931."

In his famous nomination speech ("I pledge you—I pledge myself—to a new deal") at Chicago, presidential contender Roosevelt apologized for the "dry subject of finance" but called attention to the principle of "letting in the light of day on issues of securities, foreign and domestic, which are offered for sale to the investing public." [72]

In the course of the campaign Hoover responded in kind to Roosevelt's attacks on his administration's treatment—or lack of treatment—of the public losses suffered in foreign bond issues. "The Governor," said Hoover, "does not inform the American people that there is no Federal law of regulation of sale of securities." Furthermore, "there is doubtful constitutional authority for such law . . ." President Hoover concluded his rebuttal by taunting Roosevelt as governor of the state from which most of these bonds were originally issued and which, Hoover said, had such authority over issuance itself. [73]

The failures of the Republican administration in exercising some supervision over security sales and exchanges occupied a prominent place in Roosevelt's campaign speech at Columbus, Ohio, in August. He proposed three concrete remedies: first, "truth telling" concerning the stock to be issued, and pertinent facts concerning the issuing corporation itself; second, Federal regulation of holding companies that sell securities in interstate commerce; and third, the use of Federal authority in the

[72] *Ibid.*, pp. 113, 114, 653.
[73] Myers, *State Papers of Herbert Hoover*, II, 402.

regulation of stock and commodities exchanges. In pointing to "unsound investing policies under a lax and indifferent leadership" [74] as Republican responsibility to be shouldered for the speculation boom and burst, Roosevelt provoked his opponent into a wildly improbable analogy.

"The only way . . . a President could even tilt with a boom," Hoover retorted angrily, "would be to turn himself into a blue sky law and go on the stump analyzing balance sheets and stock market prices. . . ." Impressed with such a creative image, Hoover then thrust from him "this proposal that the White House should be turned into a stock tipster's office." He could not abide, he added, that "such a form of dictatorship should ever be set up over the American people even if they do get over-optimistic." [75]

Throughout the campaign Hoover was defensive and usually content to reiterate such measures as he had already undertaken in banking legislation. Roosevelt became increasingly expansive on financial matters, and countered Hoover's generalized "wrongdoing must be punished" with specific remedies to forestall future wrongdoing. Roosevelt made manifest his concern with the individual investor and his concern for the welfare of the average purchaser of securities. The Republican nominee, while obviously speaking with great sincerity from a high moral plane, was more concerned with the punishment of immoral men and of those who had "embarrassed" his administration through the avenue of the stock market.

The public in the first year or two after the Great Crash had participated in the early tendency to diagnose "speculation" as the cause of the nation's financial ills. In later years it had, however, found room for increasing doubt that speculations furnished the chief cause for the mountainous public losses in investments. The collapse of such financial structures as those of Insull and Kreuger revealed a callous exploitation of the investor, whose financial support had been so earnestly so-

[74] F.D.R., *Public Papers and Addresses*, I, 682, 678.
[75] Myers, *State Papers of Herbert Hoover*, II, 402.

licited. The discovery that the leading investment bankers of the nation had set the urge for huge commissions far above the most elemental standards of integrity was especially shocking to a nation that had reverenced its financial leaders. Both stockholders and legions of depositors were able to glimpse the utter lack of fiduciary responsibility exercised by banks speculating with funds entrusted to them. Despite the stock exchanges' insistence on its detached role as the mere reflector of basic supply and demand, many could now see that the market forces operating were not so impersonal as depicted. Evidence of market pools raising stock prices artificially, and of inside information used to promote the gain of corporate officers, outlined more clearly the personal forces at work and their manipulative devices./Lack of editorial concern with the disclosures of the spring and summer of 1932 could not offset the cumulative impact of recurrent front-page tales of financial misdeeds.

The nation had time to reflect on the crash of fiscal empires and the resulting rubble of corrupt financial foundations. It could more readily glimpse a Congress that was determined to sidetrack serious efforts at reform in the issuance of securities, and a national leader whose occasional threats of regulation of the exchanges were obviously belied by his expressed political philosophy and the more frequent entreaties he addressed to the perpetrators. The New York Stock Exchange mirrored only too plainly the light regard in which it held political efforts at regulation. Its rule changes were chiefly innocuous ones and, in any event, were clearly devised from a viewpoint of protection for its own members rather than for the investing public or the national economic welfare.

Such regulations as the states were able to put into practice were, at best, inadequate protection against the fraudulent securities dealer who operated across a convenient state line or under the protective wing of the United States mails. An inevitable lack of uniformity effectively precluded any adequate measure of regulation unless applied by the Federal government.

It is impossible to assess, even among the millions actually defrauded or affected by stock market losses, the extent to which the individual voter was influenced by his attitude toward securities and exchange regulation. Even on a larger scale, what part of his vote reflected his anger toward the entire vague area of financial misdeeds cannot be determined. But certainly some considerable measure of outraged voter feelings, some sense of the helpless frustration he felt in the face of continued financial fraud and irresponsibility left unresolved can be seen in the votes that turned down a stubborn defense of the status quo in favor of a Rooseveltian mood of "bold, persistent experimentation," of concrete remedies to be applied over the entire field of finance.

CHAPTER TWO

THE SECURITIES ACT OF 1933

THE CROWDS that gathered on a cold and cheerless March day
in Washington to hear the first inaugural address of President
Franklin D. Roosevelt paid significant tribute to those condemnatory remarks that related to the financial scene. Greatest
applause of all was reserved for Roosevelt's insistence on "an
end to a conduct in banking and in business" that could more
properly be described as simply "callous and selfish wrongdoing." [1] Second only to this was the outburst that greeted the
grim Biblical indictment of the "money changers." So ran the
contemporary estimate.[2]

Much of the Rooseveltian stand regarding the shortcomings
of the world of finance had actually been voiced for many years,
and frequently in the face of far less applause. The broad outline of the new President's position had been visible since his
earliest political life, and the specific references to reforms in
securities issuance and in corporate integrity were gradually
sketched in over the gubernatorial years and in the first presidential campaign.

Even in 1912, as a young progressive New York State Senator,
Roosevelt's recognition that "new sets of conditions of life
require new theories for their solution" [3] was a preparation
for necessary government regulation of industry and the ad-

[1] F.D.R., *Public Papers and Addresses*, II, 12.
[2] New York *Times*, March 5, 1933.
[3] Fusfeld, p. 49.

ministrative government agency as its vehicle. In his concept of the positive role of Federal government in promoting the general welfare, Roosevelt carried on Theodore Roosevelt's "people before property" theme. In his gubernatorial efforts in the fields of utilities and banking, Franklin Roosevelt displayed the Progressive belief that "business should be subjected, through the power of government, to drastic legal limitation against abuses."[4]

Following the Great Crash of 1929, Governor Roosevelt was among those who denounced the "improper schemes and questionable methods" used in stock promotions. Echoes of anti-Wall Street populism were heard in a strong speech Roosevelt made in Chicago several months after the market collapse of 1929. A particular target was made of the merger and the holding company ideas. Too frequently, according to Roosevelt, investors' funds were solicited for such ventures solely through the intrinsic value of the holding company device, even though the affiliating companies themselves might merely be "pooling their individual debts and inefficiencies."[5]

Roosevelt's own speculations during the middle 1920's were marked by a desire to combine personal profit with public service innovations. Fairly successful ventures in photograph- and stamp-vending machines were followed by a less fortunate experience with air transport by dirigibles.[6] The Roosevelt investments included everything from wildcat oil operations to the purchase of German real estate with depreciated German marks. Stock purchases as such were a lesser part of the picture, although they included more than a few worthless issues.[7] Considered as a whole, the Roosevelt financial ventures revealed an attitude of social responsibility in regarding investments as a means of expanding productivity and public services.[8]

[4] F.D.R., *On Our Way*, p. x.
[5] New York *Times*, Oct. 26, 1929; Dec. 11, 1929.
[6] Fusfeld, pp. 110–14.
[7] Gunther, p. 78.
[8] Roosevelt's secretary for many years said he never speculated in anything while he was President (Tully, p. 110).

Roosevelt's approach to securities regulation was developed chiefly through his long study of the power and public utility problem. In his annual address to the state legislature in 1931 the financing and stock issuances of the utilities holding companies were the specific objects of the gubernatorial wrath, but the message conveyed a regard for the welfare of all investors. As a result of holding company methods of finance, Roosevelt said, "the householders and businessmen of the Nation . . . must now pay exorbitant rates, measured not in terms of reasonableness for legitimate investors but rather in terms of speculative profit." The pyramiding of capital structures behind such issues resulted in "stock which is not always represented by actual investment." By the time Roosevelt made his last annual address to the state legislature he had broadened the area of securities regulation to include all those of any kind offered to the public, and had advanced the William Z. Ripley principle of promoting truth-in-securities issues through the glare of publicity.[9]

Much of the advice on financial reforms that was tendered Roosevelt before his elevation to the Presidency was in furtherance of his own ideas. Roosevelt's liberal stand on the power question drew the support and advice of an old acquaintance of his Wilson days, Felix Frankfurter of Harvard. Frankfurter's suggestions of utilities regulations were influential with Roosevelt as governor, and his recommendations on successful appointments were the basis for many similar ones in presidential days. The trio popularly known as the early Brain Trust—Raymond Moley, Adolf A. Berle, Jr., and Rexford G. Tugwell—were the builders of campaign speeches on securities regulation and stock exchange reform, but Roosevelt acted as his own architect here as in many another aspect of his political and social philosophy. Moley himself wholeheartedly agreed with Ernest K. Lindley that "Mr. Roosevelt did not recruit his professorial advisers to provide him with a point of view: he drew them to him because their point of view was akin to his own." [10]

[9] F.D.R., *Public Papers and Addresses*, I, 107, 114.
[10] Moley, *After Seven Years*, p. 13; Lindley, *The Roosevelt Revolution*, p. 7.

It was in furtherance of these long-held views, explicitly stated in the Democratic national platform of 1932 and pounded home by Roosevelt as candidate, that the newly elected President addressed the Seventy-third Congress on March 29, 1933.[11]

> I recommend to the Congress legislation for Federal supervision of traffic in investment securities in interstate commerce.
>
> In spite of many State statutes, the public in the past has sustained severe losses through practices neither ethical nor honest on the part of many persons and corporations selling securities.

Here Roosevelt drew on the advice of Huston Thompson, former Federal Trade Commission chairman, who had just drawn up a securities regulation bill. Thompson, in a note to Roosevelt the day before had listed his "suggestions in presenting the bill to Congress." It could be described, Thompson said, as one that "changes the ancient doctrine of *caveat emptor* to Let the Seller Beware . . ." [12]

As modified by the President, it became the phrase featured in most newspaper stories the following day: "This proposal adds to the ancient rule of *caveat emptor* the further doctrine, 'let the seller also beware.' "

The much abused idea of "confidence" received vastly different treatment from the new President. While Hoover pleaded for it continually in the name of the business community, Franklin Roosevelt summoned it in the name of the public, emphasizing again his belief that it was in the national community as a whole, rather than in any of its parts, that the begetting of such faith must take place. The proposed act, the President stated, "should give impetus to honest dealing in securities and thereby bring back public confidence."

Roosevelt then outlined the entire framework of the hoped-for program, and indicated the method of approach.

> This is but one step in our broad purpose of protecting investors and depositors. It should be followed by legislation relating to better supervision of the purchase and sale of all property dealt in on the exchanges, and by legislation to correct unethical and

[11] F.D.R., *Public Papers and Addresses*, II, 93–94.
[12] Huston Thompson to F.D.R., March 28, 1933, Roosevelt Papers.

unsafe practices on the part of officers and directors of banks and other corporations.

Evidence of the fiscal philosophy of Justice Louis D. Brandeis was visible in a reference to the ethics of banking stewardship. The goal of a legitimate relationship between fiduciary and depositor or investor was stated in simple Brandeisian terms, even to including the title of Brandeis' work within its context.[13]

What we seek is a return to a clearer understanding of the ancient truth that those who manage banks, corporations, and other agencies handling or using other people's money are trustees acting for others.

Here was no propitiating the financial community; the National Recovery Administration had no financial counterpart. No bankers were to write their own code of business practices, no investment houses or stockbrokers were urged voluntarily to agree on commission price levels for their services. The world of finance was not to be granted any of the self-policing privileges that business was to receive. It had something more than poor judgment to answer for; its lack of fiduciary integrity and its unethical greediness were too clearly and too recently a matter of public record.

The administration bill embodying these stern concepts was in the hands of House and Senate leaders as the President spoke. Introduced in the Senate that same day by Senator Joseph T. Robinson of Arkansas on behalf of Senator Henry F. Ashurst of Arizona, S. 875 was referred at first to the Committee on the Judiciary. After a rather testy reminder from Democratic Senator Duncan U. Fletcher of Florida that his committee had been carrying on a lengthy investigation in the field of investors and investments, the reference of the bill was changed to the Committee on Banking and Currency under the Floridian's chairmanship.[14]

The same legislation—a bill "to provide for the furnishing of information and the supervision of traffic in investment se-

[13] Brandeis, *Other People's Money.*
[14] *Congressional Record,* 73 Cong., 1 Sess., LXXVII, Part I, 1019–20.

curities in interstate commerce"—was introduced simultaneously in the House by Democrat Sam Rayburn of Texas and referred to his Committee on Interstate and Foreign Commerce as H.R. 4314.[15]

Prepared by Huston Thompson, who had been suggested for the task by Roosevelt cabinet members Cummings and Roper, the bill called for the regulation of securities by the FTC without mention of the stock and commodity exchanges. Its shortcomings in financial knowledge and in statute draftsmanship quickly became apparent to committee members in the hearings that got under way. The bill was so vaguely worded that even securities already issued and outstanding would be affected. No exemptions were provided for municipal issues or for the most inconsequential private offering of securities. Further, it flatly violated the President's warning that no such legislation could constitute a governmental guarantee of the issuing corporations' economic health.

Thompson's testimony was largely confined to the longfelt need for such legislation rather than to a specific defense of the bill under consideration. In his opinion Belgium had the best legislation for the preservation of security purchasers' rights, and he commented favorably on the strictness of similar German statutes. He stated that "the United States is farther behind than any other civilized nation . . . with respect to preserving the rights of purchasers of securities."[16] Thompson made a strong presentation for modeling legislation after the British Companies Act, impressing committee members with the case of Lord Kylsant, who had recently been sent to prison for failing to give certain information that the British Companies Act required in the issuance of securities.[17]

[15] *Ibid.*, p. 1006.

[16] House, *Federal Securities Act*, p. 9.

[17] Head of the Royal Mail Steam Packet Co., and the richest shipowner in the world, Lord Kylsant had offered a new security issue to stockholders without telling them that dividends had been paid out of nonrecurring reserve funds and that the company was actually operating at a loss (*Review of Reviews*, LXXXIX, No. 3 [March, 1934], 18).

As amended in 1929, the British act established liability for the securities issuer who made an untrue statement on the prospectus offered to customers, but the British courts sometimes interpreted this in the light of omissions of fact, as in the case of Lord Kylsant.

Another witness whose testimony was repeated before both House and Senate committees was Robert E. Healy, chief counsel for the Federal Trade Commission. The FTC itself, in a memorandum prepared by Baldwin B. Bane, indicated a preference for the House version of the bill, although Healy preferred the more stringent Senate draft.[18] Healy, an outspoken native of Vermont, and previously an associate justice of that state's supreme court, showed Congressmen that much of the corporate information required by H.R. 4314 and S. 875 was even less than that asked for by the New York Stock Exchange and the New York Curb Exchange for their membership listings. Healy put his finger on another weak spot in the proposed bill by asking the committees to give the power to apply for injunctions against transgressors directly to the FTC rather than require that agency to go through the Attorney General's office. In direct and forceful language Judge Healy questioned this unwise division of responsibility. Such a "buck-passing opportunity" meant to Healy the loss of the driving power that an effectively regulatory body must possess. Judge Healy's suggestion that required information as to corporate assets and liabilities be left up to the regulating agency to prescribe led to the flexible workings of the future Securities and Exchange Commission, and undoubtedly contributed to his selection as one of its first commissioners the following year.[19]

The wide range of shortcomings visible in the bill worried the astute chairman of the House group, Sam Rayburn of Texas. Its legal draftsmanship caused friendly committee members to question its workability, and it was clear to the chairman that it would not do the job that the President had in mind. Raised in the rural red-clay area of northeastern Texas in an atmosphere tinged with Populist thought, Sam Rayburn had no fear of economic, and particularly financial, reform, although his chief Congressional interests were in railroad and

[18] Told to author in interview with Baldwin B. Bane, Washington, D.C., July 20, 1959. Mr. Bane became chief of the FTC's Securities Division, and then moved to the new Securities and Exchange Commission as one of its division heads.

[19] House, *Federal Securities Act*, pp. 234, 241, 235.

transportation legislation.[20] He had, in fact, attempted un-
successfully some years before to introduce legislation regulating the securities issues of railroads through the Interstate
Commerce Commission. Rayburn was in accord with the spirit
and aim of the bill but worried that its workmanship might
jeopardize the results desired. A clean, new bill seemed the
best solution.

Raymond Moley, with his "roving commission to watch over
the formulation of legislation" direct from the Boss, was the
obvious source from which to request the entirely new bill
Rayburn decided on.[21] The recipient of Moley's call for aid,
in turn, was Felix Frankfurter of Harvard Law School, an old
and valued acquaintance of Roosevelt, whose stated convictions
on regulatory government and unquestioned legal abilities
made him a logical choice to supervise the drafting of such
legislation. Frankfurter appeared in Washington in early
April with two of the many protégés he was enthusiastically
to project into the New Deal. They were introduced as James
McCauley Landis, a brilliant young Harvard Law School professor, and Benjamin Victor Cohen, a young attorney with considerable skill in legal draftsmanship and a knowledge of the
British Companies Act. Work was immediately begun on the
drafting of a new bill for the House committee chairman, with
Frankfurter contributing suggestions and watchful supervision.

A Senate report on the bill under consideration in that
chamber indicated a strong committee stand for fixing the
responsibility of untruths in security issues. Having asked itself the question whether ignorance of an untruth should ex-
cuse the corporate director and thus leave the loss with the
buyer of the corporate stock, the Committee on Banking and
Currency did not attempt to evade the answer. "It is familiar
legal principle that he should bear the loss who has the opportunity to learn the truth and has allowed untruths to be
published and relied upon." Not the buyer of the stock, who

[20] Tucker, p. 49. See also *Current Biography, 1940,* p. 673; Moley, *Twenty-
Seven Masters of Politics,* pp. 242–43.
[21] Moley, *After Seven Years,* p. 166.

must rely on what he is told, but the person "who occupies a position of trust in the issuing corporation" should be the one who suffers any loss, the report concluded.[22]

By the time the Senate committee had ended its lengthier hearings and amended the bill accordingly, Rayburn's House group had received the new administration-blessed legislation and introduced it as H.R. 5480.[23] Without even pausing for further committee hearings, Rayburn whipped the new bill through the House with consummate skill and speed.

The discrepancies between the language of the Senate version and that of the new Rayburn bill were explained by Senator Fletcher to his colleagues as not denoting "any very serious difference." Chief among the existing differences were the House insistence on a thirty-day wait after registration before issuing any securities, to which there was some Senate objection, and distinctions regarding the limitation of liability to be imposed on corporate directors. The latter regulation was distinguished in the Senate version by an unlimited liability, regardless of good faith or competency, whereas H.R. 5480 followed the British Companies Act by measuring liability more in terms of the exercise of reasonable care. The Senate, at Fletcher's suggestion, appended the language of the Senate bill to the House title, and conferees from both chambers met to reconcile the two versions.[24]

Comment from press and periodical alike singled out the differences that Senator Fletcher had cautiously indicated between the Senate and House bills. They were not inclined to agree with him that such differences were not very serious, however. A strong protest was registered with the Senate by Henry I. Harriman, president of the Chamber of Commerce of the United States. The Senate measure, Harriman said, was "undesirable and impractical." Some objectionable features in the legislation, he conceded, had now been "eliminated or clarified in the House bill." [25]

[22] Senate, *Regulation of Securities,* Report No. 47 on S. 875.
[23] *Congressional Record,* LXXVII, Part III, 2838.
[24] *Ibid.,* pp. 2979, 3000.
[25] New York *Times,* May 4, 1933.

Financial writers in *Barron's* agreed that the House bill was "immeasurably better and more workable." Its attempt to "prevent and punish fraud" was lauded, while the "burden of exactions" incorporated in the Senate bill was clearly of a "punitive nature." [26]

Opponents of the proposed legislation fell largely into two categories: those who had objections to specific portions of the House or Senate bill, and those who, wanting no such legislation at all, had expressed over the years general approval of any intent to eliminate fraud while offering vociferous objections to each specific bill introduced. Organizations and individuals in the first category were given considerable opportunity to be heard by committees of both houses. Their testimony and objections were, as Senator Fletcher freely admitted, responsible for considerable revision in both bills. The Florida Senator reserved his most heated remarks for those organizations and groups that were the adamant objectors to all legislation. Prominent among these were "certain classes of so-called 'investment bankers.' " Their telegrams of instruction to their members stated in part that while the intent of Federal legislation was to be approved, both bills as drafted were to be classed as unworkable and constituting "a serious menace to industry." An organization issuing similar instructions was the United States Chamber of Commerce. As read on the Senate floor, a communication from this group prescribed to certain of its members the language in which objections to Congress should be couched:

You are in sympathy with the intent of Congress to regulate the issuance of securities but believe both bills (giving their numbers), as drafted, are unworkable and also are a serious menace to industry and business generally.[27]

Senator Fletcher asked to have his indignant letter to President Harriman of the United States Chamber of Commerce printed in the record. Since many of his colleagues had received

[26] *Barron's*, May 8, 1933, p. 10.
[27] *Congressional Record*, LXXVII, Part IV, 3801.

telegrams, Senator Fletcher pointed out that such objections had only a perpetual postponement of all such legislation as their motive, and urged quick action to get the conferees' bill on the statute books.

While both House and Senate were considering the Rayburn-Fletcher bills, another important function of the elderly Floridian proceeded at quickened tempo. Drawing more of the attention of the press because of its sensationalism, it both added and detracted from his efforts on the Senate version of the "Truth-in-Securities" bill. This was the investigation being carried on by a subcommittee of the Banking and Currency membership, also chaired by Duncan U. Fletcher, into stock exchange and allied financial practices. Its tremendous demands on Senator Fletcher's time and energies were in part fulfilled at the expense of his supervision of the Senate's bill. At the same time, the investigation's shocking headlines were very much in the public eye, and the record it was compiling of the nation's financial corruption and malpractice was of inestimable value in documenting the need for further securities legislation. The Florida Senator's dignity and tenacity in this investigation, even though its counsel received chief credit, added to his prestige on Capitol Hill.

The inquiry into stock exchange practices had been initiated by Senate Resolution No. 84 of the Hoover administration's Seventy-second Congress, and was carried on and expanded with Roosevelt's support in the New Deal Seventy-third Congress under Senate Resolutions Nos. 56 and 97.[28] Its chairman in the lame-duck days of the Hoover administration was Republican Senator Peter Norbeck of South Dakota, whose partisan status was described as that of "a prairie Republican—meaning one half Democratic, and one half other ingredients." [29] His dogged persistence in pursuing the inquiry led to the hiring of Ferdinand D. Pecora, an intense young

[28] Senate, *Stock Exchange Practices*, p. 1.
[29] Flynn, "The Marines Land in Wall Street," p. 149.

New York City prosecutor, after William A. Gray, the sub-committee's previous counsel, decided to resign in January, 1933. Pecora, who had already gained a measure of national fame in the securities field for his bucket-shop prosecutions as assistant district attorney of New York, was described as "the most brilliant cross-examiner in New York" by Bainbridge Colby, former Secretary of State in Wilson's cabinet.[30]

The tremendous tide of Roosevelt votes in the November, 1932, elections and the consequent Democratic flood in the Senate carried Duncan Upshaw Fletcher of Florida, beginning his fifth consecutive term in the Senate, to the chairmanship of the Banking and Currency Committee and its investigative subcommittee. Fletcher retained Pecora, and the inquiry into Wall Street's peculations and economic influence took on added sharpness and intensity.

The senior Senator from Florida had a background of public service at both state and municipal levels. As a young Florida liberal in 1892, Fletcher took his seat in the state legislature from Duval County, in the northeastern corner of the state. Presaging the advent of the Populist party, the Ocala convention of the Farmers' Alliance in 1890 had called for means to get credit to the hard-pressed farmers and to halt the speculative trading in commodity futures.[31] The cotton economy of northern Florida differed in no respect from that of neighboring Southern states, and membership in the Farmers' Alliance, which militantly opposed the financial domination of agriculture, composed nearly half the voting population of Florida.[32]

Although not a member of the Alliance, Fletcher sympathized with and backed their views on commodity speculation, and had distinguished himself in the state legislature by sponsoring statutes to permit the public ownership of utilities in his home city of Jacksonville. While city councilman and mayor

[30] San Francisco *Chronicle*, Feb. 3, 1938.
[31] Proctor, pp. 161 ff.
[32] Knauss, p. 304.

of that city in subsequent years, he had worked tirelessly in the field of public improvements and municipal ownership.[33] Because of this background, President Wilson in 1913 had appointed him chairman of a United States commission to study the cooperative land-mortgage banks and the cooperative rural credit unions of European countries.[34]

Now, despite his seventy-four years, Senator Fletcher aggressively pursued the investigation of the nation's finances and its more questionable financial leaders. He was motivated by more than partisan loyalties. Senator Carter Glass, jealous of any activity that trespassed on the field of banking, which he considered his own unchallengeable domain, attacked the subcommittee investigator, Ferdinand Pecora. The minutes of the subcommittee, Glass asserted, did not show that Pecora had ever been employed as counsel. Senator Fletcher, in outspoken language "punctuated by vigorous vertical swings of his right arm," astounded and impressed his colleagues and observers with his fervent defense of Pecora and with his implied criticism of the formidable Senator Glass.[35] The dramatic content of the investigation and the relentless and skillful tactics of the subcommittee's chief counsel caused the proceedings to be popularly known as the Pecora Investigation (a slip, hastily corrected, that even Tom Corcoran was guilty of in testifying before the Rayburn House Committee). Yet Fletcher gained respect and added prestige by consistently backing Pecora in the search for evidence that was to mean sitting "day after day through the greater part of fifteen months in sleepless vigilance at hearings." [36]

Less than two weeks before the New Deal inauguration date of March 4 the subcommittee had spread out before the public's shocked gaze the squalid corporate details of the National City Bank of New York. Charles E. Mitchell, the chairman, whose resignation was quickly accepted by other members of

[33] *National Cyclopedia of American Biography*, 42 vols. (New York, 1950), XXXV, 178.
[34] Congress, *Biographical Directory of the American Congress*, p. 1165.
[35] New York *Herald Tribune*, May 27, 1933.
[36] Flynn, "The Marines Land in Wall Street," p. 149.

the bank's board of directors, related how the bank officers had loaned themselves $2.4 million, largely without collateral, to make purchases of the bank's own stock.[37] These details, plus Mitchell's spurious sale to a relative in 1929 of 18,000 shares of National City Bank stock for $2.8 million in order to avoid payment of income tax, drew complete editorial silence from the leading journals of New York City. Conservative papers in Senator Fletcher's own state of Florida, such as the leading journals of Miami, Tampa, and Jacksonville, also ignored editorially the subcommittee's revelations, as did much of the national press. Journals such as the San Francisco *Chronicle* and the Chicago *Daily Tribune* carried the story of Mitchell's resignation but did not comment editorially or even report the investigation proceedings. The Houston *Post* was content to use abbreviated accounts of the income tax evasion details.[38] One of the few exceptions was the Denver *Rocky Mountain News,* which prominently reported the National City Bank's part in the sale of its dubious Peruvian bonds and its unsecured loans to bank officers, as well as the details of its president's financial activities. It was ample evidence, this journal stated editorially, to warrant pressing for amendments to the banking laws.[39]

As a home-town boy and a local institution, Mitchell and the National City Bank drew thorough coverage from the New York City press, despite the notable absence of editorial comment. Not until the closing days of the Mitchell testimony did the New York *Herald Tribune* agree that Mitchell had done right to resign. Its reasons, however, were models of euphemism: the disclosures had "impaired confidence in his stewardship"; his "errors in judgement" were simply inherent in his "good salesman" philosophy.[40] One newspaper, the *Nation* noted, evidently spoke for the many silent ones. This was the New York *Evening Post,* which reacted editorially by

[37] New York *Times,* Feb. 22–23, 1933.
[38] San Francisco *Chronicle,* Chicago *Daily Tribune,* and Houston *Post,* Feb. 22–28, 1933.
[39] Denver *Rocky Mountain News,* Feb. 23–28, 1933.
[40] New York *Herald Tribune,* Feb. 22–28, 1933.

denouncing the Senate for having "done nothing to restore public confidence." The Senate's "revelations . . . cannot be ignored," the *Post* continued, although "they break the faith of the people in their financial leaders." [41]

In any case, the Senate subcommittee inquiry continued to provoke front-page news. The trail led on to Rockefeller's Chase National Bank and its more equable president, Winthrop Aldrich. It was Aldrich, whose views showed more awareness of public and Congressional sentiment than did those of his colleagues, who was generally credited with the astute maneuvering that brought the titanic firm of J. P. Morgan and Company within range of the subcommittee's questions. He accomplished this by announcing the voluntary divorce of Chase National Bank from its security affiliate. At the same time Aldrich pointed out to the subcommittee the indistinct but tempting target of J. P. Morgan and other private bankers whose tremendous deposits were handled without any public statements or supervision of any kind.[42] Diverted by this gambit and by the magic of the J. P. Morgan name, the Senate promptly expanded its investigative powers to include the preserves of private banking as well. The subcommittee's inquiry thereby reached new heights of fame by providing the world with a picture of the second-generation Morgan in the rather intimate company of a blonde female midget, whom an enterprising circus press agent had deftly plopped into the morning-trousered Morgan lap as the hearings opened.[43] The midget, whom J. P. Morgan inscrutably regarded on the front pages of the nation's press the following day, could conceivably have been symbolic of the House of Morgan's stature after the sharp-edged Pecora queries had carved its public image down to a considerably less than colossal figure.

After trunkloads of evidence had been hauled in under Justice Department guard, the relentless questioning of committee counsel Pecora exposed the so-called favored list of

[41] *Nation*, March 8, 1933, p. 249.
[42] *Business Week*, April 12, 1933, p. 12.
[43] New York *Times*, May 24, 1933.

the Morgan "friends," containing the names of judges, political leaders, and cabinet members, as well as bankers and industrialists, who received shares of stock in the Morgan holding company, the Alleghany Corporation. The stock was distributed at the firm's cost of $20 per share at a time when the market price was $35–$37 per share. The recipient was advised in the usual accompanying letter that there were "no strings attached" and that he might sell the 1,000- or 2,000-share blocks, which comprised the average distribution, whenever he wished. Further disclosures revealed that J. P. Morgan and many of the firm had managed to avoid, through legal means, payment of income tax on many millions of dollars over a period of several years.[44] Most newspapers treated the House of Morgan with due deference, but only the Hearst papers' Edwin C. Hill carried eulogy to the point of bravely likening the thick-necked Morgan to Lorenzo the Magnificent, and of angrily comparing Pecora's examination of Morgan to that of a schoolboy quizzing Einstein on the solar system.[45]

While these were perhaps the most sensational disclosures, due partly to the eminence of the Morgan name, they largely duplicated previously exposed financial attitudes and methods. In pointing out that the securities act would effectively combat any further distribution of new securities at cut-rate prices simply by its publicity provisions, the New York *Times* had in mind the most recent such disclosures. However, it properly added that the provisions of the bill, then in its last stages of approval, were "based principally on findings from other investigations of stock and bond sales conducted by the Senate Banking and Currency Committee for the past year." [46]

The practice of watering new issues of securities based on corporate reorganizations also received further and more emphatic treatment at this stage of the investigation. In forming their newest holding company, the United Corporation, J. P. Morgan and Company had assembled securities with a market

[44] *Ibid.,* May 25–31, 1933.
[45] *Nation,* June 7, 1933, p. 633.
[46] New York *Times,* May 27, 1933.

value of $69 million and turned them over to the new corporation to be written up as assets of $122 million. This constituted, in John T. Flynn's opinion, $53 million in watered value, almost precisely similar to the operations of the elder Morgan in forming the United States Steel Corporation a generation earlier.[47]

Although many of the specific abuses in the Morgan and Company testimony were publicized only a few days before the House and Senate conferees finished the securities bill, methods to curb such practices as the artificial inflation of the assets supporting a new securities issue were already incorporated in the full publicity provisions of the new legislation. Earlier disclosures, such as the revelations the previous February of the National City Bank officers' unsecured loans, had already served to incorporate detailed accounting requirements and directorial responsibility in the legislation being prepared.

Other fields profited by what had originally started out as a stock exchange inquiry. The divorce of investment bankers from their security-selling affiliates, as dramatically announced by Chase National Bank's new head, Winthrop Aldrich, was legally consummated and applied nationally in the Glass-Steagall bill of 1933. The disclosures of legal, albeit shocking, evasions of income tax payments by Charles E. Mitchell, J. P. Morgan, and many others, were channeled into subsequent tax legislation. In addition to many specific abuses, the hearings produced an atmosphere and an aura that were of undeniable benefit to the deliberations of both Congressional committees. The accumulation of the evidence of arrogant misuse of depositors' funds, of blatant financial privilege for the favored few, and the complete absence of any regard for the fiduciary responsibility that financial leaders yet claimed as their chief distinction were anger-provoking material common to all. No one could attend the Pecora Investigation, nor could the public follow the hearings in the press, without being convinced

[47] *Nation,* June 14, 1933, p. 125.

beyond all doubt that financial leaders and spokesmen thought of themselves as distinct from the rest of the nation. Their sovereign command of finance was, quite clearly, being invaded by an unduly inquisitive and rather insubordinate Federal government. Finally, the bulk of more than 12,000 printed pages containing the evidence of the financial community's own leaders was more than any opposition could effectively overcome.[48] The investment bankers who pleaded before Congressional committees for some amelioration of the bill's restrictions found they had been damned out of the mouths of their own fellows.

In the House report supporting the new bill, committee members succinctly stated the need for such legislation in their opening words:

During the post-war decade some fifty billion dollars of new securities were floated in the United States. Fully half or twenty-five billion dollars worth of securities floated during this period have been proved to be worthless.[49]

The conferee report was quickly adopted by the House and then passed by the Senate. The original differences concerning the thirty-day period after registration and the area and extent of liability were adjusted to the satisfaction of both bodies. The Senate, which objected to the first feature, had obtained a compromise figure of twenty days that had to elapse after registration before a security issue could be offered for sale.[50] If during that time the regulating agency found some misstatement in the registration, a stop order prohibiting the sale could be issued. Although no waiting period was required in the British Companies Act, proponents of the idea reminded its critics that in Great Britain, ". . . except for a very unusual Hatry or Kylsant, the distribution of securities is a decorous, traditional business, offering its wares only to in-

[48] Senate, *Stock Exchange Practices*, p. 3.
[49] House, *Federal Supervision of the Traffic in Investment Securities in Interstate Commerce*, p. 2.
[50] *Congressional Record*, LXXVII, Part IV, 3901.

stitutions and wary family solicitors." [51] The enforced wait was considered a necessary curb on American high-pressure tactics. In addition, it enabled the agency to examine the prospectus first, rather than go through the awkward procedure of recalling a fraudulent issue later.

The Senate in turn had yielded somewhat on the severity of the liability imposed on corporate directors, but the area of the liability had been considerably expanded. A majority of the corporate directors still must sign the registration statement and be liable thereby, but more classes of persons must share their liability. Unlike its British predecessor, liability was now extended beyond the corporate directors to include "experts such as accountants, appraisers and engineers who give the authority of their names" in the registration statement.[52]

H.R. 5480 became Public Law 22, Seventy-third Congress, after President Roosevelt's signature on May 27, 1933.[53] In signing the "Rayburn-Fletcher Bill," as he referred to the Securities Act of 1933, Roosevelt called the public's attention to the fact that the measure "at last translates some elementary standards of right and wrong into law." It will not, he warned, be "insurance against errors of judgement," since this "is the function of no Government." But it will "require full disclosure of all the private interests . . . who seek to sell securities to the public," and will also "safeguard against the abuses of high pressure salesmanship in security flotations." The President predicted that further legislation would be forthcoming by referring to the new law as one of the "steps in a program to restore some old-fashioned standards of rectitude." [54]

Reaction to the bill was largely discounted in advance. Much of the comment both pro and con had been addressed to the bill as it emerged from the joint Congressional conferences, and it retained the same form when it was enacted into law.

[51] Flexner, p. 236.
[52] *Congressional Record*, LXXVII, Part IV, 3902.
[53] *Ibid.*, Part V, p. 5195.
[54] F.D.R., *Public Papers and Addresses*, II, 214.

The liberal journals of opinion, having looked upon the bill, pronounced it generally good. The *New Republic* considered it "an immense improvement" over the earlier versions, and thought it bore "marks of expert craftsmanship." [55] John T. Flynn, the flail of Wall Street, had earlier complained that what was actually needed was legislation to reveal corporate operations after their stock was sold, and not just before. However, the importance of the new bill, he thought, was based in the fact that "the burden of proof no longer lies upon the claimant for damages, but upon . . . the issuer or seller of the security." Flynn still considered that the legislation offered more protection to bondholders than to stockholders, since stock was not publicly offered but "sold to insiders" and then to the public later through the Stock Exchange.[56]

Business and financial periodicals had undergone a wide variety of reactions. The initial idea of antifraud legislation drew nearly unanimous praise. Then the perilous generalities of the Thompson version of the Senate bill had set off a chorus of alarmed outcries, which were only quieted when the final bill was seen to be largely the House version. After final passage of the act, reaction ranged from a mild agreement over the bill's principles to a restrained enthusiasm. The old and new versions of the bill were "not entirely dissimilar" in any event, *Barron's* said in an attitude expressing reasonable satisfaction.[57] *Business Week* actively welcomed the new legislation. "It wraps red tape around the issuing business but in a good cause," this periodical commented philosophically. Contrary to much adverse comment later, *Business Week* thought the Securities Act "does not seriously interfere with present [securities] marketing channels." In an attitude foreshadowing the contemporary feeling that such legislation is actually a protection for the legitimate bond houses and stock brokers, this journal also pointed out that the bill protected responsible underwriting houses from the competition of "fly-by-night gentry." In an editorial

[55] *New Republic*, May 24, 1933, p. 30.
[56] *Ibid.*, May 10, 1933, p. 364; July 5, 1933, p. 195; May 31, 1933, p. 70.
[57] *Barron's*, May 29, 1933, p. 4.

discussion several weeks later on investment banking, it reminded its readers that "the securities bill just made law the cures of certain abuses," and asked whether it went far enough.[58]

Forbes's comment earlier in the year was typical of a widespread feeling. A need for fixing responsibility, for some regulatory laws, was agreed upon, but care must be taken "to guard against strangulating legitimate new financing." The substitution of most of the House provisions regarding liability for those of the Senate drew a grudging "more workable" from the *Wall Street Journal,* and the entire legislative effort was admitted to be "passably good." [59]

Some resentment regarding the whole idea of calling corporate officials to accountability for their securities issues still remained. The New York *Herald Tribune* maintained a diehard attitude, insisting that the entire corporate structure was in jeopardy. A "misstatement" on the registration statement, the paper warned editorially, could enable a plaintiff to sue for some subsequent loss even though the company's error should be "on the conservative side." [60]

Interpreting the bill for the Wall Street clientele of Sullivan and Cromwell, one of that firm's foremost counselors, Arthur H. Dean, declared that the Securities Act was far less workable yet contained more drastic civil liability provisions than the British Companies Act. Dean, who had frequently submitted testimony at the bill's various hearings, thought the Securities Act "unduly harsh" in a provision that would permit a refund of the purchase price "if there has been an error which may only have affected the value of the securities by one or two points." [61]

Those who had played a part in getting the legislation introduced were less than fully satisfied with the results. Felix Frankfurter had written some months previously that "poignant experience has made us realize the public implications of interests treated heretofore as private." Such interests, he stated, "must be stripped of many of their past immunities and subjected to

[58] *Business Week,* May 24, 1933, p. 6; June 7, 1933, p. 6.
[59] *Forbes,* April 15, 1933, p. 3; *Wall Street Journal,* May 25, 1933.
[60] New York *Herald Tribune,* May 20, 1933.
[61] Dean, p. 101.

appropriate responsibility." However, the Securities Act as passed was to him a "belated and conservative attempt to curb the recurrence of old abuses . . ."[62] Frankfurter, whose contribution in the formation of the act was one of several acknowledged on the floor of Congress by House Chairman Sam Rayburn,[63] felt that the new act mainly required an attitude of corporate responsibility commensurate with the "rigorous liability" it imposed before it could become effective. "The Act will never protect the gullible unless it alters the premises of the sophisticated." He was hopeful, however, that the bill would aid in bringing about new business habits by this new definition of standards. The twenty-day "cooling period" particularly drew Frankfurter's praise, since "the social function of investment banking is betrayed by speed and secretiveness."[64]

Adolf A. Berle, Jr., writing on the subject of high finance several months after the Securities Act was passed, indicated a disappointment that was fundamentally directed at the financial system rather than specific shortcomings of the bill itself. To Berle, one of the original Brain Trusters, investment bankers still dominated the financial scene to an unhealthy degree, and the control of new corporate security issues that had slipped from their grasp in the 1920's had lately been regained through devices such as the investment trust and the pyramid holding company. The Securities Act as the national equivalent of the state blue-sky laws thus was inadequate, Berle thought, because it excluded only fraudulent finance. The problem of power arising from financial control exercised by investment bankers was not solved, since the fundamentals remained unchanged even though the Securities Act served to clean up many financial practices and ethics.[65]

Raymond Moley, who, as the original liaison agent for Roosevelt, brought in Frankfurter and his protégés Cohen and Landis to aid in writing the bill, considered it somewhat "unsound"

[62] Frankfurter, "Social Issues Before the Supreme Court," p. 480, and "The Federal Securities Act," p. 54.
[63] Congressional Record, LXXVII, Part III, 2916.
[64] Frankfurter, "The Federal Securities Act," pp. 109, 55.
[65] Berle, "High Finance: Master or Servant?" pp. 40–41, 42.

in a practical sense. By this he meant that although the act was "a fine job" and appropriate as a "long-time measure," it lacked the necessary sweet reasonableness that he thought might have enlisted the warm-hearted support of the corporation lawyers and bankers of the country. Moley made no mention of the liability provisions that were the chief cause of Wall Street complaint, stating merely that these groups found the act "excessively cumbersome." [66] His argument that recovery was retarded and that new stock issues were shelved solely because the country's corporation lawyers considered the act "cumbersome" lost thereby much of its effectiveness.

Although the bill was avowedly part of Roosevelt's long-range program for reform in the field of securities and banking, and had been clearly forecast as such in the presidential campaign and before, the administration lost no opportunity to link the idea of business recovery with fundamental reform as its necessary predecessor. When he signed the bill into law, Roosevelt stated this conviction:

If the country is to flourish, capital must be invested in enterprise. But those who seek to draw upon other people's money must be wholly candid regarding the facts on which the investor's judgment is asked . . . Without such an ethical foundation, economic well-being cannot be achieved.[67]

In its effectiveness the bill fell somewhere between two viewpoints. One of these was the attitude regarding the responsibilities now placed on all corporate directors and underwriters for the truthfulness of their new stock registration certificates. Arthur H. Dean expressed this in the cliché currently popular in Wall Street, remarking that "it seems hardly necessary to burn down the house to exterminate the vermin." [68] This successfully epitomized the wounded feelings of the erstwhile fuglemen of the nation's finances, who now found themselves called to accountability rather than called on to lead the way.

An opposing attitude of disappointment was that the legis-

[66] Moley, *After Seven Years*, p. 183.
[67] F.D.R., *Public Papers and Addresses*, II, 214.
[68] Dean, p. 106.

lation had not been pushed far enough. This was characterized by objections such as those of Adolf A. Berle, Jr., that measures to inhibit the control of the nation's industrial finances by investment bankers would have been more appropriate than mere excision of the fraudulent aspects of the situation. Felix Frankfurter's disappointment with the Securities Act was expressed largely in admonitory tones warning that business morals must undergo a considerable change for the better to accompany effectively the self-disciplinary portions of the act. Even Frankfurter, however, recognized that the legislation of new standards would lead to the establishment of new business practices.

Most of the disappointment from this viewpoint, however, closely paralleled John T. Flynn's. His took the form of bitter criticism of the early and poorly constructed Senate version of the act. Because of this unworkability, Flynn claimed earlier that "the bankers rewrote the bill." But even as severe a critic as he was could still express his general approval of the final results, and could detail for his readers the vast importance of shift in the burden of proof from the claimant for damages to the actual issuer or seller of the security involved.[69]

A large part of the effectiveness of the bill was due to the earnest testimony before House and Senate committees of Robert E. Healy, chief counsel for the Federal Trade Commission.[70] Healy, experienced in the huge investigative operations then being carried out in the field of public utilities, warned his hearers that the FTC did not have the power to deal with an "Insull situation." More flexibility was needed in records and accounting documents that might be required by the commission, and more direct injunctive power was necessary, Healy thought.[71] Both committees queried Healy at length on the advisability of legislating specific rules and regulation, or of giving such residual powers to the commission itself. Section

[69] *New Republic,* April 26, 1933, p. 309; July 5, 1933, p. 195.
[70] Hereafter referred to as FTC.
[71] House, *Federal Securities Act,* pp. 240, 235, 241.

19(a) of the act accordingly contained Healy's strong recommendation of the latter course of action, and Section 20(a) was written to give the commission power to apply for an injunction directly.[72]

Judge Healy's FTC experience thereby played an important part in preventing any rigidity of administrative fiat. Zealous and misguided attempts to legislate rules and regulations rather than let a regulatory body sublegislate the policy of Congress might have led to wrecking such a structure by an equally zealous reaction later. The injunctive process as it was finally written gave to the legislation a directness and a strength of action that was to set the tone for succeeding measures.

Healy was also responsible in part for the choice of the FTC as the administrating agent of the new act. The FTC did not have a strong regulatory record under the Harding-Coolidge-Hoover regimes. It did have, however, a recent outstanding investigation to its credit. This was the report in ninety-odd volumes on the activities of the nation's utilities companies and their holding company affiliates. Vigorously prosecuted by Judge Healy, the investigation general counsel, it became one of the most condemnatory reports ever submitted to Congress, and in a field dear to Roosevelt's heart. Additionally, the drafters of the Securities Act and its Congressional leaders were given the distinct impression that the administration intended to restaff and reinvigorate the FTC.[73]

The Securities Act of 1933 became the first Federal statute enacted in the field of securities regulation. As such, it was the inheritor of centuries of Anglo-Saxon experience, of numerous experimental state laws, and of the continual efforts of previous Congresses and individuals to pass such needed legislation. This heritage was transformed by President Roosevelt and his legislative and administrative assistants into one of the most carefully prepared pieces of legislation in the early New Deal, and became the important forerunner of more ambitious

[72] U.S. *Statutes at Large*, XLVII, Part I, 85, 86.
[73] Landis, "The Legislative History of the Securities Act of 1933," p. 34n.

efforts in the regulation of socially expensive securities and exchange abuses.

The new act was "not an emergency measure, but a permanent addition to our regulatory legislation." [74] This perceptive comment came from Chairman March of the FTC. It was evoked largely by the favorable trend of regulatory legislation that would, unknown to Chairman March, have an even more successful vehicle thirteen months later in the Securities and Exchange Commission.

[74] New York *Times,* May 28, 1933.

CHAPTER THREE

THE SECURITIES EXCHANGE ACT OF 1934

IT HAD BEEN the presidential intent to initiate legislation simultaneously in the fields of securities issuance and stock market regulation. The earliest drafting of a bill incorporating both measures had failed, however, because of the inability of Samuel Untermeyer, of Pujo investigation fame, and Huston Thompson, former FTC member, to work together. The latter's greatly amended efforts at securities control, which excluded any exchange regulations, formed the only legislative material ready to be acted on in the hectic Hundred Days of early 1933. Roosevelt indicated to both Congress and the public, however, that the idea of "Truth in Securities" was but one step in the general program, and should accordingly be followed by further legislation designed to supervise the nation's commodities and stock markets.[1]

Efforts toward a stock market bill originated from several sources. In the winter of 1933, Roosevelt appointed a committee through Secretary of Commerce Daniel C. Roper, which had Assistant Secretary of Commerce John Dickinson as its chairman. It included Adolf A. Berle, Jr., James M. Landis of the FTC, and two Wall Street attorneys, Arthur H. Dean and Henry J. Richardson.[2] The committee was to inquire into

[1] F.D.R., *Public Papers and Addresses,* I, 682–83.
[2] Senate, *Stock Exchange Regulation.*

the practicality of regulating the stock exchanges, carrying on its surveys concurrently with the booming Pecora Investigation and cooperating with that group. Limitation of its efforts to the stock market was the result of a memorandum to the President recommending that legislation affecting the commodities exchange be dealt with separately and shortly afterward, on the grounds that the dissimilarity of problems required different technical experts and that it would be wise not to permit any consolidation of opposition against a multiple-purpose bill.[3]

The Roper Report, as it was commonly referred to, was a mild bit of regulation on the face of it, with a definite Wall Street point of view. Landis and Berle could have been expected to temper this trend considerably, but the deciding voice then became that of Chairman Dickinson. His subsequent testimony during the House Interstate Commerce Committee hearings, in which he sharply and lengthily opposed many of the provisions of the House bill, indicated clearly that he stood with the financial fraternity in matters of regulation.[4]

Submitted to the President in late January, 1934, the Roper Report called for a Federal licensing of all exchanges. Securities regulation would be further carried out through the constitutional control the Federal government already exercised over the United States mails, and also by use of the interstate commerce clause. Heart and soul of the report was the attitude, strongly expressed, that there be no statutory detailing of proposed rules and regulations for exchanges, but that these should be prescribed instead by an administrative agency "in accordance with the broad standards of the statute." The committee stated its belief and intent thus:

to enact a measure which will provide a system embodying a minimum of specific regulatory provisions in the statute itself and a maximum of discretionary powers of regulation in an administrative agency. This conclusion is based on the fact that while it is possible to outline legislation devised to correct known wrongs, it will be of little value tomorrow if it is not flexible enough to

[3] Memo to F.D.R. from James M. Landis, Feb. 8, 1934, Roosevelt Papers.
[4] House, *Stock Exchange Regulation,* pp. 505-25, 540-58.

meet new conditions immediately as they arise and demand attention in the public interest.[5]

The proposed administrative agency, the committee stated after reflection, had better not be the FTC, or even a new arm of the FTC. "Technical specialization in financial matters might dictate as the wisest course the setting up of a new and separate authority." Administration of the Securities Act of 1933 should also be vested in the new agency. The committee further proposed that a representative of the stock exchanges be drawn into the administrative agency "since the field covered is decidedly technical." [6]

The mildness of the report's suggestions evoked an equally mild response from spokesmen within the financial community. The New York Stock Exchange was "impressed with its temperate tone." Regarding the creation of a new Federal agency, the Exchange "had little to fear in such supervision," having already met the necessary requirements through its own rule changes.[7]

First glimmers of a new and beneficial role for such an agency again came from those large commission brokers who, with branch offices throughout the country, were more concerned with and more aware of public reaction to the business of purchasing securities than were the floor traders and specialists headed by Richard Whitney. This group recognized "confidence" as the feeling that the public normally held for its financial leaders, an attitude that had been severely battered by the recent disclosures of the Senate Banking and Currency Committee investigation. But the public, this group reasoned, would regard a government agency as a policing body that would guard against the recurrence of such abuses. "Just as the Hughes investigation into the insurance business twenty-five years ago was followed by a return of a public confidence in life insurance, the enactment of a bill establishing an agency

---

[5] Senate, *Stock Exchange Regulation*, pp. v, 6.
[6] *Ibid.*, p. 7.
[7] New York *Times*, Jan. 30, 1934.

to supervise the stock market might cause a similar revival in the securities markets." [8]

Another approach to new legislation came from the small group originally called on to draft the Securities Act. James M. Landis was a member of this group, which included Benjamin V. Cohen and a former Wall Street lawyer, Thomas G. Corcoran. Corcoran, a young Providence, Rhode Island, Irishman, had been a brilliant student at Brown University and Harvard Law School. As a favorite of Felix Frankfurter, he was able to achieve several worshipful years as legal secretary to that towering personality, Justice Oliver Wendell Holmes. He had also spent six years with a prominent Wall Street law firm before being recruited into the ranks of the New Deal as a Reconstruction Finance Corporation counsel. Benjamin Cohen was a sensitive and silent young man, an associate general counsel of the Public Works Administration, and already accounted a superb legal draftsman. Reputedly his association with Wall Street had been an entirely successful one; he had made a considerable fortune in stocks and then stepped out before the Great Crash. Corcoran's enthusiasm and legal brilliance paired with Cohen's masterful statutory draftsmanship made a formidable combination, and the team was increasingly called on by the administration to draft legislation and furnish aid and advice to hard-pressed administration leaders in House and Senate.

Raymond Moley relates that he called on Corcoran and Cohen to begin work on securities exchange legislation some time prior to the second session of the Seventy-third Congress.[9] Three other sources, however, are agreed that the bill-writing team was called in by Max Lowenthal of Pecora's staff.[10] John T. Flynn, who also worked for Pecora as a member of his investigating staff, relates that work began in late 1933, with preliminary drafts by two young lawyers, I. N. P. Stokes III and

[8] *Ibid.*
[9] Moley, *After Seven Years*, p. 284.
[10] Flynn, "The Marines Land in Wall Street," p. 150. See also "SEC," *Fortune*, p. 120; Alsop and Kintner, "The Battle of the Market-Place," p. 75.

Telford Taylor. In the ensuing revisions and rewriting Corcoran and Cohen—particularly Cohen—played major roles, with Landis as the most prominent adviser, aided by Pecora, Lowenthal, Flynn, and David Schenker.[11]

Early work on a securities exchange regulation bill included various legal briefs in which the constitutionality of the proposed legislation was tested and found to be valid. In briefs prepared by Noel T. Dowling and Walter Gellhorn of Columbia University and by the team of Thomas Corcoran and Benjamin Cohen, ample constitutional foundation was discovered. Both briefs referred to *McCulloch* v. *Maryland* as attesting the fiscal powers of the Federal government. The Dowling-Gellhorn memorandum cited John Marshall and the scope of the commerce clause as used in the national interest. The brief of the Corcoran-Cohen duo stressed the constitutional power to exercise necessary and proper control over credit practices that affect the activities and instrumentalities of the Federal government itself. Both reflected the Justice Holmes view that the Supreme Court "must consider what this country has become" in the interpretation of the Constitution. This is not a mechanical process, the Corcoran-Cohen brief averred, but rather the adaptation of organic law to the changing conditions and needs of a nation. Both memoranda exuded supreme confidence in the constitutional validity of legislation regulating the stock exchanges.[12]

On January 30, 1934, the Senate Banking and Currency Committee disclosed that it had directed Counsel Pecora to draft a bill regulating the stock exchanges, to be ready as soon as the current inquiry into the Detroit bank crash was concluded. A request by Richard Whitney that the committee hold separate conferences with stock exchange officials was declined. Asked whether the proposed bill would be along the lines of the presidential committee's report, Chairman Fletcher replied that such a decision rested with the members of the Senate

[11] Flynn, "The Marines Land in Wall Street," p. 151.
[12] SEC, "Memo Concerning Power of Congress . . . to Regulate Security Exchanges," pp. 3, 12, 13.

Banking and Currency Committee. Many of them, he added—referring to the idea of a separate agency with wide discretionary powers—were for direct and mandatory legislation.[13]

When President Roosevelt addressed a recommendation for such legislation to Congress in early February, he reminded its members that they had already performed useful services in protecting the investing public in its acquisition of securities. But there remained yet unchecked speculation that ran the scale from the individual's meager savings risked in a margin transaction to a "pool of individuals or corporations with large resources, often not their own, who sought by manipulation to raise or depress market quotations." Since the exchanges and their customers were in every part of the country, their business was a national one and a broad policy of national regulation was therefore required.

It is my belief that exchanges for dealing in securities and commodities are necessary and of definite value to our commercial and agricultural life. Nevertheless, it should be our national policy to restrict, as far as possible, the use of these exchanges for purely speculative operations.

I therefore recommend to the Congress enactment of legislation providing for the regulation by the Federal government of the operations of exchanges dealing in securities and commodities for the protection of investors, for the safeguarding of values, and so far as it may be possible, for the elimination of unnecessary, unwise and destructive speculation.[14]

The bills introduced into the Senate by Duncan U. Fletcher of Florida and into the House by Sam Rayburn of Texas were the fruits not of the Roper committee deliberations but of the Corcoran-Cohen-Pecora writings and conferences. They specifically referred to the FTC as the administrating agency, contained stringent prohibitions against manipulation of prices ("jiggling"), segregated the functions of broker, specialist, and dealer, and provided for 40-percent-margin requirements. Sena-

[13] New York *Times,* Jan. 31, 1934.
[14] F.D.R., *Public Papers and Addresses,* III, 90, 91.

tor Fletcher nevertheless referred to S. 2693 as a "moderate and middle-of-the-road program." Conceding that it would not seem so to many financial interests, he still considered that it contained "a number of measures less advanced than those favored by many members of Congress," and included himself among the latter group.[15]

The legislative restrictions proposed drew the immediate fire of a large segment of the press. The Pittsburgh *Post-Gazette* protested editorially that the provision for a segregation of investment bankers from the brokerage business would "force out of business the great majority of bond and brokerage houses." [16] The provisions for administration by the FTC drew heavy blasts. The "autocratic meddling" of an agency that the New York *Times* considered "not in the highest esteem of observant citizens" was regarded as purely mischievous. The "intricate machinery" of the stock exchanges, according to the *Times,* could only be supervised by those whose long experience in the securities field could be relied on to choose the regulations to be exercised.[17]

Both the Senate and House bills (which were the same) [18] were widely regarded as impractical and as deliberately punitive. The bills were "purposely made drastic" in the opinion of *Business Week,* although the periodical was the first to point out that this stringency left plenty of room in the bills for horse trading in their future modification.[19]

The New York Stock Exchange president, Richard Whitney, registered his institution's objections to the legislation in a variation of the carrot-and-stick technique. He announced ominously that following publication of the terms of the Fletcher-Rayburn bill, several Stock Exchange firms had refused to negotiate extension of their leases for their lower-Manhattan offices. Also, Whitney stated, trading was sure to

[15] *Congressional Record,* 73 Cong., 2 Sess., LXXVIII, Part II, 2265–72.
[16] *Ibid.,* Part III, p. 3024.
[17] New York *Times,* Feb. 12, 1934.
[18] House, *Stock Exchange Regulation,* p. 559.
[19] *Business Week,* Feb. 17, 1934.

be curtailed, and brokerage firms would have to reduce the number of their employees.[20]

Offsetting the tone of these statements was a personal memo to President Roosevelt informing him of several new regulations that the powerful Law Committee of the Exchange would recommend for immediate adoption.[21] Several days later Whitney publicly announced the adoption of these new Stock Exchange rules. In the future, members would not be permitted to take part in pool operations; no specialist might acquire any stock for which he was the specialist broker, nor could the specialist disclose information in regard to an order entrusted to him.[22]

The transgression of these regulations, however, and evidence in appalling detail of the Stock Exchange's unwillingness to regulate itself, were being offered the public that same day as a part of the Pecora Investigation. Under the circumstances President Whitney's statements can only be seen as an exercise of incredibly poor judgment or incredible arrogance, or more likely a combination of both.[23]

Ferdinand Pecora, attempting to get the New York Stock Exchange to take some action to restrict the pool operations of its own members, had received only a grudging promise to investigate. Several weeks later the Senate subcommittee received a letter from Exchange President Whitney stating that his investigation showed "no material deliberate improprieties" in transactions of the securities in question. Nor could the Stock Exchange investigators find any evidence of "activities

[20] New York *Times,* Feb. 14, 1934.

[21] Richard Whitney to F.D.R., Feb. 8, 1934, Roosevelt Papers.

[22] A specialist is a broker who confines his activities to a particular stock or to a few particular stocks, buying and selling only these securities. Other brokers who have orders either to buy or sell his stock place them with the specialist for execution. With his knowledge of existing bids and offers before they were executed, the specialist thus had inside information of enormous advantage. If he traded for his own account or for the account of pools with which he was associated, he was in a position to make a personal profit with a minimum of risk.

[23] A Capitol correspondent reported that he had learned from the Brain Trusters that "the stock exchange representatives are considered the dumbest business group, with the bankers next" (*Magazine of Wall Street,* March 31, 1934, p. 607).

which might have stimulated improperly the activity of these stocks." [24] The incredulous Pecora thereupon turned his own staff to the problem, picking as a prototype the stock of American Commercial Alcohol, which had undergone violent and suspicious fluctuations in the summer of 1933. Using records and files readily available to Stock Exchange authorities, Pecora's staff turned up ample evidence of the complete inability of the Stock Exchange to police itself and its members. This material was presented to the Senate subcommittee in public hearing on the same day Richard Whitney was uttering further soothing self-regulatory promises.

The outstanding disclosure of improper activities came from Russell R. Brown, chairman of the board of American Commercial Alcohol Corporation, who appeared before the Senate subcommittee with his associates and testified that four of the company's officials had acquired 25,000 newly issued shares in their own company without cost through dummy corporations. Enlisting the aid of a Wall Street brokerage firm and a renowned pool operator, "Sell 'Em" Ben Smith, the group stimulated a burgeoning activity in the stock. This was accomplished by the feat of numerous selling orders and buying orders, all, however, executed by the same group. In the public view this constituted unusual and hopeful activity; in reality it was simply a series of "wash sales"—transfers from one pocket to another. This frenzied stimulation proved later to have accounted for six times as many shares changing hands in the market as were in the entire company capitalization. With the use also of planted "estimates" of the stock's future earning power, the pool group drove up the price of American Commercial Alcohol from 20 in May, 1933, to about 90 in July. The group unloaded their own share of the stock near the peak, and the market price, with the pool support withdrawn, promptly sank back to under 30 in the space of four days, leaving the public holding the bag.[25] It was a well-publicized part of the summer market plunge that sent a flurry of letters

[24] Senate, *Stock Exchange Practices*, p. 56.
[25] *Ibid.*, pp. 57 ff., 61.

and telegrams to the White House, the general tenor of which was to demand the closing not only of the Stock Exchange but the grain exchanges as well to prevent further stock and commodities speculation.[26]

The sworn evidence implicating the Stock Exchange, its members, and many corporate officials was inescapable, Senator Fletcher told his colleagues on the Senate floor. Fletcher ridiculed Stock Exchange claims of self-regulation, pointing out that the market-rigging practices just revealed took place in 1933, "a year of alleged penitence and reform." A fellow committee member, millionaire Republican Senator James Couzens of Michigan, protested that Stock Exchange President Whitney had already sent out communications to some 875 industrialists and 1,370 brokers urging them to protest enactment of the bill. "There is just one central organization of propaganda," Couzens said, "and the propagandizing is being carried on before any hearings have really been had on the bill itself." [27]

Whitney warmly protested labeling the campaign he had inaugurated as propaganda. Regarding the minor crash of 1933, he insisted that speculation in alcohol stocks had nothing to do with it. Security prices actually rose "as a result of the abandonment of the gold standard." The collapse did not even start in the stock market, Whitney said, but in the grain market, where "prices had reached an unsound level." Their decline then "unsettled the stock market." [28]

The opposition to stock exchange regulation, for which Whitney acted as field marshal, was summoned up in widespread and formidable array. Not since the opposition to the railroad legislation of 1903, or to the Federal Reserve legislation of 1914, Raymond Moley wrote, had such a comparable conflict or such a mobilization of forces developed. The Stock Exchange president organized his forces through the thirty principal wire houses of the Exchange and their branches, and then through the presidents of the eighty outstanding com-

[26] Various communications to F.D.R., July, 1933, Roosevelt Papers.
[27] *Congressional Record*, LXXVIII, Part III, 3141.
[28] Washington *Post*, Feb. 24, 1934.

panies on the big board. Two essential points were made in the message relayed: that the FTC would be able to control all corporations in the United States, and that the bill itself would lead to the nationalization of all industry.[29]

The lower echelons were reached through the bogey of unemployment. A typical broker's message was that of Livingston and Company of New York City:

Re the Fletcher-Rayburn bill:

Are your employees alive to the fact that with the passage of this bill a great many of them would be out of employment?

Are they writing their Senator or Representative? If not, they should do so at once, using their own note paper, not the firm's paper, and writing in their own way, protesting the passage of the bill which will rob them of employment.[30]

Appeals to reconsider the entire idea of stock exchange regulation, or at least to modify the Fletcher-Rayburn bill drastically, quickly besieged both House and Senate committee hearings. Senator Hamilton F. Kean of New Jersey recorded a communication from the president of Monsanto Chemical Company warning that Monsanto stock would be withdrawn from its stock exchange listing if such legislation were passed.[31] Rayburn's group received a formidable resolution from the Cleveland Committee on the Fletcher-Rayburn bill, which listed nearly 150 Cleveland industries united to protest vigorously against enactment of the bill. Each of the member groups significantly listed the number of its employees, and the M. A. Hanna Company, with the largest number of employees—12,000—provided the group's chairman. The National Association of Building Owners and Managers wrote to Chairman Sam Rayburn that the drastic regulations envisioned would not only "endanger the transaction of many legitimate enterprises" related to the securities business, but would have "a ruinous

---

[29] Moley in *Today*, April 21, 1934, p. 5.
[30] *Congressional Record*, LXXVIII, Part VII, 8433.
[31] Senate, *Stock Exchange Practices*, p. 6570.

effect upon property accommodating financial institutions" throughout the nation.[32]

Dire warnings of unemployment in all departments of the financial world served to bring additional complaints before the hearings. The specialists of the New York Stock Exchange added a postscript to their protesting resolution to the effect that they were "assisted in their labors by 1290 employees who support 2481 dependents." [33] The branch of the Telegraphers' Union employed by the brokers of New York detailed their numbers and the number of their wives and progeny in similar fashion.[34] W. C. Van Antwerp, a San Francisco stockbroker, wrote to Senator W. G. McAdoo that of his "102 loyal employees," to whom he was "attached by ties of friendship," 80 percent of "these excellent men and women" would have to be discharged if the Fletcher-Rayburn bill became law in anything like its present form.[35]

Even the home state of the country's largest stock exchange entered a plea for ameliorating the proposed legislation. The state of New York, Governor Herbert H. Lehman anxiously reminded the President, was counting on $40 million in state revenue from 1934–35 stock transfers. It was hoped, Lehman wrote, that these interests "will be given careful and sympathetic consideration." To which Roosevelt genially but firmly replied that he could not encourage the governor, since the forthcoming legislation would, without doubt, cut down the number of shares transferred. But the portion lost, President Roosevelt pointed out, was the purely speculative element, and larger sums would be saved if these reckless and unnecessary ventures were eliminated. "It is just too bad from one point of view but all to the good from the bigger point of view." [36]

Such institutional and organizational protests received by

[32] House, *Stock Exchange Regulation*, pp. 939, 659.
[33] Senate, *Stock Exchange Practices*, p. 7750.
[34] House, *Stock Exchange Regulation*, p. 648.
[35] Senate, *Stock Exchange Practices*, p. 7412.
[36] Governor H. H. Lehman to F.D.R., March 24, 1934; F.D.R. to Lehman, March 27, 1934, Roosevelt Papers.

the two hearings groups far outweighed the approval of those few individuals who urged on the legislators to greater lengths. The Senate committee received occasional irate communications referring to securities purchased on the "recommendations of Wall Street crooks" who subsequently "robbed millions of people of their money." Some of the smaller brokers and some financial employees took exception to the correspondence suggested to them by the Wall Street leaders. The Swartwout Company of Cleveland supplied a refreshing corporate change by describing the modest distribution of its own stock and suggesting that despite the bill's severity, they saw no reason why their operations would be harmed by such legislation.[37] Senator Fletcher himself, in an article reminiscent of earlier Populist demands, suggested that "the monetary policy of this nation be administered by the federal government, wholly independent of the control of speculators, bankers, and all vested interests." [38]

The weight of an organized and well-financed campaign, however, was overwhelmingly apparent. A revision of some of the more drastic provisions of the original bill was begun after the hearings of early March, with Corcoran, Cohen, Landis, and the Pecora group again collaborating. With administration approval, representatives of the Federal Reserve Board and the Treasury Department advanced suggestions that were among those criticisms and reevaluations worked into a new bill. The revised Fletcher-Rayburn act that emerged (retitled H.R. 8720 and S. 3420) differed chiefly from its predecessor in making the margin requirements more acceptable to banks lending money on securities as collateral and in softening some provisions relating to the segregation of brokers and dealers.[39] Nevertheless it represented no repudiation of the principles called for by the President in his original request to the Congress or in his previous references to the need for such legislation. Somewhere, however, a line had to be drawn. The core

[37] Senate, *Stock Exchange Practices*, pp. 6891, 6890, 7408, 7204.
[38] Fletcher, p. 22.
[39] House, *Stock Exchange Regulation*, pp. 674 ff.

of the principle of stock exchange regulation was still safely inviolate, but continued pressure leading to further revision could penetrate even the ample protective padding remaining.

On the occasion of leaving Washington for "a few days' holiday" Roosevelt evidenced his concern for the safety of this major administration legislation. In letters addressed to Chairman Fletcher of the Senate committee and to Chairman Rayburn of its House counterpart, President Roosevelt remarked on the "highly organized drive" being made against the attempt to regulate exchanges. The letters and telegrams pouring in on the White House and Congress bore "all the earmarks of origin at some common source." However, since the people of the country "in overwhelming majority" were aware of the dangers arising from unregulated speculative excesses they would support action to ensure its prevention.

I am certain that the country as a whole will not be satisfied with legislation unless such legislation has teeth in it. . . . The bill, as shown to me this afternoon by you, seems to meet the minimum requirements. I do not see how any of us could afford to have it weakened in any shape, manner or form.[40]

The campaign carried on by financial and industrial leaders and through the conservative press was, if anything, intensified after the first small backward step in stock exchange legislation had been effected. In pointing out the change in national editorial support, Raymond Moley in the magazine *Today* said that on February 24 eight out of every ten newspapers supported the Fletcher-Rayburn bill. Day by day the ranks of its supporters had thinned, Moley continued. "There have been complete rights-about-face, perhaps the most interesting of them that of the *Miami (Florida) Herald*." This paper thoroughly approved, said Moley, on February 24. By March 28, however, it had evolved a new theory that enabled it to join in the chorus against the pending regulation. This theory, according to Moley, was that national prosperity was to be achieved through gambling; that any damper on margins would

[40] F.D.R., *Public Papers and Addresses*, III, 169, 170.

keep grain and cotton prices low, and thus perniciously influence commodity prices generally.[41]

The White House had prepared an even more comprehensive tally that reflected the same shifting of opinion. Compiled by Press Secretary Steve Early from 219 papers, the data on the stock exchange bill showed a tremendous decrease in affection for the proposed legislation from January through April, 1934. As of the latter month, even those 77 journals that still favored regulation exhibited a strong tendency to discount the need for stringent measures, and most suggested changes to be made in the bill. Those papers that simply urged modification showed a generally unfavorable attitude toward the idea and purpose of the Fletcher-Rayburn bill. The Philadelphia *Record* stood practically alone in demanding stock market regulation from the beginning and in continuing to uphold the administration in its insistence on regulating that would actually regulate. It was also a fact, the memo noted, that the press demand for "moderation" appeared before the bill was introduced in Congress February 9.[42]

The campaign of pressure to modify further the Fletcher-Rayburn bill continued in full force. Notably, however, complaints centering about the margin requirements and the segregation of broker and dealer functions appeared to be approaching the bedrock of Congressional resistance. More and more emphasis in the financial journals veered toward the creation of a new agency to take over the problem of stock exchange regulation. The trend was moving back toward the form of control recommended in the Roper Report, *Business Week* reported. Such a movement, this periodical said, reflected an attitude "which has met with the approval of all but the most violent anti-Wall Street group." [43] This was true, in part, where the Senate Committee on Banking and Currency was concerned. Flooded with amendments, the Senate committee had seized on the idea of a separate commission as the most

[41] Moley in *Today*, April 21, 1934, p. 5.
[42] Memo to the President from Secretary Early, April 16, 1934, Roosevelt Papers.
[43] *Business Week*, March 17, 1934, p. 33.

comprehensive answer to the complaints of the financial and business world. This provision, under the guidance of Senator Carter Glass of Virginia, was incorporated into S. 3420 over the protest of its chairman by a vote of 10 to 8.[44]

Any suggestion that this change was at the behest of Wall Street was warmly refuted by the peppery Virginian. There would be no exchange representatives on the considerably different body that he proposed, Senator Glass promised, and the amendment as drawn "textually prohibited" its members from having any connection, direct or indirect, with any of the stock exchanges. Another member of the committee disclosed an additional reason for favoring a new agency. Under the FTC, Senator Barkley of Kentucky stated, administration of the new act would merely be "sort of a lean-to under the commission's original activities." Also, Senator Barkley said, it was felt that instead of adding three men to the FTC as first proposed, it was entirely possible for the President to pick five new men equally well qualified to administer the law. Further, "public attention would always be focused upon that separate commission." [45]

On the other side of the capitol, the Fletcher-Rayburn bill had metamorphosed into its ultimate form, retitled H.R. 9323. Reporting the bill to members of the House of Representatives, the committee stated the philosophy behind their efforts:

The bill is conceived in a spirit of the truest conservatism. It attempts to change the practices of exchanges and the relationships between listed corporations and the investing public to fit modern conditions, for the very purpose that they may endure as essential elements of our economic system. The lesson of 1921–1929 is that without changes they cannot endure. . . . The repetition in the summer of 1933 of the blindness and abuses of 1929 has convinced a patient public that enlightened self-interest in private leadership is not sufficiently powerful to effect the necessary changes alone— that private leadership seeking to make changes must be given Government help and protection.[46]

[44] *Congressional Record*, LXXVIII, Part VIII, 8411.
[45] *Ibid.*, p. 8162.
[46] House, *Securities Exchange Bill of 1934*, p. 3.

The House bill retained a moderate 55 percent figure for margin requirements. The act was to be administered by a special division to be created within the FTC, the agency that the House favored, which was to be enlarged by two additional members. The question of the segregation of the functions of dealers and brokers was treated partly by discretionary agency powers, but depended mainly on an investigation and a report to Congress by the Commission in January, 1936.[47] The bill represented but slight deviation from preceding efforts, yet had passed over suggestions for sterner provisions. One such would have allowed the President at his discretion to make public the income tax returns of issuers of securities if it were deemed necessary in the public interest. This suggestion sought to provide a mesh to net those smaller corporate fish that might simply delist their securities in order to avoid registration under the act. As an afterthought this memorandum added that "politically it might be necessary to raise the exemptions indicated [$5 million in outstanding securities] so as to include only the very biggest, and hence most unpopular, corporations." [48]

Following presentation of the amended bill to the House, Chairman Rayburn of the Interstate and Foreign Commerce Committee gave evidence that the campaign of pressure from the financial community had not only reached but passed the point of diminishing returns. No bill ever introduced in all his years in Congress had ever been attacked "as viciously and in many instances as senselessly as this legislation," Rayburn told his colleagues. Referring repeatedly to "the most vicious and persistent lobby every known," Rayburn read letter after letter from brokers' employees forced to sign petitions against the bill and even compelled to contribute fifty cents each for lawyers' fees to oppose it. Many communications now received from financial firms announced covert support for the amended

[47] *Ibid.,* pp. 17 ff.
[48] SEC, Untitled compilation of mimeographs and photostats . . . relating to the Securities Exchange Act of 1934, Item 35.

bill. Several of Rayburn's colleagues recorded letters from business associations that not only withdrew their opposition after hearing the legislation discussed thoroughly but now expressed themselves in favor of the latest revision.[49] Chairman Rayburn scored a telling blow against the "insidious" influence of Wall Street having penetrated even "the veil of governmental authority" by relating a damning incident.

Mr. George Houston, the actual head of the so-called "durable goods committee of the code authorities under the NRA," admitted that a formal memorandum of proposed changes in the bill to satisfy business, presented to me as the official work of the committee, was at least physically mimeographed at 2 o'clock in the morning on the machines of the New York Stock Exchange lobby in the suite of Mr. Whitney's lawyers in the Willard Hotel.[50]

President Roosevelt's views favoring the administration of the Securities Exchange Act by the FTC—to which he had recently appointed James McCauley Landis, one of the bill's authors—were known. He reiterated them publicly in a press conference in May, praised the margin requirements of the House version, and communicated this attitude to Sam Rayburn.[51] Roosevelt later made a personal survey in "a small average community of up-state New York" that revealed the fact that 108 families out of 150 had been in the market on margin in 1929. A recent checkup, he wrote to Representative John W. McCormack of Massachusetts, showed only six families in the market on margin. This fact, Roosevelt indicated, led to the query whether "it is a good thing for the Nation to have any margin speculation at all." [52]

However, judging from the reaction of Senator Glass, Roosevelt must have given at least tacit support to the idea of a separate commission. Glass insisted to the press that President Roosevelt had told him that the administration would favor a special

[49] *Congressional Record,* LXXVII, Part VII, 7694–7700.
[50] *Ibid.,* p. 7696.
[51] New York *Herald Tribune,* May 17, 1934.
[52] E. Roosevelt, *F.D.R.: His Personal Letters,* III, 721, 722.

commission. The President had a right to change his mind, the ruffled old Virginian commented tartly, but "he should have told us so." [53]

A similar understanding was voiced by Senator E. P. Costigan of Colorado, who wrote the President that "the impression prevailed in the Senate that you desired a new commission." But progressive sentiment both Democratic and Republican, said Costigan, strongly preferred the FTC as the supervising agency. Again the President indicated the Federal Trade Commission was his personal preference.[54]

To smooth over the angry waters in the Senate, the White House hastily had to remind the public that the President had also said that the bare question of who was to handle the regulations was "not frightfully important," even though he still favored the FTC.[55]

This favoritism was further hedged several days later in correspondence with F.D.R.'s old running mate, James M. Cox of Ohio, the 1920 Democratic nominee for President. Writing to his vice-presidential campaign companion of fourteen years earlier, Cox advanced a yet different reason for using a new agency rather than the FTC. The small businessman and the man in the street "look on stock exchange operations as gambling . . . ," Cox assured the President. Such activities should not, therefore, be "mixed up with the business of the country through its administration by the FTC." Replying in a friendly "Dear Jim" letter, Roosevelt indicated that his choice of the latter agency was by no means final.

I am not permanently or irrevocably wedded to my preference for the FTC over a new commission but the FTC has a large part of securities and other corporate data anyway and a new commission would necessarily do a lot of duplication. My combination of Scotch and Dutch blood jumped at the chance to save about $100,000 a year.[56]

[53] New York *Herald Tribune,* May 17, 1934.
[54] Senator E. P. Costigan to F.D.R.; F.D.R. to Costigan, May 15, 16, 1934, Roosevelt Papers.
[55] Washington *Post,* May 17, 1934.
[56] James M. Cox to F.D.R.; F.D.R. to Cox, May 19, 24, 1934, Roosevelt Papers.

When the differing House and Senate versions moved on to a joint committee of conferees, press surmises on the resulting compromise were fairly accurate. The Senate idea of a new securities commission would be retained, observers thought, since the President and the administration seemed willing to yield on this point in order to facilitate an agreement. House conferees, on the other hand, would give up the FTC feature in order to retain the margin standard of the House version, and put further margin provisions under the Federal Reserve Board control.

The conference report issued on May 31 bore out the press and political speculation. A separate commission was agreed upon, with the Senate suggestion of "Federal Securities Exchange Commission" shelved and the more comprehensive title of "Securities and Exchange Commission" replacing it. Administration of the Securities Act of 1933 was removed from the FTC and placed under the new agency, a move that now had the nearly unanimous approval of all viewpoints. Instead of the House standards for the guidance of initial margin requirements, the Federal Reserve Board was entrusted with complete administration of margin provisions under a compromise starting date of three years later. Another expression of the administration's conciliatory gestures was agreement on several amendments to the Securities Act of 1933, which were appended as Title II in the suggested conference version of the new bill. These provided for less stringency in the civil penalties of the original act plus measures to prevent using the bill as a vehicle for damage suits far in excess of any losses actually suffered.[57]

The conference report, citing the amended legislation as "The Securities Exchange Act of 1934," was passed with overwhelming oral approval in both House and Senate.[58] When President Roosevelt signed it as Public Law No. 291 on June 6, 1934, a correspondent who wrote that it was directed at the

[57] House, *Securities Exchange Act of 1934*, pp. 5, 25–29, 31.

[58] *Congressional Record*, LXXVIII, Part IX, 10185, 10269. Final versions of the two separate bills had previously been passed in the House by a vote of 281 to 84, and in the Senate by a margin of 62 to 13.

evils depicted in Brandeis' book *Other People's Money* also noted that two disciples of Brandeis (Cohen and Corcoran) "stood beside the President as he signed." [59] Ferdinand Pecora was present at the ceremony, as were the two Congressional leaders of the bill, Fletcher and Rayburn, and Rayburn's "allies"—Representative Carl Mapes, Republican, of Michigan, and Representative Clarence Lea, Democrat, of California.

Under the new act, twenty-two national securities exchanges plus the New York Stock Exchange were required to register with and be subject to the regulations of the new commission. Six others, too small to be considered, were exempted. Nine exchanges that could not meet the requirements closed, including a one-man stock exchange with offices in a Hammond, Indiana, poolroom.[60]

Certain manipulative devices of the stock exchanges were prohibited entirely, such as wash sales and matched orders, both of which had been commonly used to give false pictures of stock activity. Effective measures were taken to prohibit planted stock tips, even though the information might prove true, if they originated with brokers, dealers, or stock exchange employees. False and misleading statements by brokers, dealers, sellers or buyers became a penal offense.

The act effectively dealt with corrupt practices of corporate "insiders." Any officer, director, or stockholder holding more than 10 percent of any class of a corporation's stock was required to file a report of his holdings, plus monthly reports reflecting any changes that took place. Any profit made by selling the stock of one's own company within six months of the purchase date reverted to the company itself, and any stockholder might bring suit to recover such profit for the company. All directors, officers, and major stockholders were expressly forbidden to sell short the stock of their own company.[61] Prevention of abuses of one's official position were fondly termed by

[59] New York *Herald Tribune,* June 7, 1934.
[60] Rodell, p. 116.
[61] U.S. *Statutes at Large,* XLVIII, Part I, 881 ff.

the Pecora staff as "anti-Wiggin" provisions, to commemorate the exploits of the Chase National Bank's former president.[62]

Furnishing misleading information through deceptive balance sheets was stopped by requiring certified periodical audits for any corporation listing its securities on a national exchange, with discretionary power over the form and details of such reports vested in the new commission. Further stock waterings such as the classic Morgan examples were impossible under the strict accounting standards required by the act; and additional explanatory details were to be furnished if deemed by the Commission to be in the public interest.[63]

The Securities Exchange Act of 1934 as it became law was a strong and effective instrument capable of dealing with the problems that precipitated it. In view of this fact the suppositions that the strength of the act was "traded" away to secure its passage were largely unfounded. Many sources embraced the viewpoint that the bill was deliberately made too drastic in order to afford ample opportunity for trimming.[64] From the vantage point of a half dozen years later Raymond Moley also adopted the view that Thomas Corcoran made this a profitable habit in writing further legislation.[65] In making this assertion Moley failed to consider that some of the most vital sections of the act, such as the segregation of broker-dealer functions and bankruptcy reorganizations, had to be given up temporarily and inserted in the bill only as subjects for future study. Yet the continued intensive effort to get these important points into legislative form—both finally effected several years later— belied the attempt to label the bill's major provisions as deliberately intended to be simple political sacrifices. And in connection with the Securities Exchange Act of 1934, at least, Moley's viewpoint overlooked the existence of much more stringent bills concurrently considered. If the final legislative result had been planned under this trimming formula, the

[62] Pecora, *Wall Street Under Oath*, pp. 268–69.
[63] U.S. *Statutes at Large*, XLVIII, Part I, 881 ff.
[64] Lindley, *Half Way with Roosevelt*, p. 110. See also "SEC," *Fortune*, p. 112; *Business Week*, Feb. 17, 1934, p. 9.
[65] Moley, *After Seven Years*, p. 303.

administration would have done better to embrace H.R. 7924 as offered by Democratic Representative A. J. Sabath of Illinois. This was a far more restrictive bill, drawn up by a Congressman who had labored for years to have such legislation adopted. Sabath's bill, for example, would have outlawed short selling completely.[66] Other uncompromising amendments drew strong support, such as a senatorial drive to do away with marginal purchases altogether.[67]

The real trader, if trading there was, remained Franklin D. Roosevelt. The President and his advisers had long favored the FTC as the administrating agency. One of its commissioners, James M. Landis, recently appointed by Roosevelt, was one of the authors of the House and Senate bills that put the exchange regulation under the FTC. When the controversy over the legislation was nearing its peak, Roosevelt publicly announced himself for the FTC in preference to the separate commission idea adopted by the Senate. At this point it was apparent to many that whether Roosevelt appointees were to function under FTC or some sort of stock exchange commission, the designation in itself would have little bearing on the policies to be carried out. The only exception to this was the die-hard Wall Street community, which expected that its continuing pressure would bring about a newly formed commission susceptible to the banker and broker point of view.

Actually Roosevelt's views on the nature of a regulatory commission were definite and forthright. They had the added benefit of having hardened in the mold of pressure during his two terms as governor of New York State. In Roosevelt's fight to develop electrical resources on the St. Lawrence, his views on the Public Service Commission were the subject of a state-wide radio address in 1930. In this instance Roosevelt was dealing with utilities regulation, but there was no doubt as to the principle stated. A regulatory commission, Roosevelt said emphatically, was created

[66] *Congressional Record*, LXXVIII, Part VII, 8028–30.
[67] New York *Times*, May 4, 1934.

to act not as a court as between the public on one side and the utility companies on the other but to act definitely and directly for the public, as the representative of the public and of the Legislature, its sole function being to supervise the utilities themselves under definite rules. That is a very clear statement of the common law principle which goes back hundreds of years in the civilization from which we spring.[68]

Consequently Roosevelt's public plea for retention of the FTC was the means of getting a political something for nothing. Further softening of the bill was avoided, yet the make-up of the new commission revealed that the President's regulatory ideas remained quite unaffected.[69]

Even in the amendments to the Securities Act of 1933, which became Title II of the new legislation, administration aims remained inviolate. The changes made were in response to flaws that appeared in actual operation. The most pertinent comment regarding the intent and background of the amendments was furnished by *Business Week,* which pointed out that "they were written by Trade Commissioner Landis, who has supervised the administration of the act up to the present time." [70] They represented no essential or significant withdrawal from the intent of the original act, despite the intensive campaign for wholesale change.

Although the onslaught on the entire concept of regulating the stock exchanges was largely a massive frontal assault by the combined financial and corporate strength of the nation, several flanking attacks on the emerging legislation were carried out also. These were rooted in and directed toward the feelings of the contemporary business community, and attempted to obstruct and undercut the Securities Exchange Act as a bill devised by "young theoreticians," essentially "unworkable."

Raymond Moley delivered a vigorous rebuttal to the first

[68] F.D.R., *Public Papers and Addresses,* I, 239.
[69] A majority of three out of the five new commissioners were appointed from the FTC: Landis, Mathews, and Healy. No one questioned the viewpoint of a fourth appointee—Ferdinand Pecora.
[70] *Business Week,* April 21, 1934, p. 37.

of these attacks. From the experience of one who "knew the facts at first hand" he was able to point out that "at least a dozen men—old and young, and certainly not inexperienced—drafted the legislation." Protection of stockholders from exploitation by insiders "came from the partner of one of the most conservative law firms in Wall Street, who has himself taken credit for being the 'foster father' of the provision. (Name furnished on request.)" [71] Further, Moley reminded critics, the bill was gone over word by word by Treasury and Federal Reserve experts "including Governor (of the Federal Reserve Board) Black, who as yet has been suspected of no Moscow affiliations."

One of the chief architects of the bill, Thomas G. Corcoran, left little doubt in the minds of the House Committee on Interstate and Foreign Commerce as to his qualifications. Called as a witness and asked to state his "past connections," Corcoran was able to say:

I spent six years in Wall Street, with one of the very best law firms up there, handling promotions, stock pools, listings, and blue sky matters, and then . . . as counsel for two of the very best brokerage houses in New York. [72]

Others active in designing the legislation, such as James M. Landis and Ferdinand Pecora, were revealing to the public and to Congress by active administration and demonstration that their fitness could not be questioned. Even from a viewpoint of several years later, however, the "young theoretician" gambit was still employed. *Fortune,* in discussing the origins of the SEC, published a patronizing account of how "private capital's men" Roland Redmond, W. A. Harriman, and Arthur Dean helped to "whack the reform theories into practical form," though it added that they did not wholly succeed. [73]

The charge that the bill was "unworkable" was frequently uttered. Faced with the possibility of legislation that substituted

[71] Moley in *Today,* April 14, 1934, pp. 5–6. The individual Moley refers to is probably Arthur H. Dean, who was a member of the Roper bill-writing committee.
[72] House, *Stock Exchange Regulation,* p. 82.
[73] *Fortune,* XXI, No. 6 (June, 1940), 91.

genuine authority for the lip service of self-regulation, the bill rapidly became known as "unworkable" in the jargon of the lower-Manhattan canyons. Wall Street dwellers, accustomed to legislation through which they could drive a span of corporation lawyers with great ease, were unable to find any loopholes in the bill. The act was drawn with this inevitable onslaught in mind, and "so perfect was its draftsmanship that it was passed by the House of Representatives without changing a single comma." The chief draftsman, Benjamin V. Cohen, was characterized by Paul Mallon as "a man of exceptional ability, as any lawyer who has tried to break through the Securities Act and the Stock Market Regulation bill now will testify." [74] Charges that the chief defect of the Securities Exchange Act, like its sister act, lay in its "unworkableness" and "cumbersomeness" proved unsuccessful and unimpressive. Such trivial complaints scarcely did justice to the genuine ability of the Wall Street and corporation lawyers who had built up, in holding companies and investment affiliates, some of the most formidable and complex legal structures known to the American financial world.

The strength of the Securities Exchange Act lay not only in its explicit provisions bringing remedial and preventive action to the field of corrupt stock exchange and corporate practices. It resided also in the tremendous discretionary powers vested in the new Securities and Exchange Commission to request further such preventive action as the occasion demanded. In addition, the act contained certain built-in provisions for dealing with problems that could not be treated in the act itself, either because its drafters lacked sufficient knowledge or because they recognized the need for political expediency.

The provision for segregating the public functions of a broker from the personal trading of a dealer, rather than permit their combination in the same firm or individual, was one that drew considerable fire. It received only partial treatment in the bill, but Section 11(e) called for a study of the feasibility of complete and final action on this problem. The results were

[74] Mallon, p. 20.

to be in the hands of Congress by January 3, 1936. Additionally, the act provided for a study and recommendations regarding the rules of national securities exchanges "with respect to the classification of members, the methods of election . . . and . . . disciplining of members." The act concluded with Section 211, authorizing study and investigation into the functions of "protective and reorganization committees in connection with the . . . liquidation or consolidation of persons and properties . . . ," a field to which the attention of the Senate investigating committee had been drawn by investment banking's control practices and exorbitant fees.[75] The important fact was that each of these studies was to be carried out by Securities and Exchange Commission personnel, with results and recommendations presented to Congress for further legislative extension of Commission duties. In other words, these portions of the act constituted a self-levering bootstrap action for raising the regulatory limits of the new agency.

The creation of the Securities and Exchange Commission was brought about as a New Deal reform, confidently stated as such in the Democratic platform of 1932, confirmed in the past utterances of the presidential nominee, and increasingly restated by Franklin Roosevelt in his first two presidential years. It was carried through to completion by the able shepherding of Senator Fletcher of Florida and Representative Rayburn of Texas, aided by a group of devoted and industrious young men, who would have wholeheartedly subscribed to Senator Fletcher's statement that "the new deal" was not so much a political slogan as it was "a moral attitude in government action." [76] Senator Fletcher, particularly in his wrathful defense of Ferdinand Pecora against the acrimony of fellow committeeman Carter Glass, was reminiscent of the William Jennings Bryan battles with the ogres of Wall Street. Representative Sam Rayburn, whose attitude in financial legislation was definitely more Main Street than Wall Street, was more-

---

[75] U.S. *Statutes at Large*, XLVIII, Part I, 892–909.
[76] *Congressional Record*, LXXVIII, Part VII, 8161.

over an unswervingly loyal partisan follower of Franklin Roosevelt.

Carried through as it was by active New Dealers, the act creating the new agency yet required the tremendous assistance of public and Congressional favor, and was aided in no small measure by the blunders of the rabid supporters and officials of the New York Stock Exchange.

The American public, subjected to continuous injunctions regarding the pursuit of sturdy independence and rugged individualism, had thriftily saved and invested. The average citizen had made his investments in good faith, although his greed had been inflamed by financial salesmen and the national speculative frenzy. The terrible crash of 1929, the sickening depression years following, and then the first revelations of the corrupt behavior of financial and business leaders brought about a shocked and furious reaction. By 1933, Joseph Dorfman wrote, "the general public was in a receptive, and indeed demanding, mood with regard to the need for substantial reforms in banking, investment markets, and corporate practices." [77]

Congressional temper was affected in some degree by the impressive academic arguments used, but Congressmen were far quicker to take account of the investigation results before them and to take into consideration widespread public losses of a very general character. Financial periodicals of the less reactionary type were under no illusions as to Congressional feelings. "If the fight becomes acrimonious," reported one, "Congress is bound to line up, pro-Wall Street and anti-Wall Street. There could be no doubt of the issue then; a drastic bill would pass in a whoop." [78]

The spokesmen of Wall Street demonstrated a completely irresponsible approach and an intransigence scarcely credible. "Give the Stock Exchange time to do those things which are wanted of it . . . ," was a typical reaction. If it seemed that enough time had already lapsed, then one had to remember,

[77] Dorfman, V, 652.
[78] *Business Week,* March 3, 1934, p. 36.

said a writer, "that no lightship was ever anchored to a shoal until several ships had foundered there, that no railroad crossing was ever guarded until several people had lost their lives." [79] The social aspects of regulation meant merely that in the future, "bootblacks, barbers and charwomen" would be barred from the market place.

To avoid any regulation whatever, Stock Exchange spokesmen uttered ever new regulations, many of which were thoroughly discredited by sworn testimony almost before they had an opportunity to become effective. The proposed legislation to regulate the exchanges became the first New Deal act to face the combined business and financial resources of the nation, and was generaled largely by the New York Stock Exchange. The drive was interspersed with shrill warnings that "rude hands" would utterly wreck the "delicate mechanism" of Wall Street, and with covert and overt threats to move the entire "mechanism" to the more favorable climate of Montreal. This campaign of intimidation showed very little understanding of the actual issues involved or any willingness to treat them. Writing to Adolf A. Berle, Jr., several months after the act's passage, Roosevelt could diagnose "the fundamental trouble with this whole Stock Exchange crowd" as complete lack of elementary education. This meant, he explained, "just an inability to understand the country or the public or their obligation to their fellow men." [80]

But Wall Street far overplayed its hand in an effort to equate its own regulation with that of the entire corporate economy. Discussion and the publicizing of the act's specific provisions offset the Stock Exchange's use of deliberately horrifying generalities. The campaign eventually boomeranged when businessmen discovered they would not actually be placed in thralldom to FTC, when Wall Street employees wrote Congress protesting their coercion, and when some responsible brokers were heard to say that with some regulation the public might very well reenter the market more readily. The Stock Exchange

[79] Clifford, p. 48.
[80] F.D.R. to Adolf A. Berle, Jr., Aug. 15, 1934, Roosevelt Papers.

itself, however, admitted *Business Week*, "continued fighting tooth and nail against any regulation whatsoever." [81]

Finally, there remained only the White House announcement of the appointments to the Securities and Exchange Commission. Although Wall Street spokesmen had originally pressed for just such a new and separate agency, with high hopes of naming some of its initial personnel, their bitter campaign had left them with little hope for a commanding voice in its counsel.

[81] *Business Week*, April 28, 1934, p. 36.

---◆---

CHAPTER FOUR

THE FIRST COMMISSIONERS

THE WIDE discretion granted the members of the newly created Securities and Exchange Commission made it obvious to all that with the President's appointees rested the choice of either a vigorous prosecution or an amiable and lax interpretation of the Securities Exchange Act. The ensuing pulling and tugging, wrote Ernest K. Lindley, was "reminiscent of the struggle which preceded Mr. Roosevelt's selection of a Secretary of the Treasury prior to the inauguration." [1]

Rival sections of the press pelted each other with names and qualifications of their favorite candidates, as well as with the names of those whose appointment would undoubtedly bring utter disaster. "Wall Street," said the *New Republic* bitterly, "would like to see Mr. John M. Hancock, of the firm of Lehman Bros., and Mr. John Dickinson, Assistant Secretary of Commerce, on the Commission." "Appointments like these," John T. Flynn warned, "would practically nullify the whole purpose of the Exchange Bill." Instead, Flynn suggested the two young attorneys who had played a major part in drafting the legislation, Benjamin Cohen and Thomas Corcoran, and also his erstwhile employer, Senate investigator Ferdinand Pecora.[2]

Editorializing on the Commission possibilities, the New York

[1] New York *Herald Tribune*, June 6, 1934.
[2] *New Republic*, May 30, 1934, p. 71.

Herald Tribune considered that appointment of Landis and Mathews from the FTC seemed "both logical and reasonable." But at least one member of the new board should have "a banking background," and one other commissioner should have "a knowledge of the mechanics of the stock market." The *Herald Tribune* accordingly proposed Thomas F. Woodlock and George W. Hodges of the Better Business Bureau.[3]

Two of Wall Street's own were frequently mentioned in the rumors of the day. But James Auchincloss, a Stock Exchange member, and Dean Witter, an investment banker, would likely not be on the winning side of any Commission vote, one columnist pointed out, even if they were selected.[4] The Far West entry, according to Ernest Lindley, was Frank Shaughnessy of the San Francisco Stock Exchange. A front-running political choice was George Henry Payne of New York, who had the backing of the reasonably liberal Republican state chairman of New York, W. Kingsland Macy.[5] By the latter part of June both Landis and Mathews of the FTC were unanimous choices of the press, and both the news gatherers and the knowing political insiders of the Mayflower Hotel lobby variety had placed James M. Landis in the chairman's seat.

Brain Truster Moley's recommendations, requested by President Roosevelt, included besides those actually chosen to serve on the new board, Benjamin Cohen; Paul V. Shields, one of the more progressive Wall Street brokers; an investment banker, Gordon Wassor; and Frank Shaughnessy, of San Francisco. Hearing several days later that Ferdinand Pecora had expressed a desire to be chairman, Moley added his name to the list verbally.[6]

Roosevelt waited until the eve of his departure for a vacation trip to Puerto Rico to make the waited announcement. While speculation had it that the event was delayed until after the Senate adjourned, it was also explained that Republican leaders had consented to this move so that they might have a sample of the new officers' performances before their confirmation the

[3] New York *Herald Tribune*, June 6, 1934.
[4] *Business Week*, June 23, 1934, p. 3.
[5] New York *Herald Tribune*, June 6, 1934.
[6] Moley, "Five Years of Roosevelt and After," p. 30.

following January.[7] The presidential announcement of commission appointments included those to a new and permanent National Labor Relations Board, and statement of the transfer of several men from the old Radio Commission to the new seven-man Federal Communications Commission that replaced it.

Overshadowing these names, however, were the five appointees to the new Securities and Exchange Commission.[8] Four of them—Ferdinand Pecora, the affable and relentless quizmaster of the Senate investigation, and Landis, Mathews, and Judge Healy of the FTC—were more or less expected, but the one chosen for the fifth position created considerable surprise and some chagrin. The name of Joseph P. Kennedy, and his appointment to the top five-year term, brought widely differing reactions. The forthright John T. Flynn labeled the appointment "grotesque," and referred to Kennedy as "that worst of all economic parasites, a Wall Street operator." [9] Young New Dealers were reputed to be in a state of alarm. Pecora, after recovering from the shock, one journal reported, viewed the appointment of Kennedy as "something of a sardonic anticlimax." [10] To some sources Joe Kennedy was chiefly a close personal friend of the President, and "the largest creditor of the Democratic National Committee, next to Raskob." He was the "first allayment of apprehension" to much of Wall Street, and to Raymond Moley a sound bet for chairman as an executive, a moderator, and a knowing master of those very wiles that were to be regulated.[11]

To President Roosevelt, Joe Kennedy was, indeed, an old friend. Their acquaintance dated back to Roosevelt's Assistant Secretaryship of the Navy and Kennedy's shipbuilding activities of World War I. More recently Kennedy had been one of the earliest of the small "Roosevelt-Before-Chicago" group and a frequent passenger on the 1932 campaign train. Although it was true enough, as presidential adviser F. W. Taussig could later

[7] *Business Week,* June 30, 1934, p. 1.
[8] Hereafter referred to as SEC.
[9] *New Republic,* July 11, 1934, p. 221.
[10] Knappen, "The Rulers of the Stock Market," p. 329.
[11] *Business Week,* July 7, 1934, p. 9; *Magazine of Wall Street,* Sept. 14, 1935, p. 539; Moley, *After Seven Years,* p. 286.

write to a friend, that Roosevelt "genuinely despised the 'Wall Street crowd' whom he knows and knows about," [12] Kennedy's activities were far removed from those indictments that were aimed at many financial figures. His participation in a 1933 pool in Libby-Owens-Ford Glass Company stock was regrettable,[13] but was outweighed by a personal integrity recognized by Roosevelt and Wall Street alike.

Joseph P. Kennedy was the son of a Boston Democratic ward boss with minor banking affiliations. Not only did the young Kennedy put himself through Harvard but he was able to realize a several-thousand-dollar profit from a summer sight-seeing bus venture during his student days.[14] Control of a paternally dominated neighborhood bank with the aid of borrowed capital was followed by investment banking and shipbuilding operations. Forays into the stock market and ventures into moving picture finance brought Kennedy a large fortune. Joe Kennedy was one of the few, however, who could and did say of the frightening bank-closing days of early 1933 that he would be willing to part with half his fortune if he could be sure of keeping "under law and order" the other half. Uniquely, Kennedy continued to state the same theme after the crisis was over. To him those Wall Street leaders who had recovered enough from their fright to rail at the Roosevelt efforts toward financial reform were models of ingratitude. Much worse, they were guilty of profound stupidity in not seeing that Roosevelt had been "at pains to protect the invested wealth of the nation." [15]

Roosevelt's unique ability to choose a suitable human instrument to effect his purpose, his selecting of executive ability capable of getting a tough job done without continual plucking at the presidential coat sleeve, is nowhere better exemplified than in the appointment of Joseph P. Kennedy to the SEC. Not even the most partisan financial writer considered that Kennedy

[12] Dorfman, V, 654.
[13] "Mr. Kennedy, the Chairman," *Fortune*, p. 144. The title of the article refers not to the SEC but to Kennedy's later chairmanship of the U.S. Maritime Commission.
[14] *Current Biography, 1940*, p. 450.
[15] Kennedy, *I'm for Roosevelt*, pp. 3, 7.

would "turn Commission shells at Wall Street into duds." More likely, was the admission, "the victim who gets in the way of a fast one will be greeted with a slap on the back and a loud blast of laughter as over a good joke." A later appraisal rated Kennedy as reassuring to the brokerage fraternity because "they knew that their game would not be ruined, although the rules might be revised and strictly interpreted." [16]

The announcement that Kennedy had been given the longest term of the five staggered appointments to the new Commission was, in part, a presidential accolade for Kennedy as chairman. In addition, it was notice served that the tenure of the new and jovial ambassador to the world of lower Manhattan was sufficient to allay any fears of too-rapid transition to a less sympathetic authority. This, in spite of the "informal understanding" between Roosevelt and Kennedy that a year or so would be sufficient for the President's purpose. Such an expedient had been the uneasy rumor, and it was necessary that it be quieted.[17]

Corcoran's alleged reaction, as stated to Raymond Moley, "that four are for us and one is for business," becomes understandable in the light of press reaction, and Moley's indignation over such a "class-struggle concept" becomes less so.[18] The press and periodicals, New Deal and anti-New Deal, traced the same pattern as Corcoran did in assessing the general attitude of the new appointees. Liberal journals uniformly applauded a majority of the Commission and portrayed Kennedy's role as a repudiation of the principles of exchange regulation legislation. Wall Street periodicals advancing their candidates for the SEC regretted that too few of them would wind up on the Commission ever to become the "winning side." [19] The financial journals and the conservative press, while mostly content not to snipe at Kennedy's fellow commissioners yet, hailed him as the only genuine hope of the Wall Street fraternity and his chairmanship as reassurance that policies of the new agency would be interpreted with some understanding of the stock exchange position.

[16] Knappen, "The Rulers of the Stock Market," p. 330; Herring, p. 25.
[17] Kennedy, *I'm for Roosevelt*, p. 2.
[18] Moley, *After Seven Years*, p. 289.
[19] *Business Week*, June 23, 1934, p. 3.

One journal, whistling in the dark regarding the majority of
the Commission, recalled that Landis was no "aginner" on principle, and drew some sustenance from the fact that the chairmanship "went to Kennedy over Pecora's head." [20]

The appointments of Landis and Mathews of the FTC were
agreed upon well in advance by all shades of opinion. James
McCauley Landis, various journals related, was born in Tokyo
of Presbyterian missionary parents, and came to the United
States at thirteen. After schooling at Holland, Michigan, and
Mercersburg Academy, he followed his father's footsteps to
Princeton, where he was chiefly noted for his intellectual and
financial interests. Landis was graduated in 1921 with highest
honors in history and politics, and with a considerable bank-
roll derived from the sale of masterfully prepared syllabi that
he peddled to his less talented fellow students.[21] Close acquaintance with Felix Frankfurter at Harvard Law School led to schol-
arships for graduate work culminating in the doctorate in jurid-
ical science and a term as secretary to Supreme Court Justice
Brandeis.

Soon afterward Landis accepted an assistant professorship at
Harvard Law School offered him by Dean Roscoe Pound. When
a special chair in legislation was created in 1928, it meant Landis'
appointment to the post as full professor. The young professor
saw something of practical politics at the city council level, and
helped his students draft model legislation, much of which was
enacted into statute.[22] Meanwhile his writings on legislation and
labor law were providing him with a growing reputation. When
Frankfurter was asked to recommend someone to help draft
securities legislation in early 1933, James McCauley Landis was
the answer.

If his critics had looked into his background more closely
they would have discovered that no one at Harvard considered
the cautious and judicious Landis a sounding board for Frank-

[20] *Ibid.*, July 7, 1934, p. 9.
[21] Mallon, p. 5.
[22] Van Arkel, pp. 237, 238.

furter, as Wall Street did. Two labels—"open-minded" and "antidoctrinaire"—remained in the memory of those who had contended with him in Harvard Law School.[23]

The four-year term on the new SEC went to Landis' fellow commissioner at the FTC, George C. Mathews. (Landis himself received the three-year term.) A graduate of the University of Wisconsin in 1908, Mathews was for many years rate expert and statistician for the Railroad Commission of Wisconsin. After several years of public accounting and a short term as professor of public utilities at Northwestern University, Mathews became director of the securities division of Wisconsin's nationally noted Public Service Commission.[24] From this post, with strong support from Senator Robert M. La Follette, Jr., he came to Washington.

A writer of the day described Mathews as a typical "Badger Teuton," referring to his appearance as "thicknecked, baldheaded, and ornate as a smokehouse." [25] Since the Securities Exchange Act of 1934 specified no more than three appointees from the same party, Mathews' label as Republican was a great convenience, inasmuch as it actually stood for the Republican Progressivism of a La Follette. Mathews' experience confirmed this. It was widely recognized that "Wisconsin was the first state to have an airtight law regulating the issuance of stocks and bonds, and Commissioner Mathews was the first administrator of that law." He was described as a zealot in preventing the flotation of fraudulent securities, but as an individual whose "enthusiasm is restrained by sound viewpoints and good sense." [26] An earlier observer accurately pictured Mathews as being of the conviction that the corporate world had brought about its own punishment through foolishly unsocial ways, yet at heart remained a person "with a naturally conservative makeup." [27]

A two-year term as commissioner went to Robert E. Healy [28]

---

[23] "The Legend of Landis," *Fortune*, p. 47.
[24] *Who Was Who in America, 1943–1950*, p. 350.
[25] Knappen, "The Rulers of the Stock Market," p. 331.
[26] Brayman, p. 118.
[27] Knappen, "The Rulers of the Stock Market," p. 368.
[28] Pronounced as though spelled Haley.

of Vermont. The other Republican on the Commission, Healy had prepared for the law by reading in a local lawyer's office after his graduation from Bennington, Vermont, High School in 1901. Admitted to the bar in 1904, Healy had been an associate justice of the state supreme court of his home state before coming to the FTC as counsel. In 1928, Calvin Coolidge was looking for someone to direct an investigation into the public utilities companies that Congress had authorized. Since Coolidge considered this investigation inexpedient, he looked for someone to head the inquiry "who would not dig deeply enough to open any wounds." [29] Judge Healy was made chief counsel of the FTC to carry out the project, an appointment Coolidge lived to regret.

In the subsequent investigation, which covered the next four years and produced voluminous evidence, Healy "went after the power companies more daringly than any reformer had previously ventured." [30] This earned him considerable enmity in investment banking circles. Healy was described in an ill-tempered magazine profile as "Catholic Irish by descent, gone 100 per cent Yankee puritan." The writer went on to compare him to Kennedy in his Irishness, arriving at the conclusion that Kennedy was the "worldly" type who had "held on to the humanistic ways of Southern Ireland." Healy, on the other hand, was the "pious" type who had "retained his faith but absorbed the New England conscience." [31]

Particularly concerned with accounting questions in regard to security issues, Healy exhibited stern moral convictions when testifying before Congressional committees on this topic. "I do not come as a member of the brain trust referred to," Healy told one group, "because I could not qualify." But he did appear, he went on, because he supposed simply that "the purpose of bookkeeping and accounting was to make a historical record of events" in corporate finance, and not to cheat stockholders or stock buyers. Vehement and outspoken, Judge Healy related to

[29] Brayman, p. 118.
[30] New York *Times*, Nov. 18, 1946.
[31] Knappen, "The Rulers of the Stock Market," p. 331.

the committee that he had been shocked to find that "you can capitalize in some States practically everything except the furnace ashes in the basement." [32] He was known as a person of stern rectitude, and even his detractors were convinced that he would "judge according to the law—not according to emotions." [33]

Both President Roosevelt and James Landis reputedly helped persuade Ferdinand Pecora to accept a one-year Commission appointment instead of the chairman's post he coveted.[34] Roosevelt's idea that the chairman must act as liaison between the SEC and Wall Street made Pecora's elevation to that post manifestly impossible. However, his unquestioned legal talents and his experience in tracking through previously unexplored financial jungles made him a valuable adjunct to the new agency.

Not without cause, the financial community reserved its chief hostility for the implacable prosecutor of its major figures. Titles such as "the hellhound of Wall Street" and "The Icy Latin" led one waspish writer to conjecture that since Pecora was "born in Sicily but is a Methodist in religion," the result was "a good combination of potential vindictiveness and austerity." [35] Yet Pecora's year-and-a-half public performance against some of the most formidable figures of the banking and investment world brought him unstinted admiration also. His former associate, John T. Flynn, called attention to Pecora's "balance, intelligence and resoluteness," and pointed out that throughout the investigation "in a field new to him, he never forgot a name, never made an error in a figure, and never lost his temper." His "unflagging industry and pertinacity" were widely admitted.[36] In the attack on the Securities Act of 1933 led by the directors of the Chase National Bank it became evident from the testimony that "Ferdinand Pecora, who is not in the banking busi-

---

[32] House, *Stock Exchange Regulation*, pp. 834, 880.
[33] Knappen, "The Rulers of the Stock Market," p. 368.
[34] Van Arkel, p. 238.
[35] Knappen, "The Rulers of the Stock Market," pp. 329–31. *Who's Who in America, 1958–1959*, p. 2155, lists Ferdinand Pecora's religion as Episcopalian. He came to this country as a child of five.
[36] Flynn, "The Marines Land in Wall Street," p. 149; *Nation*, June 7, 1933, p. 633.

ness, knew a great deal more about important Chase transactions than the two directors did." Moley, however, considered that Samuel Untermeyer would have done a better job than Pecora did.[37]

Pecora himself mildly rejected the idea that original sin was inseparable from corporate affairs. "I have never been a crusader or a romantic who imagines that the world is made up of sheep and goats, of heroes and villains." [38] As chief assistant district attorney of New York County for eight years before becoming the counsel for the Senate investigating committee, Pecora's relentless pursuit of lawbreakers convinced many Wall Streeters that his one-year term on the Commission would make early cooperation between the SEC and the financial community impossible. Although Pecora was, to put it mildly, taken aback by Kennedy's appointment, relations between the two men—as between Kennedy and the other commissioners—quickly became amicable. Several years later Kennedy revealed that both he and Pecora derived considerable amusement from the "striving for power" continually ascribed to them by the press.[39]

The actual formation of a complete agency staff chiefly involved moving the securities division of the FTC, so that the SEC not only acquired the former's staff of experts in that division but also "adopted its procedure and administrative machinery, as well as the rules and precedents developed as a result of more than a year's experience." When the September 1 date of administration change arrived, the one hundred fifteen persons engaged on securities work had already been transferred to the new agency.[40]

Not only three SEC commissioners had been transplanted from the older agency but such top administrators as Baldwin B. Bane, chief of the securities division, were brought in to head the new SEC registration division.[41] From Pecora's highly spe-

---

[37] *New Republic*, Dec., 20, 1933, p. 152; Moley, *After Seven Years*, p. 177.
[38] Pecora, "Wall Street Under the Flag," p. 61.
[39] Kennedy, "Shielding the Sheep," p. 65.
[40] FTC, *Annual Report*, 1934, pp. 10, 11.
[41] Told to author in interview with Baldwin B. Bane, Washington, D.C., July 20, 1959.

cialized staff of investigative assistants came David Saperstein to prepare the report on the government of securities exchanges that the Securities Exchange Act directed. David Schenker, Pecora's legal assistant, was recruited as counsel.

William O. Douglas, Sterling Professor of Law at Yale, was appointed by Chairman Kennedy to direct the Commission report on the reorganization of corporations as called for under Section 211 of the act. Douglas had written of the Securities Act of 1933 that it was symbolic of the shift of political power from the bankers to the masses, and from the promoter to the investor.[42] As a noted authority on the legal aspects of finance and a keen analyst of bankruptcy procedure, Douglas' particular talents were to be employed in the Commission's study of investment bankers' activities in bankruptcy reorganization proceedings.

Kennedy and Landis collaborated in obtaining the services of John J. Burns as SEC general counsel. The brilliant Burns had become judge of the Massachusetts Superior Court three years earlier at age thirty, and had been made full professor at Harvard Law School just a month before his elevation to the bench. Burns's appointment was typical of the talent that enabled Kennedy to say several years later that the SEC "had a staff whose competence was never challenged." [43]

A statement of the official policy to be pursued was, of course, eagerly awaited after Kennedy's chairmanship of the Commission became known. It was facetiously suggested that the Stock Exchange should either suspend operations between two thirty and two forty-five on the afternoon of July 25, or provide a loudspeaker to broadcast Kennedy's first scheduled talk to members on the floor.[44] The vital importance, to finance and government alike, of Chairman Kennedy's carefully considered opening address was apparent in its front-page treatment by both the New York City and Washington press. The consensus of the thou-

[42] *Newsweek*, July 28, 1934, p. 30.
[43] Kennedy, *I'm for Roosevelt*, p. 99.
[44] New York *Times*, July 25, 1934.

sands of Wall Streeters who did gather to listen in their offices was generally stated in one word—"reassuring." [45] Kennedy had, indeed, worked hard to give notice that the SEC intended to make "an effort to develop the financial market," and could not concern itself with "grudges" or vindictiveness. The tenor of Kennedy's first speech was strongly affirmative, friendly yet firm. The SEC was cast in the role of aiding recovery by showing the public that its investment dollars would be channeled henceforth into an honest market. It was encouraging to financial circles to hear the new chairman state that "we of SEC do not regard ourselves as coroners sitting on the corpse of financial enterprise. On the contrary, we think of ourselves as the means of bringing new life into the body of the securities business." [46]

Kennedy promised that there would be no "political publicity of any sort." He gave warmest encouragement to the "domestic tranquility essential to business." Strict supervision would be no hardship except to the crooked, and renewed public confidence would bring investment funds back into the market again. In the end, the new chairman assured his listeners, "a New Deal in finance will be found to be a better deal for all." [47] Kennedy's first speech as chairman had additional significance in that, as a joint policy to be carried out by the New Deal's newest agency, it was carefully read and edited by the other commissioners and administration sources.[48]

A large part of the early months of the SEC were occupied with erecting permanent administrative machinery and inaugurating the several studies and reports called for by the Securities Exchange Act. After a series of informal conferences with Stock Exchange officials, the commissioners and chief SEC administrators paid their first official visit to the New York Stock Exchange. With President Richard Whitney escorting Chairman Kennedy, and Vice-President Allen L. Lindley guiding Commissioner Pecora, the group moved about among the trading posts, studied the operation of the money desk (for broker's bor-

[45] Washington *Post,* July 26, 1934; *Newsweek,* Aug. 4, 1934, p. 27.
[46] Kennedy, *Address to the National Press Club,* p. 3.
[47] *Ibid.,* p. 5.
[48] *Literary Digest,* Aug. 4, 1934, p. 37.

rowings), and asked numerous questions, which Stock Exchange members "answered readily, even eagerly."

At noon the combined forces lunched in the exclusive Stock Exchange Luncheon Club, parading through the lobby past the ornate three-ton bronze figure of a bull and bear locked in mortal combat, done to order originally for Thomas W. "Frenzied Finance" Lawson by I. Bonheur, cousin of painter Rosa Bonheur.[49] The following day the tour covered the Curb and Produce exchanges, and offices of representative brokerage firms. A "greater cheerfulness was apparent" after this mutual inspection, financial journals reported. The general feeling was that this "more intimate contact with the commissioners seemed to have produced confidence that the new SEC rules will involve no unnecessary harshness." [50]

In publicly expanding the SEC policies, Kennedy was a jauntily confident ringmaster, alternately cajoling and admonishing varied segments of the business and financial world through numerous speeches and interviews. He brushed off charges of "government interference" and "radicalism" in pungent detail, and impatiently dismissed propaganda directed against the Securities Exchange Act as coming from "unthinking reactionaries." [51] The Union League Club of Chicago provided a convenient platform from which Kennedy voiced his displeasure over the "indifferent response" of corporate officials in filing with the SEC the amount of their security holdings. "I urge upon you the wisdom of being properly advised concerning your duties." [52]

Yet Chairman Kennedy never lost an opportunity to remind his listeners of the Better Business Bureau aspect of the SEC. His talks were frequently keyed to the theme that the new agency functioned as a protector of the businessman from fraudulent dealers and stock swindlers. In this respect the agency was a partner of the honest securities dealer and the prosecutor of dishonesty in the financial world.[53]

[49] *World's Work*, LXI (April, 1932), 29.
[50] *Magazine of Wall Street*, Oct. 2, 1934, p. 34.
[51] *Collier's*, July 27, 1935, p. 14; Kennedy, *I'm for Roosevelt*, p. 96.
[52] Kennedy, *Address to the Union League Club of Chicago*, p. 7.
[53] Kennedy, *Address to the Boston Chamber of Commerce*, p. 3.

Alternately prodding and cracking down where necessary, Kennedy called the business world "cowardly" for not "getting out and fighting for prosperity." At one business group Kennedy hurled several lines of Milton on "loathèd Melancholy" to describe the foolish pessimism of the financial world, and drew on an Elihu Root speech of twenty years earlier to defend administration law as a democratic device for needed delegation of powers.[54] As a prompt example of how wrongdoing would be dealt with, the operations of the New York Mining Exchange, based chiefly on high-pressure door-to-door canvassing among the poor with worthless "penny" stocks, were abruptly brought to an end.[55]

Joseph Kennedy was no Judas sheep leading trusting Wall Street firms into the slaughter pen of bureaucracy, as some publications darkly hinted. Rather, Kennedy was one of the few men of the 1930's whose considerable wealth was accompanied by a sense of social responsibility. The raw acquisitiveness of some of his contemporaries he found philosophically obnoxious and utterly impractical from any viewpoint of enlightened self-interest. His scorn was evident for the type of capitalist who insisted that his sizable profits as well as his capital must be fully guaranteed by government and society. Despite parental influence in his first important job and his later participation in a Wall Street pool, Kennedy's many other financial exploits showed a zest for the role of capitalist entrepreneur as a genuine taker of risks. Socially, however, there was no question in Kennedy's mind that government regulation had to be effected in order to prevent uncontrolled economic individualism from toppling the entire capitalist structure.

A conservative of independent mold, Kennedy sent his sons from Harvard to the London School of Economics to complete their education under Harold Laski.[56] Evincing a strong regard for the utilitarian and the pragmatic, Kennedy wished to put his financial knowledge to socially constructive use, and was con-

[54] SEC, Release No. 317 (Securities Act of 1933), March 19, 1935.
[55] Kennedy, *I'm for Roosevelt*, pp. 64–65.
[56] "Mr. Kennedy, the Chairman," *Fortune*, p. 144.

vinced that Franklin Roosevelt was the soundest leader that the American society could find to solve its current problems. More lone-wolf operator than top administrator, Joseph Kennedy nevertheless did a zealous and creditable job.

Although all of the commissioners joined Kennedy in presenting the SEC viewpoint to the world of finance, Landis was perhaps more articulate than his colleagues. In the first few years of the SEC Landis' speeches and articles demonstrated the development of his ideas on the responsibilities of American banking and finance. Continually pleading the benefits of a supervised self-regulation, Landis gradually shaped his distinctive philosophy of the Federal administrative agency and the administrative process.[57]

There was no question in Landis' mind that the overwhelming reelection of Roosevelt "reflected the intensity of national desire to move closer to an ideal of industrial and financial security." This mandate must be met by the fullest exercise of responsibility in finance, Landis told the Investment Bankers Association. To place the burden of an unstable market on margin requirements and antimanipulation restrictions was simply "escape ideology." Neither the financial world nor the SEC dared fail, Landis warned. The nation was so deeply determined that conditions of the late twenties not be allowed to repeat themselves, that whether through more repressive administrators or through other sanctions, "the objectives of our national life in this field will be attained." [58]

The responsibility of the exchanges and securities dealers in educating the investor had far-reaching consequences, Landis showed. Insufficient information for the buyer of stocks not only affected the fortune of the individual "but tends seriously to alter the character of the market itself." A poor quality of investment advice made an unwitting speculator out of the bona

[57] Landis, *The Administrative Process*. The dedication reads: "To Sam Rayburn of Texas, whose quiet desire to serve his country has fashioned so greatly the development of the administrative process."

[58] Landis, "The Direction of Recovery," pp. 152, 153, and "The Regulation of Investment Banking by the Federal Government," p. 17.

fide investor, and thereby injected a disproportionate element of speculation into the market.[59]

The stock exchanges were self-governing organizations, Landis pointed out. Government regulation thus welded together existing self-regulation and control by the government. Such regulation followed the lines of institutional development,

buttressing existing powers by the force of government, rather than absorbing all authority and all power to itself. In so doing, it made the loyalty of the institution to broad objectives of government a condition of its continued existence, thus building from within as well as imposing from without.[60]

Discussing the relationship of traditional concepts of law to the processes of administration, Landis stated his thesis that the agencies for the protection of the rights and liberties peculiar to modern civilization were "administrative, rather than judicial." Such agencies, created to solve problems of social control, did not come into being as a "single comprehensive philosophical conception," but rather "by a process of empirical growth." [61]

The modern administrative agency was far more than a policing agent, Landis thought, since the "mere proscription of abuses was insufficient to effect the realization of the broad objectives that lay behind the movement for securities' legislation." Neither was the administrative agency a mere extension of executive power, as some incorrectly suggested, since it differed radically in its responsibilities. The essence of this comparatively new arm of government lay in its "response to the demand that government assume responsibility not merely to maintain ethical levels in the economic relations of members of society, but to provide for the efficient functioning of the economic processes of the state." [62]

Although Roosevelt expressed some doubt about the pro-

[59] New York *Times*, May 19, 1936.
[60] Landis, "The Firing Line in the Law," p. 404.
[61] "The Mechanisms of Administration," p. 632, and "The Firing Line in the Law," p. 403.
[62] Landis, *The Administrative Process*, pp. 15, 16.

liferation of government agencies, Landis saw in them the answer to the inadequacy of the simple tripartite form of government to deal with modern problems. "Efficiency in the processes of governmental regulation," Landis stated, "is best served by the creation of more [rather than fewer] agencies." [63]

Landis was invaluable in his defense of the role of the administrative agency in modern American society. He effectively cleared the air regarding accusations of "star chamber proceedings," the alleged absence of due process, and all the other dogmatic generalizations of an older generation opposed to any infringement of complete economic individualism. But an even more valuable contribution of James Landis to the early SEC was his role of careful administrative planner. Here his great talent in the interpretation and application of statutes was combined with his feelings for the orderly growth and continuity necessary to the erection of a legal framework. Landis was convinced that the necessary approach was careful, even though time-consuming, preparation at the foundations of the administrative edifice. This attitude sometimes resulted in criticism from those more concerned with the immediate erection of a comprehensive and aggressive regulatory structure. But Landis' tireless plugging of technical gaps and his insistence on the careful polishing of each phrase of the rules and regulations to be put into public use played an important part in the respect that accrued to the agency after Wall Street attorneys had tested SEC rulings in the lower courts.

The other commissioners took an active part in soliciting the cooperation and the assumption of responsibility by banking and business groups. Addressing the National Association of Better Business Bureaus, Commissioner Mathews underscored the danger of the public's considering that governmental regulation of securities meant removal of risk.[64] This was an attitude that had caused some objection to securities legislation in the first

[63] E. Roosevelt, *F.D.R.: His Personal Letters*, III, 310; Landis, *The Administrative Process*, p. 24.

[64] George C. Mathews, "The Governmental Regulation of Securities," *Investment Banking*, IV, No. 10 (Sept., 1934), 295.

place, and consequently was a subject all commissioners emphasized.

Mathews had helped draft the Wisconsin state laws against security frauds, and a later chairman (Jerome N. Frank) described him as "a bulwark of technical expertness and highly intelligent business judgment." [65] Mathews and Healy were the two Republicans required by the SEC enacting legislation as a bipartisan minimum. Their Republicanism was such as to lead to their continued reappointment, since both Mathews' Wisconsin Progressivism and Healy's New England financial austerity meant their agreement on the New Deal financial reforms incorporated in the SEC.

A conscientious public servant with years of state and Federal service to his credit, Mathews turned down an offer in 1935 of a $35,000 salary from Associated Telegraph Utilities.[66] (SEC commissioner's salary: $10,000.) Five years later, however, Mathews regretfully informed President Roosevelt that he had an opportunity he could not refuse. He resigned in April, 1940, to join Northern States Power Company, one of the units in the holding company system of Standard Gas and Electric, which had to be integrated and simplified in accordance with the "death sentence" clause of the Holding Company Act.

Commissioner Healy's particular forte was the problem of accounting practices as they affected corporate mergers and corporate information offered to investors. Healy related his shocked surprise when he became aware of the accounting practice of certain companies that consolidated to form the Florida Power and Light Company. The property of the constituent companies appeared on their books at $25 million, but the same assets appeared on the books of the newly formed Florida Power and Light Company at a valuation of $58 million, a stock-watering operation of $32 million, or a 103 percent increase.[67] These were tactics that were effectively halted by the Securities Act and the

[65] New York *Times*, March 27, 1940.
[66] Brayman, p. 118.
[67] House, *Stock Exchange Regulation*, p. 843.

Holding Company Act. In a later speech he made clear his continual emphasis on accounting practice.

Until recently, public accountants very seldom recognized completely their responsibility to the public, and they should be charged, in my opinion, with a very large share of responsibility for some of the worst things that have happened in the security business.[68]

Healy's outlook was strongly influenced throughout his long SEC career by his intensive investigation, as FTC counsel, of the utilities holding companies and the corruption he found in the labyrinths of their interlocking financial creations. Corporate actions that deviated from the letter or spirit of the law, or holding company devices that furthered the material aggrandizement of their officers or directors at stockholder expense, were certain to draw a wrathful reaction from the Vermont judge. Healy was intent on the most scrupulous corporate integrity, and like John Adams, had a horror of the business mind that created artificial financial beings out of nothingness for use in the pyramiding of questionable profits and power. Renewed by Roosevelt and again by President Truman, Robert Healy's tenure with the SEC was ended only by his death in November, 1946.

Emphasis on the lack of corporate ethics and the decay in fiduciary relationship marked Ferdinand Pecora's few public utterances. The corporate device, Pecora declared, had been "twisted out of its original and socially useful character and has become a weapon in the hands of promoters as powerful as machine-guns in the hands of gangsters." Pecora castigated the banks for not ridding themselves of holding company control and warned that in the American system free enterprise could not continue to exist "in an atmosphere where the trust relationship is not held inviolable." [69]

At no time did Pecora give evidence of pursuing larger problems of social planning, but he was deeply concerned with putting the law at the service of society rather than at the disposition

[68] Robert E. Healy, "U.S. Civil Service Commission Training Program No. 8: S.E.C. (SEC mimeograph, n.p., 1942), p. 7.
[69] Pecora, "Wall Street Under the Flag," p. 61.

of unscrupulous financiers. His experience with a Senate sub-committee investigation that saw the Morgans, the Wiggins, and the Mitchells of the financial world exonerated by the letter of the law left him with an increased reverence for the law's substance. As a New York State Supreme Court justice several years later, Pecora continued to demonstrate this feeling. Stockholders of the Industrial Finance Corporation, appearing before him after his elevation to the bench, had sued to recover for themselves the shares with which the directors of their company had formed a separate syndicate. In awarding the entire profit of the transaction to the stockholders, including interest and accrued dividends, Pecora said of the directors' obligations, "Inevitably it is the duty of the courts to enforce all obligations implicit in that fiduciary relationship." [70]

Actually the make-up of the first Commission did not remain static for very long. Only six months after the initial five had taken the oath of office, Ferdinand Pecora resigned to fill a vacancy on the New York State Supreme Court. His appointment by Governor Lehman was unanimously confirmed by the State Senate on January 15, 1935.[71]

In September of the same year, when Joseph P. Kennedy sent his letter of resignation to the President after fifteen months as chairman, he reminded Roosevelt of their agreement that he serve only one year. Kennedy placed his further services at the presidential call, however, saying, "I shall still deem myself a part of your Administration." Roosevelt's answer verified their understanding on the length of his SEC tenure, praised his leadership in glowing terms, and heartily affirmed Kennedy's position as still "a member of my Administration." "In the future, as in the past," the President wrote, "I shall freely turn to you for support and counsel." [72]

[70] *Time*, Nov. 30, 1936, p. 58.
[71] *Commercial and Financial Chronicle*, Jan. 19, 1935, p. 408. Pecora was later nominated by both the Democratic and Republican parties for the full fourteen-year term as supreme court justice, and elected Nov. 5, 1935. See *Who's Who in America 1958–1959*, p. 2155.
[72] Joseph P. Kennedy to F.D.R., F.D.R. to Kennedy, Sept. 6 and 20, 1935, Roosevelt Papers.

Reaction in the press differed vastly from that which originally met the first chairman. Notable among those who acknowledged their initial error in judgment was Kennedy's fiercest critic, John T. Flynn. Flynn manfully retracted his earlier criticism and stated positively, "He was, I firmly believe, the most useful member of the Commission." [73] Theodore M. Knappen, who earlier had indicated in contemptuous tones the Kennedy-SEC relationship as "four intellectuals and the showman" and "four ascetics and a Sybarite," was among those who made retraction. The SEC under Kennedy, said Knappen, had carried on a "steady reconcilement" with Wall Street. The new commissioners had demonstrated satisfactorily that their discretionary power would be used constructively and "with a minimum of interference in the normal process of security issuance." [74]

Kennedy's administration as SEC chairman had won the respect of both friends and foes of the New Deal, *Newsweek* reported. In Wall Street, news of his resignation depressed stocks.[75] However, James M. Landis, whose election as chairman Kennedy had predicted, issued a reassuring statement. "Mr. Kennedy's policies are Commission policies," Landis said, "and there is no reason for changing them." [76]

It was significant that only fifteen months after the first commissioners of the new agency had taken their oath of office, spokesmen for the business world could say "the SEC was generally considered the New Deal's most successful reform." [77] In that short space of time the business and financial community found itself able to make uniformly favorable comparisons and comments regarding the newest regulatory agency. Other administrative agencies were considered variously to be somewhat

[73] *New Republic*, Oct. 9, 1935, p. 244.
[74] Knappen, "The Rulers of the Stock Market," p. 329, and "The SEC Surprises Both Friend and Foe," p. 539.
[75] *Newsweek*, Sept. 28, 1935, p. 31.
[76] New York *Times*, Sept. 24, 1935. The outgoing and the incoming chairmen collaborated some years later in *The Surrender of King Leopold* (New York: Joseph P. Kennedy Memorial Foundation, 1950), following Kennedy's service as ambassador to Great Britain. Based on the Keyes-Gort correspondence, the work absolves Leopold from much of the British and French blame for the surrender of the Belgian armies.
[77] "Mr. Kennedy, the Chairman," p. 58.

"ruthless," like the Federal Power Commission, or "tinged with politics," as the Federal Communications Commission. The SEC, however, was adjudged "highly practical" and harmonious in operation.[78]

Even after the passage of the Public Utilities Holding Company Act of 1935, the highly partisan periodical *Public Utilities* could report that the SEC was the only government agency receiving more than a 50 percent favorable response in a poll of businessmen's attitudes toward regulatory agencies. This result, the writer concluded, was traceable directly to "the practicality and reasonableness of original chairman Kennedy and successor Landis." [79]

Early critics found that after only fifteen months of existence, SEC aid in interpretation of its rulings to the Wall Street fraternity compared most favorably with the "legalistic 'upstageness' of some other administrative agencies of the Government." The reluctant dawning of an earlier truth often followed. "The Commission has in no way challenged the actual market system." [80]

The careful preparation that went into the promulgation of its rules and regulations drew early praise for the competency of the SEC staff and commissioners. It was noted that "SEC has drafted its administrative rulings so meticulously that it has thus far been challenged in the courts less than any other New Deal agency." [81] Grudging homage was frequently paid to the legal draftsmanship of the first two securities acts. With their legal talent helpless to clear the usual convenient statutory paths through the tightly worded clauses of the two acts, the financial world flexibly adjusted itself to their unassailable intent.

The initial stage of SEC success, however, must rest largely with the first commissioners, who formulated and executed early regulatory policy, and more particularly, with the agency's first two chairmen, Kennedy and Landis. A primary point of agreement between these two executives as to SEC policy was the at-

[78] Brayman, p. 116.
[79] *Ibid.*
[80] Knappen, "The SEC Surprises Both Friend and Foe," p. 565.
[81] "SEC," *Fortune,* p. 130.

tempt to encourage and employ wherever possible the use of self-regulation. It did not mean toleration of excess, but it did hold with the Landis idea of self-made restrictions freely operating within definite governmental limitations.

When Chairman Kennedy submitted a report to Congress on the government of securities exchanges pursuant to Section 19(c) of the Exchange Act, it contained numerous agency recommendations. These were made with a definite assumption in mind: "The Commission does not now suggest that legislation be enacted to bring about these recommendations. Its recommendations can be put into effect by voluntary action of the exchanges themselves without resort to legislation." [82]

It may have been true, as one writer suggested, that some part of Wall Street's confidence rested on the fact that Kennedy obviously had no bureaucratic vested interest to protect.[83] Certainly the financial world cherished no illusions regarding the strength of the Kennedy convictions. The practice of investment bankers serving on the boards of industrial corporations was a favorite Kennedy target. This custom must be stopped, he said flatly, "and I predict that it will be outlawed. It has led to excessive financing, excessive underwriting charges, excessive bonuses, improper loans, and a host of other evils which in public life would be condemned as graft." [84]

In some ways Kennedy reminded one of an erstwhile alley gamin eager to display and expose his old haunts and tricks to his newly found friends from the other side of the financial tracks. Although he undoubtedly received considerable aid and advice from his colleagues in formulating policy directives, the determined zeal with which Kennedy pursued his new duties made a favorable impression on press and financial circles alike.

The widespread approval of Kennedy's administration, coming as it did from both extremes of the political spectrum, was in one way a tribute to Roosevelt's pervasive knack for selecting the right executive instrument. But even more, it was a recog-

[82] House, *Report on Government of Securities Exchanges*, p. 17.
[83] Corey, p. 54.
[84] Kennedy, "Big Business, What Now?" p. 28.

nition of Kennedy's own native political acumen, his talent for adapting himself to various warring groups while effecting their reconciliation in the process. Kennedy's tremendous diversity of interests, particularly before his SEC career, bespeaks considerable freedom from dogma and fixed ideas. This characteristic, together with the very evident zest that caused him to value the formidable struggles of political life above the routine of business administration, were qualities of inestimable value in the early acceptance of SEC.

His successor to the chairmanship, thirty-six-year-old James M. Landis, was conscious that the SEC was still at a young and tender stage of agency growth. This realization led to Landis' demand for lengthy studies on all areas to be regulated and to his insistence that such studies be built on unassailable foundations. The Commission learned from Landis' superb legislative talents to look at their regulations in terms of eventual Supreme Court review. The proof that they built well lay in the enviable record that the SEC held in the nation's courts.

It was Landis' measured approach to the idea of maximum self-regulation that drew criticism from those who insisted that the crackdown on the exchanges be hard and immediate. In his demand for studies and more studies Landis can be likened to the field general who will not unnecessarily risk his forces until sure of overwhelming superiority. But the many studies begun by Chairman Landis—and frequently used to such good advantage by his successor, William O. Douglas—were not born of timidity. Rather, they were the outcome of an extremely judicious temperament and a realization of the need to build well for the future that enabled Landis to look beyond his critics' short-range views.

Chairman Landis later acknowledged that he had been in error in urging FTC administration of the Securities Act rather than creation of a new agency.[85] His reflections during several years of subsequent SEC tenure emerged as a strong conviction regarding the place of the administrative agency in the modern American scene. It fulfilled the demand for the new machinery

[85] "The Legend of Landis," *Fortune*, p. 46.

needed to "give old rights their intended effect." In an era of intense specialization in which the democratic processes of the judiciary would fail to keep abreast of the overwhelming demands made upon it, the administrative agency was the empirical answer for the necessary effectuation of democratic government policy. Administrative law, Landis thought, was the outstanding response of a generation alarmed by the threat to its economic democracy. The need, therefore, was for further such regulatory agencies in other critical areas of social control.

As an administrator, Landis bore out Dean Roscoe Pound's perceptive early description, "as careful and correct working under high pressure as when he had lots of time." [86] This characteristic, together with Landis' judicious approach and his concern for the long-term development of the SEC, enabled him to adhere to the view of self-regulation within firm governmental limits. "The SEC has to be both a crackdown and a cooperating agency, depending on circumstances," [87] was the succinct expression of this viewpoint. A brilliant professor of law, Landis' speeches and writings were never based on narrowly legalistic grounds. The profession of law Landis viewed from a humanistic standpoint. Lawyers were of most value to society as "mediators of human affairs," not simply as expert craftsmen of the law. Landis' point of view as constitutional expert and philosopher, one journal acknowledged, "often pitched [SEC] problems on higher planes . . . of permanent social and economic values." [88] No less important contributions to the Commission were a trained intellect and a scholarly background, with a necessary concern for the evolutionary development of American institutions. The reasonableness that disavowed any Procrustean lines of administration was rarely in conflict with the conviction that always acted as champion of the public interest.

The first two chairmen of the SEC complemented each other in effective fashion. Kennedy, conceiving of the stock market as a financial generator, was anxious to promote an atmosphere of confidence and inaugurate the necessary flow of new securi-

[86] *Ibid.*
[87] *Newsweek,* Sept. 20, 1937, p. 30.
[88] New York *Times,* Oct. 6, 1935.

ties. Landis, concerned more with the long-range activities of the new administrative agency, was eager to aid the entire field of exchanges and securities issuers to adjust itself to the necessary control of society. Kennedy ideally served as the initial contact with an apprehensive Wall Street, as the first domesticator of the bulls and bears. Landis pressed the New Deal ideals of economic democracy slowly forward, buttressed by sound studies and meticulous rulings.

The attitude of the entire first Commission reflected a shared pragmatic and undogmatic approach to early SEC problems. All were concerned with conveying to business, financial, and professional groups the need for the protection of the investor, and the positive benefits that would accrue to the business world from such a program. As members of the legal profession, both Healy and Pecora took issue publicly with the unsocial attitude of those lawyers whose talents were devoted to horrifying their clients with the imaginary pitfalls of the securities acts. Although Pecora gave evidence of more regard for the law's substance, and Healy was more occupied with the law's letter, neither could condone successful legalistic defeat of the law's intent. Healy's unyielding rectitude had its counterpart in the calm and unruffled steadiness that earned Mathews the Commission nickname of "Rock of Gibraltar."

Ferdinand Pecora, in earlier days vice-chairman of the National Progressive party from New York,[89] and George C. Mathews, a practicing Wisconsin Progressive, combined with the enlightened conservatism of Joseph P. Kennedy to give the first group of commissioners overtones distinctly reminiscent of progressive victories several decades earlier. Aided by its successful association with the more liberal element of Wall Street and the judicious policies of its first two chairmen, a dedicated and competent SEC had strongly entrenched itself in the business world through its firm yet reasonable approach to the problems for which it was created. It had, thereby, adequate strength after its first two years of existence to meet and withstand the subsequent assault of the nationally powerful private utilities and their holding companies.

[89] Who's Who in America, 1958–1959, p. 2155.

CHAPTER FIVE

THE PUBLIC UTILITY HOLDING COMPANY ACT OF 1935

In no part of the establishment of the SEC did Franklin D. Roosevelt figure so prominently as in the enactment of the Public Utility Holding Company Act of 1935, the third of the three major acts that the SEC was charged with administering.

Few pieces of New Deal legislation provoked such acrimony and produced such sharp political divisiveness. Yet perhaps no other enactment had behind it so much of the President's deepest personal convictions and drew on such continuity from Roosevelt's entire public career. Scarcely "one of the President's hobbies," as *Fortune,* with characteristic artful derogation, referred to it,[1] the entire field of public utilities and the power problem was the most important single subject in his entire political life. This concentration drew from his foremost biographer the remark that there was "no other area, even that of agriculture, in which Roosevelt undertook such extensive study." [2]

Indications of influences on Roosevelt's early consideration of the power and utilities problem have been found in his collegiate career. Daniel R. Fusfeld points out that Roosevelt, as an economics major in his senior year at Harvard, had studied the economics of corporations under William Z. Ripley, and banking under Oliver M. W. Sprague. The trust problem, the harmful effects of merger and monopoly, were major political and

---

[1] "SEC," *Fortune,* p. 123.
[2] Freidel, p. 101.

economic issues of the day. Both Ripley and Sprague were identified as strong advocates of economic reform and of Federal regulation to curb economic abuses. A major work of Ripley's, *Main Street and Wall Street,* was concerned with exposures of financial malpractice, and his continued demands for corporate "open-book" practices were strongly reflected in those portions of the Securities Act of 1933 requiring full publicity for many corporate holdings and activities. Later, at Columbia University Law School, Roosevelt studied public utilities law under Jackson E. Reynolds, an articulate proponent of the strong regulatory commission.[3]

The young Roosevelt also had as models the Progressives' attitude toward the public utility problem, particularly as exhibited by his admired cousin Theodore and his later mentor, Woodrow Wilson. Franklin D. Roosevelt, as a youthful progressive Democrat, voted successfully in the New York State Senate of 1913 to annul the previous grant of the St. Lawrence River to the Aluminum Company of America as a power site. In this action and in its continuation through his state career Roosevelt exhibited the profound distrust for concentrations of economic power on which the Progressive movement was built. In many subsequent speeches his advocacy of governmental regulation of the public utility type of corporation was a resounding echo of Theodore Roosevelt at Osawatomie.

Both before and during his gubernatorial service Roosevelt used a variety of public forums to air his views on the power and public utility problem. Writing for the Beacon (New York) *Standard* as a private citizen and a "Good Neighbor" of Dutchess County, Roosevelt foreshadowed his later "yardstick" theory. His consideration of government control of great power sites, he wrote, came from his concern with "keeping a check on prices for electric current paid by the consumer." But the idea of a detrimental concentration of economic power was of vast and underlying importance.

Electricity is of such vital and growing concern to everyone of us in our daily lives that we have a right to demand that no individual

[3] Fusfeld, pp. 33–35.

or set of individuals should ever get into a position where they can make vast fortunes at our expense.[4]

In an article that he wrote for *Forum* the first year he was governor of New York State, Roosevelt illustrated his belief that stern measures would be necessary to curb the alarming concentration of holding company wealth and protect the consumer, a belief that became only more certain with the developments of the next few years. The holding companies, Roosevelt wrote, were directly and indirectly responsible for boosting rates. Their greed made rate reductions impossible. And the inadequacies of utilities regulation in protection of the public were such that it might be necessary for either the state or Federal government to develop the larger power resources such as the St. Lawrence River and Muscle Shoals.[5]

The complete intransigence of the utilities companies in their disregard for the consumer, and the unreal capitalization on which their rate demands were based, brought a stern and blunt warning from Roosevelt, published in the utilities trade journal: "They have not been content with a fair return on their investment. They have sown the wind; they may reap the whirlwind." [6]

During his first term as governor, Roosevelt's success in stimulating public opinion via the radio had engendered tremendous support for his stand on the water-power issue. "Many Republicans, including W. Kingsland Macy and the utilities lobby, doubted the ability of the GOP to defeat Roosevelt's bid for re-election in 1930 as long as water power remained an issue." [7]

Later public utility problems of national import frequently had their counterpart in Roosevelt's gubernatorial encounters. Faced with an extremely pro-utility Public Service Commission, Roosevelt warned in his state inaugural address against the too hasty assumption that public service commissions in themselves were a sure guarantee of the proper protection of the consumer.[8]

---

[4] Carmichael, p. 140.
[5] F.D.R., "The Real Meaning of the Power Problem," pp. 327 ff.
[6] F.D.R., "How Will New York's Progressive Proposals Affect the Investor?" p. 82.
[7] Bellush, p. 217.
[8] F.D.R., *Public Papers and Addresses,* I, 78.

Such difficulty in regulation may have influenced Roosevelt toward a statutory solution, at least insofar as the later problem of holding company elimination was concerned.

The tremendous damage that a powerfully financed lobby could do, and the corruptive influence that it could spread throughout a law-making body, were lessons not lost on Roosevelt as New York's governor. The effects of public utilities companies' lobbying were visible and tangible enough in the hamstringing of Roosevelt-sponsored legislation, but actual proof only emerged several years after the act. As part of the thorough FTC investigation of the utilities companies, evidence was introduced to show that New York State Senator Warren T. Thayer was in the pay of the Associated Gas and Electric Company of New York. Thayer's valuable position as chairman of the Senate committee through which all utilities legislation had to pass became evident when letters from Thayer to his employers came to light in 1934. In a letter to a vice-president of Associated Gas and Electric written March 28, 1927, Thayer said: "I hope that my work during the last session was satisfactory to your company; not so much for new legislation enacted, but for the fact that many detrimental bills which were introduced we were able to kill in my committee." [9]

Roosevelt's actions against the public utilities, and his dramatic carrying of the fight to the people over the heads of much of the legislature, brought him national attention at a time when many other states were concerned with the same problem. Public opinion, aroused over high electricity rates and long-term private leases of state and national power sources, was moving in a favorable direction. In all those states where water power was a dominant issue, Bernard Bellush showed, the avowed champions of public control were the victors. Phil La Follette and conservationist Gifford Pinchot won the 1930 gubernatorial elections in Wisconsin and Pennsylvania respectively. An off-year in Congressional elections, 1930 saw John H. Bankhead defeat J. Thomas Heflin of Alabama for the United States Senate. Thomas Walsh of Montana and Edward P. Costigan of Colo-

[9] New York *Times,* March 30, 1934.

rado, both strong advocates of public power control, were also victorious in Senate races.[10]

Roosevelt's leadership was being recognized nationally even as he launched his campaign in 1930 for a second term as governor. Messages of support keyed to the public-power and private-utilities issue came from such disparate sources as New Market, Virginia, merchants, the Democrats of Butler County, Iowa, and the American Legion Post of Sheffield, Alabama.[11]

A wide base of national support enabled the Democratic party to take a forthright stand on the entire power and utilities issue. The national platform in the presidential election of 1932 did not only refer to the advocacy of the "conservation, development, and use of the nation's water power in the public interest." It also stated a regulatory position that acknowledged the connection between the exploitation of investors by holding companies and the excessive rates charged consumers by operating companies:

Regulation to the full extent of federal power, of
  (a) Holding companies which sell securities in interstate commerce;
  (b) Rates of utilities companies operating across state lines.[12]

As the foremost spokesman in the nation on the utilities issue, Roosevelt was superbly fitted to present his party's views from his own background of personal experience and conviction. Choosing the Pacific Northwest as an ideal site, Roosevelt devoted his entire talk at Portland, Oregon, in September, 1932, to developing his views on public utilities and the national development of hydroelectric power. The Democratic nominee pointed to the results of the current FTC investigation to show that the utilities companies, in an attempt to prejudice the public in their favor, were guilty of a "deliberate and unprincipled campaign of misinformation, of propaganda, and, if I may use the words, of lies and falsehoods." Roosevelt went back historically to James I of England to illustrate the common-law point that certain conveniences and utilities, unlike other businesses,

---

[10] Bellush, p. 217.
[11] *Ibid.*, p. 260.
[12] Porter and Johnson, p. 332.

were "vested with a public character," and that to charge excessive rates was to set up improper obstacles to the public use. Lower rates, according to Roosevelt, were prevented by selfish concentrates, such as the infamous Insull empire. The development of "these financial monstrosities" was such as to "compel inevitable and ultimate ruin" to such structures and their innocent investors alike.[13]

The first two years of the New Deal saw a considerable part of the platform regulating utilities translated into legislation. A bill to require truthfulness in the issuance of their securities had been enacted for the protection of the investor. A new agency, the Securities and Exchange Commission, had been established not only to regulate the nation's exchanges but to curb the utilities and other corporate officials in their stock-juggling activities. Creation of the Tennessee Valley Authority had partially solved the "yardstick" problem, at the same time attacking the more important areas of flood control, conservation, and land reclamation. However, the problem of the super holding company as an unhealthy concentration of wealth and power, and as a basic cause of high electricity rates paid by the consumer, still remained to be faced.

One of the lengthiest and most exhaustive reports ever called for by Congress was the one that examined this problem, a voluminous investigation finally announced as complete in the first month of 1935. Following a Senate resolution introduced during the Coolidge regime by Tom Walsh of Montana, the Federal Trade Commission made an investigation of the utilities holding companies and utilities operating companies, based on the testimony of their officers and the records and books of the companies themselves, and filled more than ninety volumes with its exhibits and statistics.[14] Drawing on material compiled over a six-year period, the investigation had been sternly and thoroughly pursued by its able general counsel, Judge Robert E. Healy, later a commissioner of the SEC.

The report left no doubt as to the menace of the holding com-

---

[13] *Ibid.*, pp. 730, 736.
[14] FTC, *Utility Corporations.*

pany on the national economic scene. Since 1920, the investigation disclosed, the problem had shifted to getting control of holding companies by still larger holding companies. Such competition, unlike the consolidation of operating companies for greater efficiency, was chiefly competition for promotional and managerial control.[15] Such structures could not be erected without the aid of investment bankers. Yet the resulting situation was one that forced increasing attention to the desires and alignments of bankers rather than to the interests of the stockholders themselves.

The tremendous size of the utilities holding companies, and their dominance in the field, was illustrated in a study of the quantity of electrical energy generated in the United States. In 1929, according to the report, the three giants—the United Corporation, Electric Bond and Share, and the Insull group—plus a dozen other large holding companies, were the source of 82.3 percent of all the kilowatt hours generated.[16] In 1932 the figure stood at 78.8 percent. However, the report considered this an understatement, since stock held in many local groups would easily increase the control to 88 or 90 percent of all electrical energy generated in the United States.

The FTC report emphasized the nature of the problem as one calling for Federal control, partly because the utilities industry had freed itself from any effective control at state level, and partly because of the dangerous concentration of wealth in the holding companies. As an example the report cited the Morgan interests' United Corporation. Its total output was given as 27 percent of the nation's electricity, but in concentrate it accounted for 63 percent of the total electrical output of the important states of New York, New Jersey, Pennsylvania, Maryland, Delaware, Michigan, Ohio, Tennessee, Georgia, and Alabama.[17]

The report scrupulously mentioned the benefits to be derived from holding companies in the form of super management and group financing, but gave as its opinion that "on the whole the

[15] Ibid., Part 72-A, pp. 60–61.
[16] Ibid., p. 38.
[17] Ibid., Part 73-A, p. 33.

detriment of the utilities holding companies to the public has exceeded, thus far, their value to the public." Their economic value was nil, since they manufactured nothing but questionable securities for a gulled public. In carefully chosen language the report declared that the operations of holding companies could not only be described in the more common terms of deceit, misrepresentation, and breach of trust but properly and suitably could be labeled as outright fraud and dishonesty. Their abuses, the FTC concluded, could be met in four different ways: by taxation, by direct prohibitive legislation, by compulsory Federal licensing, or by a permissive Federal incorporation act. It was the commission's considered recommendation that the solution could best be achieved through the adoption of the first two methods mentioned.[18]

Academically, the holding company as an institution of American economic life had been carefully and thoroughly examined by a team of Columbia University economists, James C. Bonbright and Gardiner C. Means. Writing at the same time the FTC utilities investigation was in progress, Bonbright and Means stressed the undeniably menacing aspect of holding companies that arose from their unlimited possibility of evading all forms of "social control." The Bonbright and Means work did not suggest dissolution, since their abuses did not negate the economic usefulness of the holding company device. Federal regulation must be enacted, though, before their admitted excesses caused them to be "destroyed by an angry electorate." [19]

The legislation that Roosevelt, his aides, and his administrative leaders prepared for the opening of the Seventy-fourth Congress clearly favored the dissolution of utilities holding companies, chiefly through taxation and directly prohibitive means. With his usual appreciation of the possibilities inherent in diverse approaches to a problem, Roosevelt had either authorized or suggested the three pieces of legislation that emerged. Probably the most drastic was the work largely of Robert H. Jackson,

[18] *Ibid.*, pp. 64, iii.
[19] James C. Bonbright and Gardiner C. Means, *The Holding Company* (New York, 1932), p. 339.

whose services were loaned by Secretary of the Treasury Morgenthau. Jackson's bill destroyed holding companies by means of intercorporate dividend taxes. Using both tax measures and prohibitive clauses, a somewhat less drastic bill had been prepared for Representative Sam Rayburn, chairman of the Committee on Foreign and Interstate Commerce, by Walter M. W. Splawn, the committee's temporary counsel. Splawn, an economist, was a former member of the Texas Railroad Commission, former president of the University of Texas, and officially a member of the Interstate Commerce Commission. A third bill used prohibitive measures that also outlawed the holding company but applied them with considerably more chronological leeway and some administrative latitude. This was the bill written by the New Deal legislative twins, Ben Cohen and Tom Corcoran, with aid and advice from James M. Landis and Judge Robert E. Healy of the SEC. The comparative conservatism of the latter bill was successfully urged upon the President as being the most feasible politically, although Roosevelt, probably thinking of the Insull empire, was not easily dissuaded from the most drastic of the three.

The Cohen-Corcoran bill, introduced simultaneously on February 6, 1935, by Rayburn in the House and by his counterpart in the Senate, Burton K. Wheeler of Montana, had wide Congressional support.[20] It enjoyed the prestige of presidential favor and was known to have considerable grass-roots backing. Heavy emphasis on the gradual extinction of holding companies was worked into a clause soon to be made famous—or infamous—as the "death sentence." Southern Congressmen of Populist heritage could readily join in the denunciation of great concentrates of wealth that the utilities holding company embodied. Other Southerners, whose constituents stood to benefit from the improvements and lower electric rates at hand in the valley of the Tennessee River, were fervent supporters. Liberals and radicals were drawn to the bill's support through lower rates for urban electricity consumers and for ideals of economic democracy and

[20] H.R. 5423 and S. 1725 (*Congressional Record*, 74 Cong., 1 Sess., 1935, LXXIX, Part II, 1624, 1513).

social justice. Such diverse support brought about paradoxical, if temporary, legislative alliances. One union saw rural dema- gogue and public power advocate John E. Rankin of Mississippi, and the New York City radical, Vito Marcantonio, combined in full voice for the bill's passage.

Western progressives were a strong core of unswerving ad- herents. Senator Edward P. Costigan of Colorado, once a Re- publican but now a Democrat, an advocate of public power and an active member of Senator Wheeler's Interstate Commerce Committee, had been one of the 1912 founders of the Progres- sive party. The Republican Senator from New Mexico, Bronson Cutting, whose death in 1935 was a tragic blow to the public power group, had also been a leader of the 1912 Progressives. Other stalwarts included the Progressive Republican from South Dakota, Lynn T. Frazier, in the Senate, and a small band in the House.

Sam Rayburn's home state of Texas furnished a large, able, and vocal contingent to support the bill. The entire state legisla- ture of Texas quickly put itself on record with a joint resolution addressed to the United States Congress approving the national Democratic administration's assault on the public utilities hold- ing companies. Control of these giants, the united Texans said, had become well-nigh impossible, "and under Republican rule little or nothing was being done." [21] Both Rayburn and the artic- ulate New Dealer Congressman Maury Maverick frequently took to the radio to warn or to exhort fellow Texans and Ameri- cans. Jesse H. Jones, Texas head of the Reconstruction Finance Corporation, sent a personal telegram to each member of the Texas delegation in Congress warning that support of a drastic clause outlawing holding companies was necessary to uphold the purpose of the bill.[22] Even the heavy-handed action of Vice- President Garner in appointing four staunch "death sentence" advocates among the five conferees who were to represent the Senate drew attention adversely to the efforts of this particular

[21] *Congressional Record,* LXXIX, Part III, p. 3324.
[22] Jesse H. Jones re Public Utility Holding Company Act, June 30, 1935, Roose- velt Papers.

state. Some basis for such strong Texan support may have come from the emergence of a state and regional natural gas industry. Such a thought was evidently present in the objections of Republican Representative Everett M. Dirksen of Illinois. Speaking to his colleagues at House hearings on the bill, Dirksen complained that if all utilities pipe lines could be declared common carriers by virtue of their interstate nature, then "Illinois investors and Illinois coal interests and Illinois utilities might be sacrificed upon the altar of the welfare of a State like Texas." [23]

The Lone Star State also furnished the floor leader who marshaled the Roosevelt forces in the House of Representatives behind the utilities bill. Sam Rayburn, as chairman of the Committee on Interstate and Foreign Commerce, had already shown his astuteness and masterful leadership in pushing through the two securities acts. His chief Congressional and pre-Congressional legislative interests were in the railroads, but efforts to curb the excesses in any area of the utilities field drew on his convictions as well as his partisan devotions.

As shepherd of the administration bill in the Senate, the job fell to one of the most dedicated public power advocates in either house of Congress. Burton K. Wheeler, Progressive Democrat from Montana, chairman of the Senate Interstate Commerce Committee, had a long and gallant record in the Senate and in his home state for championing the ownership of all natural resources by the people. The son of a poor shoemaker of Hudson, Massachusetts, Wheeler got as far west as Michigan in his early youth, and received a bachelor of laws degree from the University of Michigan in 1905. Pure chance found him beginning the practice of law in Butte, Montana, the same year, at age twenty-three. A persistent advocate of the farmer and of labor in the hostile atmosphere of the company-owned mountain mining states, Wheeler was part of a 1920 Non-Partisan League ticket that included a Negro and a Blackfoot Indian.[24] The Anaconda Company, attempting to cover him with as many stigmas as the mind could comprehend, charged Wheeler with loyalty to both

[23] House, *Public Utility and Holding Companies*, Part III, p. 1909.
[24] *Current Biography, 1940*, pp. 857–60.

the Kaiser and Lenin, and predicted the mines would close also if he should be elected. Wheeler didn't make it that time, or the governor's chair in 1920 (and the depression closed the mines later anyway), but the farmers, miners, and railroad men of Montana sent him to the United States Senate in 1922 and kept returning him thereafter.[25]

As a Senator, Burton K. Wheeler remained a militant dissident among the high priests of Republican prosperity in the 1920's. In 1924 he took time out to run with Robert La Follette on the national Progressive ticket, advocating public control of all natural resources and Federal aid to farmers.[26] He proudly referred to the fact that he had proposed Roosevelt for the Presidency even before the latter's reelection as governor in 1930, and he toured the West indefatigably for Roosevelt in 1932.[27] Wheeler, however, was much more at home with fellow Progressives Norris, Cutting, and La Follette, and was on bad terms with the Democratic National Committee.

Ideologically, Wheeler's approach to the utilities problem was to dispose of the evils of huge holding companies and their absentee management by smashing such structures completely and utterly. Introducing the public utility holding company bill in the Senate, Wheeler said bluntly it was "intended to whittle down and eventually eliminate the public utilities holding companies." Further, in the Brandeis tradition, "its spirit is the spirit of a bill I propose for a Federal tax on bigness, i.e., a tax on corporations based on their size." [28] Wheeler, a wily veteran with deep scars from the years of rough-and-tumble of railroad, oil, and power fights, was under no illusion as to the forces he would face, but never lacked courage and staying power. "Every 'new dealer' and Progressive in Washington knows that between the power gangs and us there can be no peace, now, in 1936, or ever," was his challenge.[29]

Opposition to the introduction of the public utility holding

[25] Creel, p. 12.
[26] *Current Biography, 1940,* p. 859.
[27] Wheeler, pp. 404–8.
[28] *Congressional Record,* LXXIX, Part II, 1525.
[29] *Ibid.,* Part III, p. 4903.

company bill from the financial press was at first lackadaisical. Congress was so certain that Roosevelt's attitude was the popular attitude, reported one editorial, that the President was sure to have his own way.[30] Some commentators considered other pending legislation more dangerous. *Barron's*, for example, indicated much more concern with the banking bill, although both bills were "concessions to the Left." Admittedly, however, the utilities holding company bill was "much closer to the Presidential heart," and its passage would represent "no mean triumph for the Reform *Ueber Alles* party." [31] Utilities stockholders were at a disadvantage, it was pointed out, in that their protests were buried under the avalanche of letters being received regarding the publicity proposed for income tax forms. The President was publicly on record in opposition to the utilities, but had been completely silent regarding the income tax publicity issue.[32]

Reaction from the New York Stock Exchange was swift, however. Three days after the public utility holding company bill was introduced, the Exchange released a statement that it had leased a large residence at 2416 Tracy Place, Washington, for maintaining close contact with the nation's capitol. Queried as to its reasons, Exchange officials cryptically replied, "Economy, and freedom from interruptions." [33] However, the "Wall Street Embassy," as the large two-story brick mansion with its colonial porticoes came to be known, represented a viewpoint and influence parallel yet definitely subordinate to the enormous resources of the nation's public utilities companies.

In addition to their admitted financial resources, the nation's public utilities companies had a considerable asset in the legacies of its master craftsman, Samuel Insull. Insull was the instigator and driving force of a movement by the nation's utilities in the twentieth century's first decade, particularly in his own state of Illinois, to establish state regulatory commissions as a matter of self-preservation. Long franchises under such an arrangement were Insull's answer to wasteful competition and the hostile

[30] *Business Week*, Feb. 16, 1935, p. 1.
[31] *Barron's*, Feb. 11, 1935, p. 10.
[32] *Business Week*, March 2, 1935, p. 10.
[33] New York *Times*, Feb. 9, 1935.

public sentiments roused over rate-gouging. Moreover, this eliminated an army of political franchise sellers from every municipality.

Forrest McDonald has shown that Samuel Insull was not only a very skillful politician, but was one of the first utilities magnates to set up a full-fledged public relations department. In addition, Insull used the idea of stock selling for "customer ownership" as an answer to municipal ownership, a campaign that he publicly launched in the 1920's.[34] This proved so successful that, as the FTC report demonstrated, rate reduction proposals were violently attacked by members of the community acting in their new-found capacity of capitalistic shareholders. Their attitude ably bore out that part of the satirical jingle that proclaimed "Men may call us robbers, sinners—but they'll never vote agin' us." [35]

The idea of the state commission had later served the utilities and their spreading holding companies in good stead. Their activities across state lines served as a warning that the state bodies could not touch them. Conversely, when Federal legislation seemed in the offing, the holding companies pointed to their component parts and invoked the doctrine of the powers reserved to the states. Meantime, they were regulated largely in theory. By 1935, however, much favorable public sentiment had been alienated through failure of the holding companies even to follow Insull's example of putting through judiciously modest rate reductions to head off extremes of public reaction. In addition, drastic declines in utilities stock values had somewhat tempered the militant spirit of ownership among the mass of stockholders.

Contemporary voices of criticism from within the utilities ranks were lacking or were ignored. C. F. Blanchard, public utilities editor of Standard Statistics Company, warned bankers of the detrimental influence that investment banking exercised over holding company policy. Speaking to the National Association of Mutual Savings Banks, Blanchard strongly opposed

[34] McDonald, pp. 241 ff.; Ramsay, p. 263.
[35] FTC, *Utility Corporations*, Part 71-A, p. 12; Ramsay, p. 263.

putting mutual savings bank funds into the holding company "hierarchy which dominated the industry," and frankly labeled the utilities holding companies as "something of a racket." [36] His advice was not taken, however, since Representative Maury Maverick of Texas in a radio address two years later specifically referred to the permanent lobby of the National Association of Mutual Savings Banks as being "against every piece of financial legislation designed to clear up conditions for investors that has come before Congress in these last three years." [37]

Committee hearings on the bill to regulate interstate utilities activities and eliminate their holding companies got under way on February 19, 1935. By that time the utilities had organized committees on everything from their executives to their investors, and rushed some of their ablest spokesmen into the fight. One of the latter was Wendell L. Willkie, forty-two-year-old president of the Commonwealth and Southern Corporation, a holding company in the upper reaches of the Morgans' United Corporation structure. An able and articulate speaker, and a persuasive and resourceful witness, Willkie emphasized the holding companies' role in financing and expanding the giant utilities industry. The utility companies were depicted as largely concerned with "technical development," their energies wholly consumed in engineering and construction problems, and blissfully unaware of questions of political control. The utilities' spokesman insisted that a better solution would be to simplify holding company structures by transferring and consolidating their stock issues, and attempted to lead legislative action back into paths of state regulation. Willkie commended Walter Splawn's suggestion to eliminate those stock taxes that currently blocked such an approach, calling Splawn's theory "the outstanding constructive thing" reported to the committee.[38] When the reprehensible practices and unscrupulous individuals in the utilities lobbying campaign were later revealed in a Senate in-

---

[36] New York *Times*, May 26, 1933.
[37] *Congressional Record*, LXXIX, Part IX, 10223.
[38] House, *Public Utility Holding Companies*, Part II, p. 587.

vestigation, Willkie's own administrative record, his frankness as a witness, and his likable personality all tended to divorce him somewhat from the proceedings. In retrospect, the image that the public retained of Willkie was that of a genial and rather innocent emissary of a ruthless gang.

Strongest emphasis from the utilities holding company side was placed on the sad state of innocent investors owning utility stocks, and particular attention was drawn to those stockholders of little or no other means. A favorite reminder was the plight of husbandless mothers and their unprotected brood of little ones. Utilities speakers took to the radio with this theme, and the mournful voice of the widows and tots was heard in the land. Philip H. Gadsden, chairman of the newly formed Committee of Public Utilities Executives, discussed this aspect on a national radio hookup. "My fellow executives and I are, of course, going to suffer," Gadsden admitted. "But that is not the important thing," he went on bravely. "There are not so many of us. But there are five million individuals who own the securities of public utility holding companies," Gadsden said, and the bill "will very largely destroy the value of these securities." [39] To this Senator Wheeler retorted that those investors have "already been plucked—legislation or no legislation," [40] and inquired in a radio address why investors should trust those who sold the stocks at $100 and then manipulated them down to $2. Congressman Maverick also reminded a "widow constituent," in a subsequent broadcast, that her utility stock had dropped from $65 to $5 long before the government proposed regulatory legislation. [41]

One of the more persuasive arguments against the bill counseled moderation; regulation rather than elimination of the holding companies would do the trick. Coupled with this argument was what might be termed the "barn-burner" theory. The abuses were those of a mere handful, Hugh S. Magill, president of the American Federation of Utilities Investors, declared to

[39] New York *Times,* April 10, 1945.
[40] *Congressional Record,* LXXIX, Part III, 2432.
[41] Washington *Post,* April 3 and 12, 1935.

the House committee, and it was "entirely unjust in striking at the abuses to kill many of the investors." Magill eagerly made known to the committee his board of directors, which included Charles C. Kerwin, treasurer of the Catholic Church Extension Society: Sol Kline, president of the Jewish Charities of Chicago: and Luther E. Todd, secretary of the Board of Finance of the Methodist Episcopal Church, South. "Millions of dollars" were represented by these names, Magill assured the Representatives, and a large part of it was in utilities securities.[42]

All of the most vehement objectors touched on a similar conclusion: that in addition to all its other obvious failings, the bill was aimed at eventual nationalization of the nation's entire capitalist structure. Once the utilities industry was mastered, *Forbes* editorialized, "then logically . . . the President would proceed to attack all industrial organizations having far-flung properties." Obviously the ambition of the administration was "to tear our most useful corporate enterprises limb from limb." [43]

Utilities-inspired correspondence directed at Congress attained a volume and intensity by mid-March that angered the President and endangered the Wheeler-Rayburn bill's success. Using the transmission of his National Power Policy Committee report to the Congress as the occasion, Roosevelt defended the administration objectives and denounced the character of the utilities propaganda campaign. The committee that formulated the report was an interdepartmental group appointed by Roosevelt in 1934, with Secretary of the Interior Ickes as its chairman, including Judge Healy of the SEC, Frank R. McNinch of FPC, General E. M. Markham, War Department Chief of Engineers, and David E. Lilienthal of TVA. It had been set up to develop a unified national power policy, and much of the present legislation, as the President added in his message, incorporated the recommendations of this report.

These recommended objectives, Roosevelt said, were not intended to "destroy legitimate business or wholesome and productive investment." But utilities holding companies, which

[42] House, *Public Utility Holding Companies,* Part III, pp. 1753–54.
[43] *Forbes,* March 1, 1935, p. 7; May 1, 1935, p. 8.

served no useful function except as a means of financial control for a few, and which derived their income from such questionable sources as contrived service contracts imposed on their subsidiaries, had no reason for existence.

The disappearance at the end of 5 years of these utility holding companies which cannot justify themselves as necessary for the functioning of the operating utility companies of the country is an objective which Congressional leaders I have consulted deem essential to a realistic and farsighted treatment of the evils of public utility holding companies.[44]

The activities of the utilities in influencing Congress and the public against the Wheeler-Rayburn bill drew scornful comment from the President:

I have been watching with great interest the fight being waged against public utility holding company legislation. I have watched the use of investors' money to make the investor believe that the efforts of government to protect him are designed to defraud him. I have seen much of the propaganda prepared against such legislation—even down to mimeographed sheets of instructions for propaganda to exploit the most far-fetched and fallacious fears. I have seen enough to be as unimpressed by it as I was by the similar effort to stir up the country against the Securities Exchange bill last spring.[45]

The drive to curb the utilities holding companies furthered one of Roosevelt's oldest and most firmly held convictions, and he was determined to keep the issue before the public. Particularly was this true in the face of a propaganda campaign that had been previously described by the FTC as one unrivaled except by the government itself in wartime.[46] In Roosevelt's first "fireside chat" of 1935, a "fear is vanishing, confidence is growing" speech, the President asserted that the elimination of unnecessary holding companies in the public utility field was "a positive recovery measure." A business that lost the confidence of its customers

[44] F.D.R., *Public Papers and Addresses,* IV, 99–100.
[45] *Ibid.,* p. 98.
[46] FTC, *Utility Corporations,* Part 73-E, p. 65.

and the good will of the public, the President explained, could not be on a sound basis for recovery or continue to be a good risk for the investor. Far from destroying values, the new legislation would protect the actual value of utility properties owned by thousands of investors who had had little protection under the old laws.[47]

Roosevelt's modest attributions of recovery to the Wheeler-Rayburn bill were far outstripped in the opposite direction by the bill's adversaries. Wendell L. Willkie, in a Washington, D.C. address, made a wildly extravagant claim:

if the electric utility business were freed from these threats it would do more to lift this country out of the depression, take more men out of bread lines and off relief rolls than any other industry, and with the multiple effects of restored confidence and expanding credit . . . do more than the Government itself can do with all its expenditures.[48]

Widely differing opinions were continuously propounded both by the administration leaders and the utility representatives seeking public support via the radio. Sam Rayburn, leader of the Wheeler-Rayburn bill's forces in the house, emphasized the lack of local control inherent in the holding company system that led to local utility decisions being made by "big bosses" in remote cities. Also, Rayburn reminded his national audience, "the holding company device is so clever that a school girl cannot use her curling iron—without paying indirect tribute to the holding company through artificially raised rates."

Philip H. Gadsden, chairman of a potent utility lobby group, addressed a national audience with many of the utilities' counter-arguments. Gadsden neatly reversed the local control idea by reminding his listeners that "State public service commissions, intimately familiar with local conditions, must hand over their authority to a remote bureau in Washington." [49] The influence of the holding company device pictured by Rayburn was offset by the utility spokesman with an even more balefully influential

[47] F.D.R., *Public Papers and Addresses*, IV, 139.
[48] Washington *Post*, May 2, 1935.
[49] *Congressional Record*, LXXIX, Part III, 2432.

image. "If this bill passes," Gadsden proclaimed dramatically to the schoolgirls and housewives of America, "every time you use the curling iron . . . or vacuum-cleaner, you will do so under strict government supervision." [50]

Correspondence received by administration Congressmen indicated a reaction identical to that provoked by pressure of business groups from their employees in regard to the previous year's Securities Exchange Act. Senator Wheeler explained that a good part of the flood of letters was the result of tactics of firms such as Electric Bond and Share, which required its employees to write cards of protest either to the House or the Senate committee handling the bill, and to have their compositions checked at the firm's office before being mailed. Wheeler explained that his knowledge of this came from the employees themselves, and that one of his informants wrote a separate letter stating, "I am 100 per cent behind your Wheeler-Rayburn Bill, and sincerely hope you put it over." [51]

Some wrote directly to the White House to repudiate the protests they were forced to make. H. Lee Howell of Blossburg, Pennsylvania, one of eighteen employees of Pennsylvania Gas Company (a subsidiary of Pennsylvania Power and Light, which was a subsidiary of Electric Bond and Share), related that all were furnished stationery and stamps to write approximately fifty letters apiece to Congressmen. Most employees, Howell believed, shared his rejection of the required protests.[52]

But for every such letter in April or May, 1935, indicating even tacit approval of the proposed legislation there were four or five strongly opposed to "destruction" of holding companies, most of them from stockholders. Organized dissent expressed itself forcibly, as in the group of telegrams to the President from Columbus, Ohio, denouncing the "modified" Wheeler-Rayburn bill as "unamerican" (sic) and a "step toward" communism.[53]

[50] New York *Times,* April 10, 1935.

[51] *Congressional Record,* LXXIX, Part V, 4903.

[52] H. Lee Howell to F.D.R. re Public Utility Holding Company Act, April 8, 1935, Roosevelt Papers.

[53] Telegrams to F.D.R. from Columbus, Ohio, re Public Utility Holding Company Act, April 17, 1935, Roosevelt Papers.

Individual letters in the press showed a wide diversification of sentiment. To an editorial page created particularly for this expression, W. E. Deppe of New York City wrote that the Insull disclosures showed the utilities had only themselves to blame. Homer Stimson of Royce City, Texas, warned that destruction of holding companies might be warranted but that the ultimate cost of the operation would still be levied on the consumer. W. Lee Harris of Miami, describing himself as "an owner of public utility stocks and a businessman," insisted that "the most ignorant, benighted and frequently vicious class of men in American business today are in charge of our public utilities." A writer who stated that he was an eighty-year-old retired clergyman with utilities stock as his only resource argued that "abuse of privileges does not warrant destruction." [54] Although careful editorial balancing precluded any deductions by the reader as to the exact strength of pro or con sentiment, it was noticeable that many of those opposed to the utilities holding companies nevertheless hesitated before the idea of their complete elimination.

Details of the unrelenting pressure by utilities companies on Congressmen during the spring and early summer months only came fully to light toward the end of the session. Denis J. Driscoll, Democratic Representative from the Twentieth Pennsylvania District, testified before a Senate special committee that the bales of telegrams he had received from his district were so much alike in formula and were so weighted with correspondents' names beginning with A, B, and C, that he investigated.[55] After receiving no reply from several and having a number of wires returned with the Western Union notation "cannot be located," Driscoll pursued his inquiry through Western Union headquarters only to find that the originals of the telegrams had been burned by a company employee at the request of an Associated Gas and Electric official. A Western Union messenger made newspaper headlines by accounting for at least eighteen cents of the utilities' alleged propaganda millions. Elmer Danielson of Warren, Pennsylvania, a nineteen-year-old messenger, whom the

[54] *Forbes,* May 1, 1935, p. 22.
[55] Senate, *Investigation of Lobbying Activities,* Part 1, pp. 62 ff.

newspapers promptly christened "Little Elmer," revealed that the Associated Gas and Electric Company was paying messengers three cents for each signature they were able to solicit, but that he had only been able to gather six signatures from his family circle and friends.[56]

The special Senate committee named to hear these charges, headed by Democratic Senator Hugo L. Black of Alabama and overwhelmingly anti-utility in make-up, reserved some of its severest grillings for the utilities' chief disbursers of propaganda funds. Philip H. Gadsden, chairman of the newly formed Committee of Public Utility Executives, admitted that the expense of bringing "influential friends" from all over the United States to talk to their Congressmen was paid for by the utilities holding companies. Revenue of the holding companies that paid such expenses, Gadsden reluctantly agreed under the prodding of chairman Black, was derived entirely from the operating companies, that is, from the public that bought the commodity itself.[57]

Witness Gadsden accounted for the expenditure of $300,000 in the utility campaign, chiefly for "lawyers' fees," derived from assessments levied on a basis of the number of electric meters operated. The entire question of sizable funds [58] raised by an industry to influence Congress provided more than one such heated exchange:

Senator Schwellenbach of Washington: I asked you whether you thought it was proper to spend between a half million and a million dollars to attempt to influence legislation on one bill in the Congress of the United States?

Mr. Gadsen: If it is legally spent, open and above-board, I think it is all right. You must bear in mind I am dealing with the threatened destruction of 12 billions of property.[59]

[56] *Ibid.,* pp. 92 ff.
[57] *Ibid.,* p. 23.
[58] New York *Times* box score based on "public disclosures, House and Senate investigations" revealed a detailed total of $1,059,662 at the halfway point in the lobbying investigations (July 26, 1935).
[59] Senate, *Investigation of Lobbying Activities,* Part 1, p. 24.

Pressure from administration aides on reluctant legislators during the torrid months of pulling and tugging over the Wheeler-Rayburn bill also became known later through Congressional investigation, centering largely about the activities of Tom Corcoran. In his presidentially approved role of legislative adviser, shared with his friend and colleague, Ben Cohen, Corcoran was a rallying point for many of the earliest and most zealous New Dealers. The Corcoran apartment in Washington was the scene of frequent sessions of strategic and tactical planning, and the group of young New Deal lawyers included many SEC personnel, present and future. William O. Douglas, a departmental head, who was to be appointed a commissioner in 1936 and become chairman of the SEC in 1937; Jerome Frank, who was to be appointed to the Landis vacancy in 1937, and was to follow Douglas into the chairmanship when the latter went to the United States Supreme Court; and Leon Henderson, who was to be appointed to the Commission in 1939 to fill the vacancy left by Douglas' resignation—all were an integral part of the small gatherings that conversed, argued, and debated the political moves of the future.

The House of Representatives, in a testy mood over administration pressure, devoted its lobbying investigation almost entirely to the question of whether Corcoran had improperly attempted to influence the vote of Congressman Brewster of Maine on the holding company question. Allegedly the leverage used was a threatened loss of patronage control over the administration's Passamaquoddy power project in Brewster's home state.[60] The resultant sessions disclosed simply that the actions of Representative Brewster in voting with the utilities, after a career of public service as governor and Representative in opposition to them, were inexplicable to say the least; and that Tom Corcoran, petulant over wasted political patronage, had been guilty only of excessive and injudicious zeal. Charles Beard, in a contemporary survey, summed up the House investigation of the Brewster affair as one that "simmered down to a question of

[60] House, *Investigation of Lobbying on the Utility Holding Company Bills,* Parts I–III.

veracity, in which the weight of evidence, if not conclusive, was on the side of the administration." [61]

In the critical stages of an issue that had been for so long an important part of his public career, the President himself did not hesitate to exhort or thank friends in the Congress. Roosevelt, after an antiadministration amendment offered by Senator Lonergan of Connecticut had been beaten down with the aid of Senator Francis T. Maloney of the same state, wrote to "Dear Frank" to say: ". . . how much I personally appreciated your fine stand on the Holding Company Bill. Before we get through the average voter will understand the justice of it." [62]

To "Dear George" (Senator Radcliffe of Maryland), Roosevelt wrote in June: "I do hope you will go along with the Utility Holding Company Bill—I *promise* you it will save the *investor!*" [63] But Senator Radcliffe, usually an administration supporter, deserted the ranks to vote for a hotly contested pro-utility amendment offered by Senator Dieterich of Illinois, which was narrowly defeated, 45-44.

Although much of the pressure both for and against the Wheeler-Rayburn bill was far below the surface of recorded events, the disposition of the President presented a telltale sign to some press correspondents. Commenting on Roosevelt's even temper, fully in check while referring to the Supreme Court's "horse and buggy" NRA decision, the utilities bill was described as the only occasion for presidential irritation. Once, a question on the Wheeler-Rayburn bill's progress provoked what was thought to be a "capricious and unfair retort"; a second time, press questions set off "the sharpest attack on lobbying ever heard in the White House." There was something about the utilities question, the writer concluded, "which touches a raw nerve in Mr. Roosevelt. It seems to be the one subject which rocks his poise." [64]

By the latter part of July, however, a shift of sentiment toward the presidential stand became noticeable. Press opposition was

[61] Beard, p. 520.
[62] E. Roosevelt, *F.D.R.: His Personal Letters*, III, 488.
[63] *Ibid.*, p. 483.
[64] Clapper, pp. 17–18.

still loud and bitter in Hearst papers like the San Francisco *Examiner*. This journal offered up front-page thanks to the Almighty after an early defeat of the "death sentence" clause in the House of Representatives. Using block letter capitals to cue its readers as to where proper emphasis should be placed, the *Examiner* explained that this vote was "AGAINST the theory and practice of DICTATORSHIP!" It went on to denounce administration "liaison men" and their activities as "ABHORRENT TO AMERICANS." [65]

But friendlier journals such as the Scripps-Howard San Francisco *News* soberly cited numerous specific instances of Congressmen attempting to answer "constituents'" objections, only to have their correspondence returned by the post office or Western Union marked "addressee unknown." The *News* also noted that many Congressmen who had made flying trips back home found themselves in trouble for voting with the utilities.[66]

This evidence of grass-roots support for the Wheeler-Rayburn bill was also born out by a July turn in the tide of White House correspondence. Increasingly these letters became expressions of "all the way" support and "don't give up" encouragement. Many begged for more radio talks "to let the public know the truth" and counteract public utilities propaganda. Significantly, a large proportion listed themselves as utilities stockholders. Further organized support appeared in the form of group letters from Democratic clubs in New York, Pennsylvania, and other states upholding presidential backing of the Wheeler-Rayburn bill.[67]

The Senate investigation into the lobbying activities surrounding this legislation was particularly effective in moving popular opinion toward the administration stand. The public was treated to garish exposures of the holding companies' huge slush funds, their ruthless arm-twisting of employees, and a variety of unscrupulous propaganda methods. In some ways a small-scale reminder of previous disclosures in the world of finance,

[65] San Francisco *Examiner*, July 2, 1935.
[66] San Francisco *News*, July 20, 1935.
[67] Letters re Public Utility Holding Company Act, July, 1935, Roosevelt Papers.

the specific facts and figures of the Senate's utility lobby investigation far outweighed in the public mind the hazy and dubious account of administration pressure that was revealed by the House probe into lobbying.

The two versions of the Wheeler-Rayburn bill that emerged from the Senate and House of Representatives in June, 1935, differed widely enough to insure two more tempestuous months in the joint conference entrusted with effecting some reconciliation. Both bills prepared machinery for the registration of utility companies with the SEC, and specifically brought their securities issues within the regulation of that agency. Both bills had also been amended to avoid encroachment on the jurisdiction of state utilities commissions and to avoid duplication of securities acts' provisions. The Bonbright and Means thesis of regulating the excesses out of the holding company so as to retain its usefulness was pushed to the background in favor of practically complete but gradual elimination of the holding company under the terms of the Senate bill. "Simplification of Holding Company Systems," as Section 11 was decorously titled, was nevertheless translated by the utilities into a dramatic "death sentence," with definite ogrelike connotation, and happily caught up as such by the nation's press.

The House of Representatives, more susceptible to utilities' blandishments, to administration pressures, and to telegrams— spurious and genuine—from constituents, had tortured the so-called death sentence into a vaguely discretionary power vested with the SEC. Section 11, which was the controversial heart of both bills, became in the House version a watered-down option for the SEC to require holding company operations to be suitably integrated unless "not necessary in the public interest." [68]

Strong objection to this stand from within the House committee was expressed in a minority view written by Representative Edward C. Eicher of Iowa, who, three and a half years later, was to become a commissioner of the SEC. Eicher, representing

[68] House, *Public Utility Act of 1935*, p. 6.

a fairly widely held House viewpoint, complained not only of the emasculation of the original intent of Section 11 but of the form that the substitution took. This wide latitude of discretion, Eicher said, "could hardly include a more constitutionally dangerous, indefinite delegation of power to a regulatory commission." The minority report struck out at the vagueness of the discretionary powers to be exercised as a tactic that shifted Congressional responsibility to the SEC without any real declaration of the policy the agency was expected to follow. If Congress hadn't the courage to state a definite policy regarding the breakup of such economic concentrations, then, Eicher warned bluntly, "no administrative commission can fairly be expected to resist the pressures which would inevitably be brought against it." [69]

Senate members of the joint conference, it was widely rumored, were deliberately stalling so as to achieve maximum benefit from the reactions to the disclosures of the Senate lobby investigation concurrently in session. House conferees insisted that "outsiders" (meaning administration adviser and drafting expert Ben Cohen) be excluded from the conference room proper.[70] Viewpoints were disparate enough and tempers sufficiently exacerbated, in any event, to require lengthy efforts at compromise. Much healing of political wounds was credited to the amiable exertions of Senator Barkley of Kentucky, while Commissioner Landis of the SEC drafted legislative changes to reconcile the House and Senate versions. Landis' suggested substitution was based on the premise that regulation, in itself, could not meet all abuses, and that the power to dissolve holding companies was the only possible recourse. To satisfy both sides, however, regulation—under stiff conditions statutorily imposed—must be given a chance, "if regulation then demonstrably fails, the substitute empowers the Commission to proceed to compel total dissolution." [71]

The unruly House of Representatives consistently rejected

[69] *Ibid.*, pp. 45–48.
[70] New York *Herald Tribune*, August 2, 1935.
[71] SEC, Untitled compilation of photostats and memoranda relating to the legislative history of the Public Utility Holding Company Act of 1935 (n.p., n.d.), Exhibit A, p. 8.

reconciliation with the Senate and administration viewpoints. Both Republicans and Democrats seemed prepared to carry the issue to the country, and splits within both parties were feared. On August 21 the President sent a note to Sam Rayburn regarding the hotly debated Section 11. Representing the closest Senate approach to administration wishes that could be expected, it had been prepared for the presidential signature by Senators Wheeler and Barkley and forwarded in a confidential memo by Tom Corcoran to Roosevelt:

> From the point of view of the House, this proposal certainly constitutes a most generous concession on the part of the Senate conferees.
> From my point of view, it represents a greater concession from the Senate bill than I should like to see made.[72]

This assurance that the President had thus publicly recorded his own compromises, plus a stern warning to the House by Speaker Joseph W. Byrns that any further recalcitrance would project the issue to the forefront of the 1936 campaign, brought a complete reversal and the bill's final passage.

Signed into law August 26 by the President, the Public Utility Holding Company Act of 1935 provided for the registration of all utilities holding companies, and brought their securities issuance and financial reports under the scrutiny of the SEC. The famous Section 11 had been modified, partly by removing the deadlines that were previously a stipulation of holding company dissolution, and partly by retaining those low-level holding companies that the SEC adjudged predominantly intrastate or of sufficiently contiguous interstate operation. However, holding companies beyond the second level were mandatorily dissolved, in a subsection that New Dealers dryly referred to as "the great-grandfather clause." Insertion in the bill of a clause requiring utilities lobbyists to be registered was an outcome of the Senate investigation into lobby pressures. Other abuses of the utilities holding companies, such as the many spurious types of service contracts and the intercompany loans, were specifically and

[72] Thomas G. Corcoran memo to F.D.R., Aug. 21, 1935 Roosevelt Papers.

statutorily outlawed. Provision for uniform accounting standards corrected another abuse widely aired both in the FTC report and the Berle and Means examination of modern corporate practice. The bill also included a section providing for the SEC "to make a study of the functions and activities of investment trusts and investment companies" to determine the "influence exerted by such trust companies upon companies in which they are interested." [73] This report and its recommendations, which investigated the claim of many holding companies to be investment companies, furnished the basis for the Trust Indenture Act of 1939 and the Investment Company Act of 1940. Thus it continued the earliest SEC practice of bringing within its purview, through agency surveys that bore Congressional approval and legislative mandate, further aspects of financial regulation.

President Roosevelt played a larger role in the enactment of holding company legislation than he did in the securities acts that initially established the SEC. This difference can be accounted for by two distinct factors. First, Roosevelt's long struggle with the power and utilities combines in the interests of the individual rate payer and stockholder was of a duration and intensity second to no other in the President's lengthy career of public service. Further, in actual number of consumers and investors affected, in the nationwide aspects of the utilities holding company problem, as well as in the nature and intensity of the struggle against such concentrated power and wealth, the opportunities and necessities for instrumental national leadership were here of greater import.

The varied aspects of the power question were among the first items to concern Roosevelt as a young Progressive alive to the convictions of Theodore Roosevelt and Woodrow Wilson. Years of doing battle with the public utilities at the state level broadened Roosevelt's concern from the initial question of ownership of natural resources. The problem amplified itself to include the rate-raising powers of the electrical combines, the economically undemocratic and dangerous concentrations of wealth that they

[73] U.S. *Statutes at Large*, XLIX, Part I, 803 ff., 837.

controlled, and the securities that such holding companies issued to the public.

With a national reputation gained from his activities in New York State, Roosevelt was the logical rallying point for the various groups and individuals each concerned with some aspect of the problem. Such diversity as represented by Democratic public power advocate, John E. Rankin of Mississippi, Progressive Western Republicans such as Lynn Frazier of North Dakota, and urban radicals like Vito Marcantonio of New York City required the Roosevelt national leadership as well as the issue's historic basis to weld a successful solution.

Much of Roosevelt's support came from those who embraced the Brandeisian distaste for bigness. Certainly administration leader Senator Wheeler, with his blunt affirmation of such a theory, was an outstanding example.[74] The President himself, however, did not subscribe to bigness as an evil per se. Writing to Norman Hapgood, a good friend of Justice Brandeis, the President clarified his position. Bigness (or smallness) in industry was not the most important question, Roosevelt wrote, but rather "who exercised the controls and for what purposes." [75] His constant use of Brandeis' fortunate phrase, "other people's money," was the key to his strongest conviction. The primary motive was to bring about fiduciary integrity, not to attack bigness. Size alone could be brought within regulable bounds. Those holding company creations set up for the purpose of exploiting investors could be demolished completely. This might actually leave the remaining utility companies more compactly efficient than before and with much of their economic power inviolate, yet shorn of their more outrageous financial practices and with their securities issues firmly controlled.

"Mr. Brandeis struggled to turn the clock backward in 1915," Adolf A. Berle, Jr., said in disassociating himself and Columbia University colleague Gardiner C. Means from this anachronistic view of bigness. It was this group, believing that social

[74] Congressional Record, LXXIX, Part II, 1525.
[75] E. Roosevelt, F.D.R.: His Personal Letters, III, 563.

control of big industry was the essential point and that its bigness was unavoidable, with which Roosevelt aligned himself. The Rooseveltian anger at the utilities holding company as "a corporate invention which can give a few corporate insiders unwarranted and intolerable powers over other people's money" was Brandeisian only as directed against financial abuses and not as against bigness itself.

The SEC played a large though unobtrusive part in effecting the new legislation that was to expand further its administrative responsibilities. Commissioners Healy and Landis were of direct aid to Congressional committees as witnesses and by virtue of their technical competence. Both aided in the preparation of the influential National Power Policy Committee report. Judge Healy was a formidable interpreter of the ninety-odd volumes of the FTC report on the utilities, which he had directed over its six-year span. Commissioner Landis provided many of the drafts that finally effected a suitable compromise on Section 11 of the bill.

The most important role the SEC played, however, was providing, by its very existence, a suitable medium of compromise and conciliation in the Congressional struggle over the so-called death sentence. Administration of some such clause by an agency looked upon with increasing respect by the financial and business world seemed more and more the easiest solution for harassed Congressmen. The rising tide of business objections had largely flowed around the new agency. This was, in part, because the financial community found more to busy itself with in efforts directed against dangerous and as yet unenacted legislation. Partly, the new Commission's exercise of a pragmatic approach rather than of a dogmatic spirit had created an extremely favorable attitude. Even those financial editorialists who were militantly aware of "the barbarians always waiting beyond the Hudson to pillage Wall Street," as one of their number expressed it, extended grudging admiration toward the SEC's firm but reasonable approach.

Pressure on Representatives had mounted, coming both from

the administration forces and from the utilities' telegrams and visitations of "old friends from home." Voting on the death sentence in July, the House chose not to be officially recorded, the members merely passing between tellers who counted them. The Scripps-Howard newspapers, friendly to the administration, to offset this tactic announced that they would assemble their entire staff in the press gallery to identify members as they thronged forward to vote.[76] Despite the threat of possible identification as public opponents of the President, House members preferred to take a chance at official anonymity in order to deal the death sentence one of its temporary defeats.

The bombardment of telegrams and letters protesting the death sentence contained a large number proved to be spurious. Yet Congressmen could not help but be aware that many were genuine, even if misguided, and a substantial number of these were from investors who were unwilling to take a chance of having their utility holding stock values wiped out completely, even though the stock might have depreciated from $100 to $5 long before.

Caught between such forces, the SEC was to many Congressmen a refuge, a veritable storm cellar. The death sentence could be modified somewhat, discretionary powers added, and the SEC be made the arbiter. Public and administration pressure for the death sentence could be modified, yet the interpretation and execution of such a sentence could be placed in the hands of an agency known favorably to the major part of the financial world for its statesmanlike attitude and reasoned judgment. Thus the House of Representatives was able to come back to a modified version of the death sentence using the knowledge that the SEC was a suitable vehicle of conciliation. Its presence and its reputation preserved them from the complete annihilation of the holding company, to which they were politically unable to commit themselves. Only a little over a year in age, the SEC by its considered judgments and its reasonable administration had made permanent its services and insured its continuous and expanded growth.

[76] *Business Week,* July 6, 1935.

CHAPTER SIX

THE SEC AND THE STOCK EXCHANGES

An EARLY project of the SEC was a thoroughgoing report on the institutional nature of stock exchanges in general and the New York Stock Exchange, the nation's largest, in particular. Prepared under Chairman Kennedy's direction pursuant to Section 19(c) of the Securities Exchange Act, the results of this research were turned over to Congress early in 1935. Highly critical in tone, the report specifically denied the need for any new legislation. Instead, following the line the SEC took consistently, it was bursting with suggestions for the New York Stock Exchange to effect its own internal reform. Great emphasis was placed on broadening the responsibility for governing the Exchange's 1,375 seats by representation on the governing board for its out-of-town members, and by a provision for their use of absentee ballots. The report ably documented the tight control exercised in the country's largest securities market by a small group headed and dominated by New York Stock Exchange president, Richard Whitney. Chief element in this group was the floor traders, linear descendants of those who met under the original Wall Street buttonwood tree, most of whom traded solely for their personal fortunes. These members and their close associates among the specialists and bond brokers, popularly referred to as the Old Guard, exercised their self-bestowed privileges from the unchanging point of view that the Stock Exchange was a private club for their personal accounts and individual trading rather than an institution widely and inseparably connected with a public interest. Occupying only 48 percent of the Exchange's 1,375 seats, the Old Guard, with its private trader outlook, nevertheless held two-thirds of the posts on the all-important governing board.[1]

Easily the most vital functional class from the investor's point of view were the commission brokers, who acted as their customers' agents. Many such firms maintained nationwide offices; as a group they were by far in closest contact with the public. Also the largest numerically, with 52 percent of Exchange seats, the commission houses were represented by fourteen governors, only one-third of the exchange's governing body.[2] Increasingly aware that much of the public's resentment toward stock manipulation was directly traceable to the anachronistic regulations and private-club attitude of the Old Guard, the commission brokers were nevertheless unable to exercise a governing voice commensurate with their numerical superiority. Paul V. Shields and E. A. Pierce, heads of large commission houses, and John W. Hanes of Chas. D. Barney and Company, were commonly considered to be the spokesmen and leaders of this anti-Old Guard group.

The system of electing the governors and the important committees was strongly criticized by the SEC report, since it readily lent itself to a perpetuation of control by the "ins." Theoretically, an independent slate of officers could be offered to Exchange members by petition, but in such a staid organization a petition, the Kennedy report explained, "connotes open revolt, and subtle forms of pressure make its use in practice infrequent."[3] And unlikely of success, it might properly have added. Appointment of executive and law-making committees, including the nominating committee, was by action of the governing board. Designation of a president by the nominating committee virtually assured his election and continued Old Guard control.

[1] House, *Report on the Government of Securities Exchanges,* p. 8.
[2] *Ibid.*
[3] *Ibid.,* p. 10.

Many members resented the authoritarian nature of this control and its harsh application by an inner clique. Few, however, cared to express their resentment openly. It was common Street knowledge that the ruling powers of the Exchange were closely connected with the truly great powers of the financial world. An outstanding example of this connection existed in the president of the Exchange, and the symbol to the reverent of its might, Richard Whitney. Whitney's brother, George Whitney, was a partner in J. P. Morgan and Company, and the firm of Richard Whitney and Company frequently acted as bond broker for the Morgan partners.

The Kennedy report's criticisms of this inner-group control and its concrete proposals for some democratization of Exchange government were an open slap at the politely unyielding front that the Whitney regime presented to the new agency. Fortuitous appearance of the report in January, 1935, a few months before the biannual election of a New York Stock Exchange president, fortified the cause of the dissidents in the Exchange membership. Several months of internal struggle followed, a period of "bickering, threats, and considerable bitterness all around," as Wall Street periodicals later summarized.[4] Five years of the Whitney presidency were equated with years of descending prices and declining volume of transactions. Growing public distrust toward the Exchange and Congressional disapproval culminating in the regulatory powers of the SEC were results more and more frequently laid at the door of the Whitney–Old Guard despotic rule. Even a considerable part of the more conservative element expressed the belief that Exchange public relations could have been handled with more finesse, instead of the arrogant disregard for any such need that constituted the Whitney policy. A "young faction" favored a clean sweep in Exchange government, a sentiment reflected in many letters from out-of-town members to the Exchange nominating committee.

Results of the SEC suggestions and the months of rebellious mutterings became apparent in March, when a series of three meetings to receive nominations and suggestions was announced

[4] *Magazine of Wall Street,* April 13, 1935, p. 707.

by the Exchange nominating committee. At the first such gathering committee members disclosed that the governing board, in special session, had approved a constitutional amendment to add eight "governing members" [5] to its present forty constituents. Approximately forty names had already been suggested for the eight new places, the committee reported. Three candidates had been proposed for Exchange president. John W. Hanes, of Chas. D. Barney and Company, one of the dissident spokesmen, and Charles R. Gay, of the venerable bond firm of Whitehouse and Company, were two names placed in nomination. The third was that of the incumbent, Richard Whitney, submitted "amid considerable applause" in a meeting that included, by Chairman R. Lawrence Oakley's cautious admission, "considerable divergence of opinion." [6]

Meeting for the second time the week following, the nominating committee announced that, for undisclosed reasons, John W. Hanes had declined to be a candidate for the presidency. Nominations for the eight new "governing members" on the Exchange's governing committee had surged upward to a prodigious seventy-two names. The widespread concern with public relations was revealed in a strongly supported suggestion that a new office be created to handle such functions, to be filled by a man of "the type of" Louis Douglas, former director of the budget, or attorney John W. Davis, the Exchange's legal adviser. [7]

The committee's final session brought forth four more candidates for the presidency—none of them representing the dissident position—and the largest attendance of the series. The noisy meeting was characterized by Chairman Oakley as "confined largely to arguments for and against retention of the

[5] A designation to permit "office partners" to take part in Exchange administration. One of the criticisms of the Kennedy report, and of particular disadvantage to the commission brokers, was that ownership of a Stock Exchange seat in the name of a firm meant that only the "floor member" was eligible to vote, whereas the firm's "office partner"—generally a person of more influence and executive ability—was not actually on the Exchange floor and therefore ineligible to participate. See Senate, *Report on the Government of Securities Exchanges,* p. 8.

[6] *Wall Street Journal,* March 5, 1935.

[7] *Ibid.,* March 12, 1935.

present administration," with pro and con sentiment for Whitney's presidency "about equally divided." The chairman went on to deny that the SEC had made any suggestions regarding nominations. It was admitted, however, that the nominating committee's archaic method of naming its successors was about to be discarded. Suggestions for a change in this system had already been forwarded to the SEC for its approval.[8]

Almost a week before the April 8 deadline for the committee's announcement of its choice for president, a group of "prominent members" of the Exchange urged Whitney to be a candidate to succeed himself even though not selected by the nominating committee. Their private polls indicated, it was reported, that Whitney "could be elected easily." It was also widely known that Whitney's good friend, Charles R. Gay, would be the committee's official nominee for New York Stock Exchange president. Financial journals accurately predicted that Richard Whitney had agreed to accept nomination to a place on the governing board, and that no possibility existed for an "open battle" in the presidential election scheduled for May 13.[9]

Counting the votes merely bore out the predictions. Yet the 1,200 ballots cast—nearly double the previous voting record for Exchange elections—revealed several significant facts. Three Old Guard members of the previous governing committee, not included among the names put up in the nominating committee's clean sweep, ran as independents and were elected. SEC urging that the out-of-town faction be represented on the governing committee was finally answered with the election of William McChesney Martin, Jr., of the St. Louis brokerage firm of A. G. Edwards and Sons. And although no name appeared in opposition to that of Charles R. Gay as president, the name of Richard Whitney received a numerically higher number of votes approving his seat on the governing board.[10]

The 1935 elections were an "upheaval without precedent," as reported, yet considerably less than a revolution. The replace-

---

[8] *Ibid.*, March 19, 1935.
[9] *Ibid.*, March 23 and April 8, 1935.
[10] New York *Herald Tribune*, May 14, 1935.

ment of "Richard Whitney of Manhattan, clubman and master of fox hounds," by "Charles Richard Gay of Brooklyn, gardener and amateur photographer," [11] did not mean either monumental change in Stock Exchange policy or the implied abdication of an aristocracy to the bourgeoisie. Rather, it revealed that the Shields-Pierce-Hanes group of commission houses could help bring about lesser changes, but simply did not have the votes to elect one of their number president. Liberalizing amendments enlarging the governing board and introducing the absentee ballot provision were passed without difficulty, and some minor results of these efforts were visible. But the new faces on the board, with one exception, were not those of the "radical left," as a financial journal shudderingly referred to the Street's younger element.[12] The solid majority on the governing committee was composed of the "moderates," who wished as few changes as possible, and many erstwhile backers of Whitney. All were aware that the new balance of power in the Exchange's 1,375 seats lay with two groups: those whose seats represented brokerage firms of other cities, and those heretofore inactive in Exchange administration. With the introduction of the absentee ballot and the admission of "office partners" to Exchange affairs, no inner core could install a president of its own choice and control the governing committee as well. The out-of-town insistence on a clean sweep had to be answered at least with new faces on the board and a president not closely identified with the insiders. Complete intransigence could provoke a combination that might bring about more cataclysmic change. The Old Guard might not reign, but it could still govern.

In large part, the 1935 Stock Exchange election represented no more than a demand for a change in the Exchange attitude toward the public and press. This problem President Gay attacked enthusiastically and energetically. In the next two years the Exchange's public relations effort included an administrative troupe on tour, available at municipal and professional gatherings for speeches explaining the function and practices of

[11] *Business Week*, March 7, 1936.
[12] *Wall Street Journal*, March 12, 1935.

the nation's largest securities market. For the first time in its 144-year history the New York Stock Exchange advertised itself. A pamphlet called *The New York Stock Exchange—Its Function and Operation,* furnished free on request, was brought to the attention of the readers of some four hundred daily papers throughout the country. Establishment of a house organ was under serious consideration.[13]

Externally the Stock Exchange's self-consciously refurbished façade represented a shift of some consequence. Internally the shift was minor. Gay's occasionally applied title of the Exchange's "New Deal" president merely reflected a precarious relativity with the more reactionary members of the Old Guard. The powerful Law Committee, a permanent subcommittee appointed by the governing board to determine Exchange policy, was still very much a Whitney organ. And Richard Whitney's numerically higher vote for a governing board seat illustrated a continued commanding position that President Gay tacitly accepted in the two years following. Although friendly to chairmen Kennedy and Landis, Gay's stubborn defense of the Stock Exchange position was later seen most clearly in the Exchange's lax enforcement of the new trading rules that it accepted from the SEC. Gay's unchallenged reelection attested to the support of his view that, with a peacefully efficient popular image, the Exchange might calmly pursue its own course. The New York Stock Exchange, having smoothed out its internal squabbles, once again presented a serene face to the public. It was inwardly serene also, as subsequent events were to show, in the knowledge that its inner workings and private-club philosophy were still inviolate.

Officially, the SEC settled back to await results from Exchange acceptance of its newly suggested governing and trading rules. Some time necessarily must elapse before their effect on Exchange internal reform could be determined. Unofficially, however, James McCauley Landis, in his 1935–37 tenure as chairman, never ceased working toward weakening the stubborn re-

<hr>

[13] *Business Week,* March 7 and Sept. 26, 1936.

sistance of Old Guard rule. Within the Stock Exchange itself Landis tirelessly cultivated the dissident faction led by the Pierce-Shields-Hanes commission houses. The aims and benefits of the SEC posture were constantly pointed out, and the superior character of change wrought from within was stressed persistently. Considerable aid in maintaining strict standards came from conscientious administrative nonmembers such as J. M. B. Hoxsey, executive secretary of the Stock List Committee, who was sincerely desirous of doing as competent a job as Exchange policies would permit his staff to do.[14]

Externally a wealth of anti-Old Guard sentiment remained to be exploited. Feelings similar to those that the out-of-town members of the New York Stock Exchange manifested in the 1935 election reappeared in allied quarters. John J. Bergen, an investment banker of 40 Wall Street, wrote to President Roosevelt that despite criticisms by investment banking heads of SEC policy, sentiment around the country echoed his feelings that the SEC had helped the investment business. In conversations with many of the nation's 2,400 investment security dealers, Bergen related, he found that "most of them who are located some distance from the New York market agree with me that the investment business today is on a more sound basis than it ever has been in the past." [15]

Often overlooked in the final result was another area where Landis' influence worked subtly to undermine the lordly Whitney position of no compromise: the nation's other stock exchanges. Although the New York Stock Exchange towered far above all others in volume of transactions, exchanges such as those of Chicago, Detroit, and San Francisco represented much of local business and were therefore of considerable political influence. These lesser centers were heartily sick of New York arrogance, and were far quicker to realize that some reform must come from within the stock exchanges or it would certainly come from without. A favorite Landis vehicle for coordinating anti-

[14] Told to author in interview with James McCauley Landis, Washington, D.C., Aug. 14, 1961.
[15] John J. Bergen to F.D.R., March 1, 1935, Roosevelt Papers.

Old Guard attitudes was the Association of Stock Exchange Firms, which included the largest commission brokers throughout the country as well as those of New York City. Moreover, the association was a financial body free of any dependence on the formidable House of Morgan, whose thunderbolts of displeasure Whitney implicitly could bring down upon any transgressor.

Although the outcome was to be postponed until Landis had been succeeded by William O. Douglas, much of the foundation that brought about reorganization of the Chicago and Detroit exchanges along SEC-suggested lines [16] several months before New York, was laid by James M. Landis. It remained, however, for W. O. Douglas as chairman to bring about the capitulation to public institutional ways of that most stubbornly defended private traders' citadel, the New York Stock Exchange.

Studies and reports authorized in the first three SEC acts were a major activity throughout the early years of the Commission's establishment, with subsequent legislation frequently the outcome of their presentation to Congress. One such lengthy survey, called into being by Section 211 of the Securities Exchange Act of 1934, was that undertaken to examine corporate reorganization proceedings stemming from bankruptcy or consolidation, in which the interests of the investor were all too often subordinated to the financial well-being of a small management minority or to the investment bankers appointed as trustees.[17] Largely responsible for Chapter X of the Bankruptcy Act and for the Trust Indenture Act of 1939, both to be administered by the SEC, this was the handiwork of an acknowledged authority on bankruptcy, Sterling Professor of Law at Yale, William O. Douglas.

Douglas, who had previously undertaken similar studies in collaboration with the Department of Commerce and had authored the article on bankruptcy for the *Encyclopedia of the*

[16] Landis interview, cited in n. 14 above.
[17] SEC, *Report on the Study and Investigation of the Work, Activities, Personnel and Functions of Protective Organization Committees.*

Social Sciences, came to Washington on leave from Yale at the instigation of Chairman Joe Kennedy in October, 1934, and was placed in charge of the survey with the staff title of Director of the Protective Committee Study. The study lasted two years and included extended public hearings on such corporate reorganizations as Kreuger and Toll, Paramount Publix Corporation, and St. Louis–San Francisco Railways. It was largely on the basis of this "so thorough and so unexpectedly devastating an analysis of financial and legal skulduggery" [18] that Douglas was appointed a commissioner in January, 1936, to fill the vacancy left by Kennedy's resignation several months before. Although Landis believed that Judge John J. Burns should have the first opportunity at a Commission vacancy (he chose instead to remain SEC general counsel), the Douglas appointment had the support and approval of both Kennedy and Landis.[19]

William Orville Douglas had been raised and educated in the state of Washington. After his father's death the family had settled in Yakima, where Douglas attended high school. Working at a variety of ill-paid jobs got the determined young man through nearby Whitman College, and graduation from Columbia University Law School followed. His enthusiasm for the study of law seemed not to have been evoked until his final years, when he became absorbed in the relationship between law and business under the guidance of Underhill Moore.

While at Columbia, Douglas was also introduced to Veblen's *Absentee Ownership* by Moore, whom Douglas regarded as "the best teacher in the entire field of law." [20] Although Max Lerner ascribed to Douglas a "mood of pitiless aloofness" as a legacy from the study of Veblen, the phrase should be applied as the measure of a coolly incisive mind rather than as denoting a lack of concern with human relationships. For Douglas the most obnoxious characteristic of exploitive finance was, indeed, "its inhumanity, its disregard of social and human values." [21] Another early influence was the writings of Louis D. Brandeis. Like

[18] Rodell, p. 119.
[19] James M. Landis to F.D.R., Dec. 20, 1935, Roosevelt Papers.
[20] Lerner, p. 270.
[21] Douglas, *Democracy and Finance,* p. 9.

Roosevelt, he employed Brandeis' pungent title, *Other People's Money*, as a unique reminder to high financiers of the actual source of their raw materials, and the Brandeis yardstick of financial ethical values was visible throughout Douglas' later writings and speeches.

After law school Douglas satisfied much of his curiosity regarding legal and financial relationships in two years with the outstanding corporation firm of Crevath, de Gersdorff, Swaine and Wood. Working under Robert T. Swaine, Douglas achieved an understanding of the complexities of corporate finance thorough enough to put it to brilliant use in his later corporate reorganization study for the SEC. Following his corporate finance practice and some lecturing at Columbia, Douglas was called to Yale Law School by Dean Robert Maynard Hutchins, where he quickly moved to a full professorship and the chair of Sterling Professor of Law.

On the Commission, Douglas exhibited a deft and discerning mind, and his utterly scrupulous regard for the letter and the spirit of fiduciary obligations frequently brought him into closest harmony with the stubbornly expressed convictions of fellow New Englander Judge Healy. To Wall Street, Douglas presented an image of blunt impatience with those stock exchange and investment banking tactics that were at utter variance with the fiduciary obligations to which financial leaders publicly subscribed. His career as the "Bogeyman of Wall Street" [22] was generally believed to date from his speech to the Bond Club in Chicago six months before assuming the chairmanship, in which Douglas dwelt on the sacrosanct practice that permitted traditional banking relationships to take precedence over competitive bidding for bond issues. He bluntly informed his audience that many tolls levied by virtue of this practice were an improper drain upon the resources pledged to the bondholders and were often entirely without economic justification. In the most precise language possible Commissioner Douglas pointed out that "the economic utility of continuity of banking relationships is

[22] *Barron's,* Sept. 27, 1937.

of unestablished value to anyone except the banker." [23] The
New York *Times,* reporting the event, detailed the standing
ovation that initially greeted Douglas, and the mere "spattering
of applause" that marked the conclusion of his speech. The New
York *Herald Tribune* in majestic understatement reported that
the speech left its hearers "grumpy." [24]

Douglas was equally candid in addressing embryo customer's
men training in the New York Stock Exchange brokerage institute.

Our educational system has been too virile in the production of
men immunized from a sense of feeling of social responsibility;
trained in the art of plunder in gentlemanly ways; imbued with
the false ideal that the American way means exploitation.[25]

These practices were "a carry over from a previous age" and
helped constitute the "financial royalism" that Douglas detested.

Such assaults were scarcely calculated to insure the welcome
of financial circles on his election to the SEC chairmanship, even
with the endorsement and blessing of Joe Kennedy. Concern
was reflected in the efforts of financial community leaders, such
as investment banker W. A. Harriman, to divert SEC chairmanship into more sympathetic hands. Harriman, as chief of the
Business Advisory Council for the Department of Commerce,
notified Secretary Daniel C. Roper that the appointment of
Landis' successor could have material effect on the confidence of
businessmen throughout the country. The Harriman letter,
passed on to the President without comment in the Commerce
Department weekly memorandum, went on to explain that the
character of the man the financial community had in mind
"would be of the type of . . . Mr. George A. Sloan . . . or
General Robert E. Wood." [26]

Douglas' succession to the chairmanship of the Commission
was accompanied by polite statements from various exchange

[23] Douglas, *Democracy and Finance,* p. 37.
[24] New York *Times* and New York *Herald Tribune,* March 25, 1937.
[25] *Time,* April 5, 1937.
[26] Secretary Daniel C. Roper to F.D.R., Sept. 18, 1937, Roosevelt Papers.

presidents and financial leaders. The strong misgivings of Wall Street, however, were never concealed. The voice of columnist Edson Blair, reminding his readers that the Street's attitude toward the SEC and Landis had changed and that the same probably would be true for Douglas, was the opinion of a lonely minority.[27] Joseph Kennedy's good opinion of Douglas was a potent factor in the latter's move to the chief executive post of the SEC, and Kennedy's convictions were respected in Wall Street. Arrayed against this fact was the warm but less welcome support of those New Dealers like Ben Cohen [28] and Tom Corcoran who considered that the Stock Exchange had been far too dilatory in effecting any genuine self-regulation. The uncompromising attitude and blunt statements of Commissioner Douglas during the previous two years were warning enough to finance and exchange circles that the tempo of SEC regulatory efforts would undoubtedly be stepped up under such a command. As Douglas interpreted for the press the continuity of the SEC's first three chairmen, it was "under Joe [Kennedy] the protection of the rights of the investor were consolidated; under Jim [Landis] we were taught how to get things done. Now we're going ahead and get them done." [29]

The object toward which Douglas' strong attribute of activism directed itself was the governing body of the New York Stock Exchange. After two years of waiting for the Exchange to adopt sterner codes of self-enforcement and make some move toward reorganization of its archaic structure, SEC officials found the negative results bitterly disappointing. The annual Stock Exchange election of May, 1937, added no assurance to the hope of an eventual move along SEC-suggested lines of self-regulation. With less than half the Exchange's 1,375 members voting, President Charles R. Gay was reelected to a third term, and the entire slate of the Old Guard-dominated nominating committee was chosen without opposition.[30] Only two of the vacancies on

[27] *Barron's,* Sept. 27, 1937.
[28] Told to author in interview with Benjamin V. Cohen, Washington, D.C., Aug. 11, 1961.
[29] *Time,* Oct. 11, 1937.
[30] *Commercial and Financial Chronicle,* May 15, 1937.

the Governing Committee were filled by representatives of the nation's large commission brokers.[31] No change or prospect of change was visible in such a repetitious pattern.

Results in the internal application of strict enforcement methods were equally disappointing. The Stock Exchange had earlier adopted at Chairman Kennedy's request sixteen trading rules, some of which were actually a clarification or codification of its own rules of long standing. However, it was in their enforcement that the Exchange still revealed the private-club philosophy that Douglas insisted must be discarded in favor of a public institutional role. The new rules used by the New York Stock Exchange to govern the trading activities of its members were the result of suggestions and joint conferences with the SEC in 1935. None had been imposed by the Commission. In fact the Commission had not promulgated its own rules even where the Exchange had failed to act, so anxious was it to encourage an attitude of self-regulation.[32] Yet evidence mounted that such an effort had not seriously been made in two years. Early in 1937 the SEC presented to the Exchange's Committee on Business Conduct detailed evidence of certain members' trading and margin violations. The subsequent report from the Exchange committee resembled a doting mother's unwilling efforts to punish a thoroughly spoiled child. Some violators received only mild rebukes, and third-time offenders were fined small amounts. Questioning the committee as to why they queried clerks and bookkeepers instead of the members involved, Douglas found out why self-regulation under such an Exchange administration was merely an exercise in futility. They did not wish to ask Exchange members questions, the committee replied, since their duty was to protect members against incriminating themselves.[33]

To Douglas the nation's stock exchanges represented scales upon which the national resources—invested capital—were

[31] The eight largest commission brokerage companies were ranked by *Fortune* as: E. A. Pierce; Fenner and Beane; J. S. Bache; Chas. D. Barney; Hornblower and Weeks; Shields and Co., Dominick and Dominick; and E. F. Hutton. See *Fortune*, "Wall Street Itself," June 1937, p. 128.
[32] Douglas, *Democracy and Finance*, p. 66.
[33] Rodell, p. 119.

weighed and evaluated. Such scales must have no concealed springs; no fat thumb might be laid upon them. The obvious unwillingness of the New York Stock Exchange to call any of its members to account for their tampering with the scale's mechanism increased Douglas' determination to reorganize the archaic make-up of the Exchange.

The complete market liquidity that the exchanges considered vital to the well-being of the nation's financial transactions represented still another area of disagreement with Douglas. Additional stability was a more satisfactory goal from the SEC viewpoint, which placed the needs of the long-term investor far above those of the quick-profit gambler. The ideal of liquidity stated in terms of volume of stock transactions was of dubious value, Stock Exchange critics maintained. On such a basis, Douglas dryly pointed out, the phenomenal market liquidity of October, 1929, with its accompanying losses of fifteen billions in stock values, approached complete evaporation.[34] An earlier SEC report had criticized the Exchange's overemphasis on market liquidity as promoting a dangerous artificiality in the financial and economic structure.[35] Further statistics compiled over a six-month period ending June 30, 1937, revealed that as high as 21 percent of stock transactions, or "liquidity," were purchases and sales by stock exchange members solely for their own speculation.[36] Here, however, as in later years, it was not simply the volume of member transactions that was critically questioned, but the dubious portion of it that consisted of deliberate market jiggling for the insider's personal benefit. Thus a large part of this internal activity accentuated a rise or a decline in stock prices that disproportionately exaggerated the relationship of the stock to its basic values and presented to the public a distorted picture of its salability.

These insiders, or "financial termites" as Douglas scornfully described them,[37] presented an enforcement problem that the

[34] Douglas, *Democracy and Finance*, p. 98.
[35] SEC, *Report on the Feasibility and Advisability of the Complete Segregation of the Functions of Dealer and Broker*, p. 98.
[36] SEC, *Third Annual Report*, 1937, p. 21.
[37] Rodell, p. 124.

SEC chairman insisted was properly the responsibility of the Exchange itself, rather than that of the SEC in the role of internal security agent. The Douglas summation of the problem had all the delightfully cryptic yet logically penetrating qualities of an *Alice in Wonderland* phrase: "It takes a snoop to catch a jiggle." [38] Superficially translated, a vigilant inside watcher was necessary to detect market manipulations. But implicit also in the idea of a "snoop" was Douglas' insistence that the Exchange, with its summary powers of expulsion over its members, was the proper agent for such regulation. Although the SEC needed more than two years of hearings and six thousand pages of testimony to expel Michael Meehan while still insuring his legal rights, the Exchange could have accomplished the same result in a matter of weeks. Further, this was precisely the type of leadership that Douglas repeatedly urged on business and industry as an alternate to the policing activities of government.[39] This would leave to government a supervisory or "residual" role, permitting it to intrude only to the extent that "business itself fails to perform its functions and make its profits in a decent way." [40]

The recession of 1937, however, offered to the Old Guard point of view not only an evasion of stricter codes applied through self-enforcement but still another lever for prying loose those regulations already clamped on them. The ill-timed effort of the administration to counter high prices by such moves as reducing pump-priming expenditures and doubling bank reserve requirements had spread a national wave of recession. In the stock market, prices, after several fluctuations, began a precipitate decline in August that continued unabated ino the fall months. Although values dropped alarmingly, it was notable that the volume of securities involved was exceedingly small in quantity, indicating there was no great public unloading of stocks.

Nonetheless, the decline afforded a convenient scapegoating formula to Stock Exchange President Gay, who lost no time in

[38] Alsop and Kintner, "The Battle of the Market-Place," p. 10.
[39] Douglas, *Democracy and Finance*, p. 54.
[40] Flynn, "Washing Wall Street's Face," p. 12.

tracking down the ills of the stock market to the "undue restraints . . . being placed upon normal, proper action, thus creating abnormal market conditions." Although admitting the possibility of other factors affecting the market, Gay insisted that "excessive regulation" was not in the public interest, since it too readily "stifles individual initiative" and "intimidates and confuses honest men so that they are unable to determine how to act when swift action is essential." The New York Stock Exchange was in sympathy with the SEC promotion of the public welfare, but foresaw "grave danger" to the common weal if regulation "destroyed" a "broad, liquid market." [41]

Collapses of securities prices brought about a minor resurgence of those public voices that insisted the blame lay with the Stock Exchange. Letters to the administration repeated earlier demands for closing the Stock Exchange (which was actually considered), for prohibition of short selling, and for further action to wipe out stock manipulation. One irate communicant accused the market policemen of the SEC of being in collusion with the Stock Exchange under Landis' leadership. What was needed was a policeman to watch the policemen, wrote Miss E. M. Myer of New York City, and offered herself for the job. [42]

Administration circles were genuinely apprehensive over the effects of the stock market drop. The possibility existed of a more accelerated and widespread reaction, and the continuing fulminations of Wall Street's Old Guard could discredit SEC and administration policy. As the New York *Post* sadly noted, "When money talks the nation listens—even if money talks nonsense." [43]

The allies of the SEC within the Exchange were sharply displeased with President Gay's effort to put the Commission on the spot for the market's ills. Such activities, if unchecked, might lose the little ground already gained and put genuine Exchange reorganization even further away. This strong desire of the public brokerage houses to work with Douglas toward reorganization, made emergent by another severe shakeout on October 18,

[41] New York Stock Exchange, *Report of the President*, Aug. 11, 1937.
[42] Various letters to F.D.R. re the Stock Exchange, Oct.–Nov., 1937, Roosevelt Papers; Miss E. M. Myer to F.D.R., Nov. 20, 1937, *ibid.*
[43] New York *Post*, Oct. 18, 1937.

culminated in a trip to the Roosevelt home at Hyde Park the following week. Paul V. Shields, head of a large commission brokerage, accompanied SEC Chairman William O. Douglas. Former SEC Chairman Joe Kennedy sat in on the conference. President Roosevelt insisted that the press interpretation of the visit's grave importance was unwarranted. The talks with Douglas and Kennedy were "routine stuff"; Shields was simply one of several persons who "drifted in." [44]

There were, nevertheless, matters of moment to be discussed. Supposedly, a chief topic was the recently completed SEC study on the market effects of short selling.[45] Two appointments to the Commission were currently under consideration. And whatever the order of business transacted, the conference included appraisal of Douglas' proposed tough line with recalcitrant Exchange officials, presidential approval of which quickly became evident.

Returning from Hyde Park, Douglas held his first extended conference with Stock Exchange officials and representatives of the large commission brokerage houses. Joe Kennedy again was present at the October 29 "surprise meeting." Although now chairman of the U.S. Maritime Commission and soon to become United States ambassador to London, Kennedy was still regarded by Wall Street as the most suitable liaison agent between the New York Stock Exchange and any administration agency. In addition to Paul V. Shields, another representative of the larger commission brokers was Gayer G. Dominick, who also occupied a seat on the governing committee. Attending the discussion for the Exchange were E. H. H. Simmons, a past president of the Stock Exchange, and William Jackson, the Exchange counsel. New York papers, although unable to report precise details of the conference, could truthfully relate that Stock Exchange officials, on leaving, "did not appear exuberant." [46]

Reason for a lack of exuberance became widely circulated within the weeks following: the SEC, dissatisfied with Exchange

[44] F.D.R. press conference, Oct. 26, 1937.
[45] New York *Herald Tribune,* Oct. 27, 1937.
[46] *Ibid.,* Oct. 30, 1937.

efforts to date, was going to draft its own rules for trading practices. The Commission had full powers under the act of 1934,
financial papers warned, to formulate rules making Stock Exchange members directly responsible to the SEC rather than to
their own exchange.[47] Actually, much of the discord between
the two bodies centered about attempts to draw up an official
communique to the SEC by Stock Exchange officials outlining
prospects for reorganization. At SEC suggestion, such a letter
would include a mutually acceptable reference to the severe
market decline. The SEC could then reply approvingly and co-
operatively, and the business of reorganization could move along.
Charged with this communicative function was the Law Committee, still very much a Whitney–Old Guard stronghold. Members of this body were extremely uneasy regarding any admission
that might be construed as a Stock Exchange responsibility for
the market plunge, and the final version underwent several drafts
as the committee labored to avoid the appearance of any guilt
clause.[48] The matter of reorganization was gently put aside in
temporizing generalities, reflecting the Old Guard point of view
that changes would be made "all in good time," but not at the
moment, since then they "would be regarded as the admission
of an error in the past." [49] In the eyes of Wall Street's elders any
threats from the SEC could safely be disregarded as pure bluff.

As a consequence the last of the Stock Exchange proposals
to be tendered to the SEC was an obviously unacceptable document that wholly ignored the critical issue of a nonmember
president and staff. Borne to Washington by the Exchange counsel, William Harding Jackson, it was carefully read by Douglas
and the Commission and resulted in a reported dialogue on November 22, 1937: [50]

Jackson: Have you read the last draft of our proposed statement?
Douglas: The SEC has read it and it is not satisfactory. The
negotiations are off.

[47] *Ibid.,* Nov. 20, 1937.
[48] New York *Times,* Nov. 23, 1937.
[49] *Wall Street Journal,* Nov. 24, 1937.
[50] Gesell, p. 54.

Jackson: Well, I suppose you'll go ahead with your own program?
Douglas: You're damned right I will.
Jackson: When you take over the Exchange, I hope you'll re-member we've been in business 150 years. There may be some things you will like to ask us.
Douglas: There is one thing I'd like to ask.
Jackson: What is it?
Douglas: Where do you keep the paper and pencils? [51]

With the unanimous approval and backing of his fellow com-missioners, Douglas issued a sharp and unequivocal ultimatum to the Stock Exchange on the following day. No longer could the SEC tolerate operations carried on as if in a private club for members only; for an institution "so vested with the public interest, this traditional method has become archaic." No ele-ment of the private gambling casino could be permitted to re-main, Douglas warned. Likewise, a management based on the private-club theory could scarcely be expected to enforce against its members regulations necessary to protect the public. There would be greater public confidence, the message stated, "in ex-changes which recognized that their management should not be in the hands of professional traders but in fact, as well as nominally, in charge of those who have a clearer public responsi-bility." Finally, the decision rested between such responsible self-regulation by the exchanges or "an immediate and more persuasive administration by the Commission." [52]

Faced with a public stand in language that clearly stated the SEC determination to administer the affairs of the Stock Ex-change if no reorganization was forthcoming, President Gay capitulated. He named a committee to submit recommendations for a reorganization, with C. C. Conway, chairman of Continen-tal Can, as its head.[53] The Conway Committee included an ad-ministration figure, Adolf A. Berle, Jr., and a high proportion of nonmembers in its make-up. Secretary of the committee was the young partner of a respected St. Louis bond house, and the

[51] The conversation as quoted "is substantially correct" (letter from Associate Supreme Court Justice William O. Douglas to the author, March 11, 1960).
[52] New York *Times,* Nov. 24, 1937.
[53] *Business Week,* Dec. 18, 1937, p. 4.

favorable publicity attending the committee's efforts soon lifted thirty-four-year-old William McChesney Martin, Jr., to the post of first salaried president of the New York Stock Exchange. In an atmosphere gradually veering toward reorganization, the Conway Committee began drawing up its report. January, 1938, saw an announcement from a smaller exchange, the Chicago Stock Exchange, of a complete reorganization that not only included a simplified governing system and a salaried management but also created an advisory committee to represent listed corporations and the public.[54] Two days later the Conway Committee's published report incorporated recommendations for all the major points suggested by Chairman Douglas, including direct representation of the public on the Exchange's board of governors. When the Stock Exchange governing board met on January 31, Richard Whitney and the floor traders' representatives proposed further evasion by the method of agreement "in principle," but to President Gay the handwriting finally was visible. It was he who persuaded Whitney to abstain rather than vote "no," and the report recommendations were approved.[55]

The Stock Exchange Old Guard, however, with its majority of seats on the governing board [56] and its willingness to look to Richard Whitney for leadership, was still in a position to influence strongly the means of achieving reorganization. The head of this group, Richard Whitney, was to much of the financial world the symbol and epitome of Wall Street's and the New York Stock Exchange's importance in the scheme of things. A man of imposing and dominating personality, blessed with a self-confidence that frequently attained arrogance, Whitney had been a member of the Exchange since 1912 and continuously active in its government. He drew additional awed respect from his relationship with J. P. Morgan and Company, for which he acted as bond broker, and from the fact that his brother, George Whitney, and his good friend Thomas W. Lamont were Morgan

[54] Douglas, *Democracy and Finance*, p. 65.
[55] Alsop and Kintner, "The Battle of the Market-Place," p. 11.
[56] Gesell, p. 53.

partners. It was to this stately and unyielding figure, to whom the Pecora Investigation and all subsequent efforts to regulate the affairs of the Stock Exchange had been sheer *lèse-majesté*, that the exponents of resistance to all change had rallied.

At the time the Conway report recommended a departure from the obsolete traditions of the past, however, the world of Richard Whitney's eminence was crumbling from within as well. Years of concentration on his official Exchange duties, coupled with rash and uniformly unsuccessful promotional ventures in everything from an applejack distillery to Florida peat humus, had brought Whitney to the systematic misappropriation of his customers' securities. A rumor caused a routine Stock Exchange questionnaire to be sent to Richard Whitney and Company and led to the eventual knowledge that the firm had been insolvent for three and a half years.[57] In an effort to restore his finances Whitney had also pledged improperly over a million dollars in securities and cash belonging to the Stock Exchange Gratuity Fund, of which he was a trustee. Like Chaucer's merchant, "so estatly was he of his governaunce," that no one suspected Whitney's fraudulent predicament. Yet his borrowings, widely known in Wall Street circles for several years, had reached the staggering total of $8,284,000, and had been made on forty-two occasions from thirty-one different Exchange sources, mostly on an unsecured basis.[58] A considerable amount was still outstanding when President Gay rang the gong that stopped Stock Exchange trading in order to make the announcement March 8, 1938, of Richard Whitney and Company's insolvency.

The personal attitude of this sleek and stately bellwether of the Old Guard flock had been that publicity regarding his misconduct would have a disastrously detrimental effect on the New York Stock Exchange. His urging that a reasonable basis for withdrawal of charges against him could be achieved through a simple transfer of his membership was indicative of the belief

---

[57] SEC, *In the Matter of Richard Whitney et al.*, I, 1. Actually the company was a limited partnership in which Richard Whitney held 52 percent of the stock. He testified that "the firm was mine . . . and I had a right to do anything I wanted" (*ibid.*, II, 58).

[58] *Ibid.*, I, 48–49, 179.

shared alike by Whitney and many of those who loaned him unsecured funds that neither the Stock Exchange nor his brotherly
connections in J. P. Morgan and Company "would let him
down." Arrested on two indictments of grand larceny in the
first degree, Richard Whitney pleaded guilty and was sentenced
April 11 to serve from five to ten years in Sing Sing on each
count.[59]

In the SEC report of the extensive public hearings that followed Whitney's insolvency and expulsion, the testimony amply
proved the assertion that the Old Guard was characterized by a
"tenacious clinging to the past when even sound business judgment indicated a contrary course." [60] Beset from within by the
commission houses' insistence on change and from without by
SEC determination, the Old Guard at best could have waged
only a foredoomed campaign of stubborn and grudging resistance to reorganization. With the public discrediting of their
idol and leader, their resistance ended with a complete and shat-
tering finality. On March 17 an overwhelming vote by the members brought in the SEC-suggested reorganization embodied in
the Conway report, including public participation, a paid technical staff, and a genuine equality of representation in Exchange
government.[61]

The democratization of the New York Stock Exchange had
its symbolic sequel. In the subsequent proceedings that saw the
personal assets of Richard Whitney auctioned off, his elegant
custom-built limousine, once the tangible evidence of the Whitney status, was triumphantly driven away by its new owner, a
Bronx delicatessen entrepreneur.[62]

William O. Douglas' philosophy, which was so instrumental
in fashioning SEC policy during his chairmanship, included a
concept of governmental regulation remarkably free of emo-
tional or partisan bias. These important years of consolidation

---

[59] *Ibid.*, pp. 77–78, 2.
[60] The SEC was apprised of the affair the day before its announcement on the
floor of the Exchange. Hearings were held April 6–June 29, 1938. See *Ibid.*, p. 164.
[61] New York *Times*, March 18, 1938.
[62] Gesell, p. 63.

benefited from the Douglas view that once such policies "have been enacted into statutory law, the business-government relationship moves out of the realm of controversy and debate and moves into the province of the technicians." One of the most effective aids to a harmonious relationship, Douglas felt, was the continued extension of self-government by the group to be regulated, such as the stock exchanges. This would relegate the governmental agency to the role of a protective shotgun, kept well-oiled but behind the door.[63] In spite of the difficulty in getting the New York Stock Exchange to accept adequate self-enforcement, the SEC persisted in the same course with the still unorganized group of over-the-counter brokers and dealers. "I wholly agree with you," Roosevelt wrote to Douglas, approving his decision to use the same pattern of self-regulation.[64] Once properly organized, over-the-counter brokers could then police their own operations, with the SEC standing by in a supervisory capacity. Such a policy of "working with industry, running our Commission on the basis of a service station," also led Douglas to suggest to a senatorial committee that those private utilities attempting holding company integration be exempted from the capital gains taxes on stock transfers, since they then became inequitable and punitive.[65]

"Mankind, not the corporation, comes first" was the Brandeisian theme on which Douglas sounded many variations.[66] To Douglas, keeping the investment banker out of industry control meant that finance kept its proper place as the servant, and never the master, of a healthy and balanced economy. Douglas shared with Roosevelt a fear of the concentration of economic power in the hands of a privileged few. This "predatory finance" dealt the most serious blows to capitalism by its disregard for the simple virtue of honesty in trusteeship, and by its usurpation of control from the individual investors, those "orphans of the financial economy." To this end, Douglas recommended some type of national organization that could supply paid professionals or

[63] Douglas, *Democracy and Finance*, pp. xi, 82.
[64] F.D.R. memo to William O. Douglas, Feb. 1, 1938, Roosevelt Papers.
[65] Senate, *The Reserve Act of 1938*, pp. 71, 73.
[66] Douglas, *Being an American*, pp. 35 ff.

public directors to sit at corporate council tables and speak for the voiceless stockholder.[67]

Reorganization of the New York Stock Exchange did not bring all of Wall Street to the side of Douglas and the SEC. Sentiment relating all stock market ills to regulation, and even an irrational belief that Richard Whitney's downfall could be traced to "government interference," was still commonly heard. Yet increasingly the many voices of those who had soberly evaluated the Exchange reorganization in terms of investor confidence were heard also. Wetmore Hodges, writing to newly appointed SEC Commissioner Jerome N. Frank, expressed the sentiment of many. Regarding the "clean sweep" in the Stock Exchange, Hodges wrote, the SEC had so handled itself "as to be gaining backers among the decent crowd in the Street every week." [68]

Public recognition of the SEC stand was forthcoming also. Several months after the Stock Exchange reorganization, Chairman Douglas was unanimously voted the annual award of the National Association of Accredited Publicity Directors. Its wording aptly summarized a Douglas principle:

Through his efforts and rulings this year he has given more prominence to the value of adequate and accurate publicity than any other public official or private person. He has interpreted publicity in the sense of its good to the public, which is an aspiration we all profess.[69]

Douglas received from James Landis the legacy of a sound body of administrative regulation and high standards of technical competence and performance. He furthered the success of the SEC administration by his formula of independence from, yet official sympathy for, the group being regulated. An idealist in aiming at a 100 percent goal in ethical performance by financiers and the exchanges, Douglas realistically admitted he would be "damned lucky" to achieve even 51 percent of such a program. Emulating the pragmatic approach of the agency's first

[67] *Time*, April 5, 1937, p. 71.
[68] Wetmore Hodges to Jerome N. Frank, March 24, 1938, Roosevelt Papers.
[69] National Association of Accredited Publicity Directors to William O. Douglas, Sept. 9, 1938, Roosevelt Papers.

two chairmen, Douglas added to it a dimension of firmness and activism that availed itself of Wall Street cooperation yet relentlessly extended the boundary of SEC supervision. With the reorganization of the New York Stock Exchange and similar changes in the other major exchanges, the SEC had extricated the nation's securities trading from its status of exclusive club members' private dealings. This major portion of the country's investment facilities, the public interest now acknowledged, was to operate in the future under the strict codes of self-regulated exchanges, with the SEC established in its persistently sought role of watchful supervisor.

CHAPTER SEVEN

THE YEARS OF CONSOLIDATION

IN THE execution and judicial interpretation of the securities acts during the first few years there were relatively few cases of enough importance to attract wide attention. Two exceptions were the Michael J. Meehan and J. Edward Jones cases, both of which helped to clarify the position of the SEC in the financial community. The Meehan case illustrated that the SEC had every intention of moving against transgressors firmly and persistently. "L'affaire Jones," as some chose to term it, evoked a rebuke by the Supreme Court for the SEC's zealous prosecution, but furnished no constitutional comfort for the agency's critics.

Michael J. Meehan, of earlier Pecora Investigation fame, was involved in the first case of stock manipulation on a major exchange to be dealt with. Not only was the case of considerable importance for this reason but also because it involved a nationally known broker. Meehan was charged in late 1935 with market manipulations in the stock of Bellanca Aircraft and with corporate errors in its registration statement. Edward J. Flynn, New York's secretary of state and the Democratic leader of the Bronx, was retained as Meehan's counsel,[1] and hearings and appeals occupied almost two years. In August, 1937, Meehan was ordered expelled by the SEC from his memberships in the New York Stock Exchange and the New York Curb Exchange on

[1] New York *Herald Tribune*, Nov. 7, 1935.

grounds of stock manipulation.[2] No attempt was made to appeal this administrative adjudication to a decision of the courts.

A dealer in oil royalties, J. Edward Jones of New York City, was the first litigant to test the SEC securities registration powers. In 1936, Jones made up a series of oil royalty certificates for public sale and submitted an account of the issue for registration with the SEC. Thought to contain fraudulent matter, the issue was held up and Jones subpoenaed for a hearing. Instead, Jones decided to withdraw the issue from public sale, and therefore refused to heed the subpoena.

The question relating to withdrawal of an applicant's registration once it became apparent a hearing might disclose fraud had arisen early in SEC experience. Should the applicant be permitted to escape the consequences that might ensue by the simple device of withdrawing his statement of registration? The statute itself was silent on the matter of withdrawals, but if the intent of the act was to be accepted as valid, then the "exercise of discretion to deny withdrawals . . . seemed appropriate." Thus the Commission soon had adopted the practice of denying withdrawals wherever there appeared to be "deliberate, material misstatements" by the registrant.[3]

The SEC persisted, therefore, in requiring Jones and his business records to appear at a hearing to determine whether the withdrawn registration statement contained fraudulent information. Jones insisted he was being unduly persecuted by the government. His attorneys, appealing service of the subpoena, fought the case through district and circuit courts to the Supreme Court on grounds that since no statutory provision specifically covered the situation, Jones had a perfect right to withdraw his registration statement without obtaining SEC consent.

The Supreme Court, at the height of the period during which it struck down eleven major pieces of New Deal legislation, also delivered a stinging rebuke to the SEC. On the first traditional Monday decision day in April, 1936, Justice Sutherland's opinion for the majority soundly condemned the agency's over zeal-

[2] SEC, *Third Annual Report*, 1938, p. 71.
[3] Landis, *The Administrative Process*, pp. 137 ff.

ousness as a transgression of its authority. Chairman Landis'
wire to President Roosevelt, on board the U.S.S. *Potomac,* told
how the "grandiloquent tirade of Sutherland (who did not hear
the arguments) against Commission procedure" likened it to the
Star Chamber of the Stuart monarchs.[4] Where the majority opinion decried "investigation not based on specified grounds," the
dissenting trio of Cardozo, Brandeis, and Stone felt that permitting "an offending registrant to stifle an inquiry by precipitate retreat on the eve of his exposure is to give immunity to
guilt; to encourage falsehood and evasion." The statute then
"becomes the sport of clever knaves." Nor could Cardozo resist
poking fun at the use of such an unlikely "sanguinary simile"
as the Star Chamber to describe the SEC's due-process pursuit of
Jones.[5]

In citing the necessity of guarding against the "appropriation
of unauthorized power by lesser agencies,"[6] and in reminding
the SEC that the grand jury was always available for criminal
prosecution, the Supreme Court made apparent its mistrust of
the modern administrative process. Clearly such delegation of
powers by Congress meant some limitation of the courts' adjudi-
catory authority. Despite the evident intent of Congress, the pre-
1937 Supreme Court did not regard with favor the use of administrative justice as an agent of the legislative body, nor did
it hesitate to go beyond the constitutional technicalities under
consideration to attack the entire philosophy of the administrative process.

Although the only setback the Commission received from the
court, it in no way questioned the constitutionality of the securities acts or the SEC itself. Unfortunately, however, the ruling—
and particularly the rhetoric in which it was couched—gave aid
and comfort to the enemies both of the SEC and of any delegation of Congressional powers to administrative agencies. The

---

[4] Naval message, James M. Landis to F.D.R. on U.S.S. *Potomac,* April 6, 1936,
Roosevelt Papers.
[5] *Securities and Exchange Commission v. J. Edward Jones,* 298 U.S. 27–33
(1936).
[6] *Ibid.,* 24.

denunciatory fervor with which Justice Sutherland's majority opinion assailed the exercise of regulatory powers as tyrannical was welcome language to many, and for months thereafter the cry of "Star Chamber tactics" was raised at each agency attempt to proceed against fraudulent promoters. To Chairman Landis, the "effect if not the purpose was to breed distrust of the administration," and thereby greatly hamper the cause of good administration.[7]

The severest legal test for the SEC came with the Public Utility Holding Company Act. The Commission wished to avoid any appearance of unreasonableness in its exercise of the new act's undoubted powers, and was anxious not to endanger recovery prospects through a pitched battle with the entire utilities industry.

In his first speech as chairman of the SEC, James M. Landis drew public attention to the importance of the new Holding Company Act, and reassured both utility investors and the holding companies themselves that the SEC was fully aware of the stature of its new administrative duties. "We assume our responsibilities," he told a national radio audience, "in an atmosphere still surcharged with passionate feelings and unreasoning fears aroused by the legislative battle that preceded passage of the Holding Company Act." [8] Chief concern of the SEC, Landis went on to say, was to insure the protection of this great national investment and its efficient and uninterrupted functioning. A trial of constitutionality from among the utility holding companies was welcomed, but the plea was made that it be limited to an individual case, so that the industry might proceed with needed expansion meantime. To further such a trial the SEC issued a release providing that holding companies might register, yet expressly reserve their constitutional and legal rights to challenge the act's provisions if they chose to do so later.[9] Punitive intent was as absent from SEC administration as it had been

[7] Landis, *The Administrative Process*, p. 140.
[8] SEC, Release No. 3 (Public Utility Holding Company Act), Sept. 28, 1935.
[9] SEC, Release No. 6 (Public Utility Holding Company Act), Oct. 9, 1935.

after the two securities acts, Landis assured the utility holding companies.

The moves of the next two months indicated that Landis' offering of an olive branch went largely unheeded, and that only a number of the smaller utility holding companies intended to observe the act's provisions. When the December, 1935, deadline for holding company registration had passed, not one of the giants of the utilities industry had elected to comply. Convinced of the act's unconstitutional provisions and supremely confident of ultimate judicial vindication, they chose flatly to disobey their new legal obligation, despite repudiation of such lawlessness by prominent business advisers.[10] Instead, the larger utilities holding companies instituted a harassing assault of some fifty-odd suits against the Commission, and acted to forestall any agency attempt to enforce the act by the use of mass injunction proceedings.

Faced with the prospect of defending itself on a multiplicity of fronts against a variety of suits, the Commission elected instead to become the aggressor in order to insure both a target and a constitutional approach of its own choosing. Benjamin Cohen and Thomas G. Corcoran, chief drafters of the act, together with special counsel Robert H. Jackson of the Treasury Department, Chairman Landis, and General Counsel Burns of the SEC settled on the best known and perhaps largest of all the utilities holding company systems, Electric Bond and Share Company, as the most logical subject for the act's testing. Its pyramiding of holding company atop holding company was shown in a chart that illustrated how Electric Bond and Share, with the "comparatively small investment of $212 million in common and preferred stocks and bonds, dominated numerous intermediate holding and operating companies whose utility assets aggregate $2,458 billion." [11] Its operating companies, construction companies and service companies, with its many subsidiaries and intermediate companies functioning through interlocking

---

[10] Roger Babson's public letter to utilities officials. See Washington *Daily News*, Dec. 4, 1935.

[11] New York *Times*, Jan. 30, 1937.

directorates at interstate levels throughout the United States, presented a diversified spread of operations that touched on the act at virtually every point.

The Public Utility Holding Company Act had been carefully formulated to permit the challenging of one or several sections without interfering with the exercise of the remaining provisions. The powers within the registration sections were demonstrably within the constitutional prerogative of Congress. Other provisions became effective on registration and were contingent on these sections, yet they could stand alone. Electric Bond and Share's refusal to comply with the registration provision (Sections 4[a] and 5) was the charge in the SEC suit, therefore, and the crux of the matter was the separability of the registration sections from the balance of the act and judgment rendered solely thereon. From the agency's viewpoint, the courts must be requested to consider only the sections involved, and not attempt an "omnibus decision" on the entire act based on any contingent and hypothetical action of the remaining provisions.

Headquarters of Electric Bond and Share were in New York, which was given as the reason for filing the agency bill of complaint in that district. A further compelling cause for the choice, however, was the Commission's desire to bring the SEC suit before the extremely able and respected Federal judge, Julian W. Mack of New York City.[12] After hectic sessions of preparation the suit was quietly rushed into Federal district court for filing at one hour before midnight on November 25, 1935, five days before the act's registration deadline.[13] Although Owen D. Young, director of an Electric Bond subsidiary, had been brought in to join C. F. Groesbeck, Electric's chairman of the board, in conferring with SEC officials the day before, they had had no intimation of the action. Officers of Electric Bond and Share admitted they were "taken completely by surprise," since they had planned to seek injunctive relief themselves.[14]

Now the Commission acted to narrow the field down to the

[12] Told to author in interview with James M. Landis, Washington, D.C., Aug. 14, 1961.
[13] Barron's, Dec. 2, 1935, p. 5.
[14] New York Times, Nov. 27, 1935.

chosen target, and to eliminate any possibility of equity suits against the SEC on grounds of irreparable injury done the holding companies by enforcement of the act. To quash the proliferation of injunctions against the SEC, United States Attorney General Homer Cummings and SEC General Counsel John J. Burns filed a motion with the Supreme Court of the District of Columbia requesting a stay in all such proceedings until the constitutionality of the act could be decided on by the highest court or "otherwise terminated," since numerous suits on the same issue were a waste of time and money.[15] With the ultimate granting of this motion, all such actions pending against the agency were brought to a complete halt. Additionally, the Attorney General instructed all United States district attorneys that the Federal government would not become a party to any further suits brought by utility company stockholders to prevent their managements from registering with the SEC.[16] An impenetrable barrier was thereby erected against the passage of any test of constitutionality other than the SEC's own carefully selected choice, Electric Bond and Share Company.

There still remained the problem of removing grounds for equity suits based on injury resulting from the act's denial of mail and interstate commerce privileges to those unregistered. With the cooperation of Federal officials, this possibility was eliminated. The United States Attorney General instructed all United States district attorneys not to attempt to enforce the interstate commerce provisions of the act until its constitutionality was assured. In similar fashion, the Postmaster General advised all postmasters that utilities holding companies illegally unregistered were nevertheless to have the right to use the mails until the Supreme Court should have finally determined the validity of the act.[17] With removal of the threat of enforcing these provisions until the court's decision was known, even against those who refused to register, classical grounds for seeking legal relief were completely undercut.

[15] Washington *Post*, Dec. 8, 1935.
[16] New York *Times*, Dec. 8, 1935.
[17] "Procedural Aspects of the Litigation under the Public Utility Holding Company Act," *Harvard Law Review*, Feb., 1937, pp. 658–59.

By adroit legal maneuvering, the SEC and its Federal allies had effected the limitation of suits that the Commission originally called for, but that the utilities industry had ignored in favor of a many-sided campaign of judicial harassment.[18] Electric Bond and Share, willy-nilly, had been made the champion of the utility holding company cause. At the same time, the SEC had made abundantly clear its *bona fides* regarding uninterrupted functioning of the utilities industry. Holding companies were promised that their registration in no way prejudiced their legal and constitutional right to challenge the act's provisions at a later date. Grounds for equity proceedings were disposed of when, in the interest of reaching a decision on the act's constitutionality, its enforcement was held in abeyance even against the illegally unregistered. All then rested upon the outcome of the sole case in the legal arena.

Voluminous briefs filed with the district court by SEC emphasized that registration would not impair the registrants' right to contest the act's provisions, and attempted to direct the court's decision to a consideration only of the constitutionality of the sections in dispute and their severability from the remaining provisions of the act. The defendant's attack conversely centered on the registration sections as unconstitutional and disavowing their separability. A cross-bill, or countersuit, further alleged that the provisions of the entire act were unconstitutional. Robert H. Jackson, now moved to Assistant Attorney General, made the main argument for the agency case, while Benjamin V. Cohen attacked the cross-bill seeking to prove the act wholly unconstitutional.

The verdict of the Southern District Court of New York, Judge Julian W. Mack presiding, delivered January 29, 1937, was understandably headlined a "Victory for Roosevelt." [19] The court had espoused the SEC line of attack at every point, and rejected forcefully each Electric Bond and Share argument. The defendant's initial contention that enforced registration would,

[18] New York *Times,* Dec. 8, 1935.
[19] *Ibid.,* Jan. 30, 1937.

in any case, have deprived them of the right to contest the validity of the act's other provisions was quickly overturned by Judge Mack, who said, "Any doubt as to this is clearly dispelled by a rule of the Commission, issued pursuant to its rule-making powers under the Act, which permits registration with an express reservation of any constitutional or legal rights." [20]

Constitutionality of the registration sections was readily admitted. As to their separability, Judge Mack stated, "It seems clear, and indeed does not seem seriously to be contested, that the registration provisions in and of themselves could constitute a workable regulatory device." Mack also cited Congressional debates and hearings to uphold the point that Congress clearly intended to have the various sections of the statute stand by themselves, even if others—such as Section 11, the "death sentence"—were declared invalid. Nor could the court find any merit in the contention of the cross-plaintiffs. Since they had not registered, the constitutional validity of the other provisions was not in controversy, and no judicial pronouncement could be rendered on such a speculative basis.[21] Defendants and affiliated holding companies, therefore, were enjoined from carrying on any activities in interstate commerce forbidden to unregistered holding companies until they had complied with the registration sections.

SEC Chairman Landis reacted most strongly against the utilities' persistent belief that registration would mean waiving their legal rights to contest the act further. After carefully publicizing the SEC stand committing itself to the contrary, this portion of the utilities' complaint could only be regarded as "utter nonsense." No such waiver was involved, Landis repeated, pointing out that "every court in the country where this issue was raised has upheld our view." The SEC chairman assailed the costly legal fights as coming from "spurious legal advice" of "highly paid lawyers," and a waste of stockholders' money. The great mass of such suits, Landis said hotly, arose from the "mad advice of Liberty League lawyers." [22]

[20] 18 Fed. Supp. 131 (S.D.N.Y. 1937), p. 136.
[21] *Ibid.*, pp. 137–39, 148.
[22] Washington *Post*, Jan. 31, 1937.

Press description of the Mack decision was largely that of a "clear-cut victory" for the SEC, with the result that Electric Bond and Share must register, and with the prediction that the agency's elaborate planning would ensure an early test in the Supreme Court.[23] The holding company chose next to refer its cause to the circuit court of appeals, however, where the rulings of the lower court were unanimously affirmed.[24] Arguments before the United States Supreme Court were not begun until February, 1938.

Electric Bond and Share Co. v. *Securities and Exchange Commission* arrived before the Supreme Court in an era when the court's post-1937 outlook reflected far more sympathy than previously toward administrative justice as a proper arm of the legislature. The intent of Congress to resolve an army of controversies over private rights outside of the overburdened courts had found a more favorable reception than that which greeted *J. Edward Jones* v. *Securities and Exchange Commission,* and by 1938 the court exhibited near unanimity in upholding the exercise of Federal regulatory powers. Particularly was this true where the clarity of Congressional intent was unchallengeable. In make-up the court had undergone only one change that affected the Electric Bond decision: the replacement, some four months earlier, of the resigned Willis Van Devanter with New Deal Senator Hugo L. Black. Only seven justices could decide the case, however, since newly appointed Justice Stanley Reed's name appeared on the SEC brief as solicitor general, and because Justice Cardozo was suffering from the illness that was to claim his life the following summer.

SEC arguments and their proponents followed much the same pattern successfully employed in the lower courts. Assistant Attorney General Robert H. Jackson, whose vigorous conduct of the government's income tax case against former Secretary of the Treasury Andrew W. Mellon had been cited originally in his choice as special counsel,[25] bore the brunt of the main argu-

[23] New York *Times,* Jan. 31, 1937.
[24] 92 F.2d 580 (2d Cir. Ct. App. 1937).
[25] New York *Times,* Nov. 27, 1937.

ment. Benjamin Cohen, chief legal architect of the Holding Company Act, again refuted Electric Bond's cross-bill attacking the entire act's constitutionality. Additional names on the SEC brief included Attorney General Cummings, Assistant Solicitor General Bell, and Special Assistant to the Attorney General Thomas G. Corcoran.

Again, on each disputed point the court's satisfaction with the government's case stood out sharply and distinctly. In the Supreme Court's 6-1 verdict of March, 1938, upholding the lower court's ruling,[26] the constitutionality of the registration sections emerged unquestioned, their severability undeniable. And, in refusing to adjudicate on the act's remaining provisions, the Supreme Court declined to make of itself a battleground for the clash of hypothetical issues. Throughout the decision appeared numerous evidences of the court's gratification with the clarity and precision of legal craftsmanship with which the intent of Congress was made known.

Writing the opinion for the majority,[27] Chief Justice Hughes addressed himself first to Sections 4(a) and 5, the registration provisions. There existed "no serious controversy," the opinion stated, that the activities of the defendant company and its affiliates brought them "within the ambit of Congressional authority." Having satisfied itself on this score, the court found "no reason to doubt" Congressional authority to demand the "fullest information as to organization and financial structure" for regulatory purposes. Validity of the penalty clause, Section 4(a), must likewise be sustained. Those who refuse to submit to registration "to supply information which Congress is entitled to demand" must bear the imposition of the penalty prescribed.[28]

The Supreme Court reserved some of its most forthright expressions of satisfaction for the act's wording where the question of separability was concerned. The majority opinion followed

[26] *Electric Bond and Share Co.* v. *Securities and Exchange Commission,* 303 U.S. 419 (1938).
[27] Chief Justice Hughes, Justices Black, Butler, Brandeis, Roberts, and Stone. Justice McReynolds dissented without opinion.
[28] *Electric Bond and Share Co.* v. *Securities and Exchange Commission,* 431, 442.

the line of SEC argument that insisted that if, for example, Section 11 (the "death sentence") was adjudged invalid, there was no inherent reason why other regulatory provisions could not be enforced as Congress provided. There was no practical difficulty in the separability and independent enforcement of Sections 4(a) and 5, the opinion agreed. In fact, "the administrative construction of the statute was formulated in that view." Nor was there any doubt that this divisibility was the intent of Congress. Pointing out the "explicit declaration" of the statute's clauses, the court found it "unnecessary to review the details of arguments or the cited statements from the legislative halls. The Act speaks for itself with sufficient clarity." [29]

The cross-bill, with which defendants sought judgment on every provision of the act as unconstitutional, presented to the court "a variety of hypothetical controversies which may never become real." Benjamin Cohen's contention that other provisions of the act could be decided only if there were specific cases testing them was fully accepted in the Supreme Court decision: "We are invited to enter into a speculative inquiry for the purpose of condemning statutory provisions the effect of which . . . cannot now be definitely perceived. We must decline that invitation." [30]

The complete SEC victory, which the court's verdict represented, was the product of statutory workmanship, astute legal maneuvering, and a high regard for the uninterrupted functioning of the economy. It was based on an act meticulously drafted, and on a carefully planned judicial course of action guided by a sense of responsibility for the continuity of national recovery. The Supreme Court that underwrote this victory was a judicial body embarked on an era of peaceful coexistence with the New Deal, and it had veered toward the Holmes viewpoint that social and economic policy formulated by legislatures should have the freest possible range of constitutional interpretation. The court's chief concern should be faithfully to give effect to the legislative will, and to accomplish this the language of the statute

[29] *Ibid.*, 435, 438.
[30] *Ibid.*, 443.

must give a graphic image of purpose impossible of misinterpretation. Precise legal draftsmanship, therefore, was of welcome importance after the hastily dawn and ineptly worded statutes of earliest New Deal days. No longer could Justice Stone, speaking of such legislation, complain that "the laxity with which the Government is proceeding in carrying out the legal details of the New Deal has been pretty shocking." [31] The Public Utility Holding Company Act, meticulously drafted in terms of hard legal realism to specify the intent of Congress, was a far cry from the carelessly structured and frequently exhortatory statutes of early 1933. The Supreme Court's approval of this precision and clarity of intent was obvious throughout its decision.

Careful planning in the court testing of the act was essential. The survival of the Holding Company Act, the effectiveness of the SEC, and the prestige of the administration could be greatly influenced by the outcome. The agency's strength would have been completely dissipated had it assigned counsel to each of numerous cases filed in what was commonly held to be a utilities-inspired plan. As columnist Arthur Krock explained, the SEC rightfully concluded that the many suits were designed actually to prevent the agency from making an adequate defense of the broad issue itself.[32] Advantages that accrue to an offensive campaign had, therefore, to be seized, and the smaller forces of the agency deployed with judicious strategy. While a stay in the many injunction proceedings brought these duplicate tests of constitutionality to a halt, the decision meantime not to enforce the act until a verdict could be rendered eliminated the possibility of any suits in equity being opened. Like a champion golfer removing each alien blade of grass in the path of the ball to the cup, the agency could then concentrate unmolested on the final stroke.

The SEC had hoped to convince the utilities industry to adopt a "register now, sue later" policy, so to speak. Public commitment to this course would lend more weight of evidence to the SEC policy of regulatory reasonableness. The utilities industry could continue its expansion unhindered at the same time the act was being constitutionally tested, and the Commission would not be overwhelmed by the tireless challenges of the holding companies' legal staffs. Although failing in this approach, the agency's willingness to permit later suits on the act in order to keep the industry from halting merely while it observed its own legal efforts was impressive to the judiciary. Both the lower courts and the Supreme Court took note of the scrupulous care with which the SEC expressly reserved the utilities' constitutional and legal rights to sue later, despite being required to register first. Such notice greatly added to public recognition of the SEC's pursuit of reasonableness rather than vindictiveness. Belief in this policy and in the act's durability were both given added proof when, eight years later, the Supreme Court upheld as constitutional the controversial death-sentence section in two unanimous decrees of 1946.[33]

On the same day the court handed down its decision of March 28, 1938, rejecting Electric Bond and Share's appeal, several of the larger unregistered holding companies filed their notices of intent to register. With few exceptions, the remainder of those unregistered then followed suit, rushing their registration forms to completion in obedience with the final verdict.[34]

The period during the agency's preoccupation with its court defense was also used to good advantage in carrying forward additional studies and surveys for further legislation, and in projecting tirelessly SEC aims and policy to the world of finance and the general public. In consolidating itself in both of these areas the SEC enjoyed the aid of a succession of conscientious and well-qualified commissioners.

An early associate of Chairman Douglas was James D. Ross, also from Washington State, and known throughout the Pacific Northwest as the developer in Seattle of one of the most success-

[33] *North American Co.* v. *Securities and Exchange Commission,* 327 U.S. 90 (1946); and *American Power and Light* v. *Securities and Exchange Commission,* 329 U.S. 90 (1946). The former was unanimous; the two judges who dissented in the latter decision did not do so on any question of the statute's constitutional validity.

[34] SEC, *Fourth Annual Report,* 1938, p. 6.

ful municipal power plants in the country. A Canadian of Scottish ancestry and little formal education, Ross demonstrated a strong belief in public service ideals by turning over his innovations in electrical design to the American Institute of Electrical Engineers rather than patenting them.[35] His strong advocacy of public power brought him an appointment to fill Pecora's vacancy immediately after the passage of the Public Utility Holding Company Act in 1935, a move that was generally received "as an indication of the aggressive attitude which the Federal agency is supposed to pursue in its new duties." [36] Ross shared the Roosevelt views that the reduction of electric power rates was the best way to tap the enormous potential demand for electricity, and he presented an able statistical support of his views to the 1936 World Power Conference.[37]

Following J. D. Ross's departure to head the new Bonneville Dam project in 1937, a Wall Street broker and a trio of New Dealers were appointed to the Commission over the next few years. The broker was John Wesley Hanes, a young North Carolinian of liberal views regarding exchange and securities reforms. The successor to Kennedy in respect to his stock exchange and financial connections, Hanes was more than "the good friend at court" that Wall Street saw in his occupancy of a commissioner's chair. A member of a wealthy and patriarchal family that boasted extensive textile manufacturing interests as well as the original ownership of Reynolds Tobacco Company, Hanes divested himself of a senior partnership in Chas. D. Barney and Company to assume the SEC post.[38] Although he had opposed Roosevelt in 1932 and 1936, Hanes modified his views considerably thereafter. His active and continued opposition over a period of years to Whitney and the Stock Exchange Old Guard furnished much of the basis for his strong recommendation to the President by both Kennedy and Douglas.[39] During his short tenure with the

[35] "It Can't Be Done, Can't It?" *Collier's*, pp. 28, 36.
[36] New York *Herald Tribune*, Aug. 24, 1935.
[37] Ross, VIII, 403–43.
[38] Newman, pp. 18–19.
[39] *Newsweek*, May 23, 1938, p. 12. See also Newman, p. 19; Alsop and Kintner, "The Battle of the Market-Place," p. 77.

Commission, Hanes successfully duplicated the Kennedy image as liaison man between financial circles and the administration. Actually, Hanes fell somewhere between the John D. Flynn description of a traitor within the gates and the *Herald Tribune*'s lavish vision of him as Wall Street's Joan of Arc.

The appointment of a Stock Exchange member was, in this case, administration recognition of outstanding support of administration views. O. Max Gardner, Democratic leader in Hanes's home state of North Carolina, wrote Roosevelt that "since his appointment he has been in constant conference with leaders in finance and business" and initiating "mutual discussions regarding the need for closer and more cooperative efforts with the national government." [40] There was no doubt in Gardner's mind of Hanes's genuine value to the administration. His appointment served as an excellent example of the means by which the New Deal brought public recognition to those who shared its views on financial reforms. At the same time Hanes, as the lone connection with Wall Street, was adequate testimony that the New Deal did not intend to permit domination of the agency by the group to be regulated.

First to reach the Commission of the trio committed to the New Deal ideology was Edward C. Eicher of Iowa, whose Congressional experience as an active member of the House Committee on Interstate and Foreign Commerce furnished valuable background for his SEC career. Described as a "one hundred per cent New Dealer from a normally Republican district," Eicher took an active part in the passage of the Holding Company Act and was the sponsor of a bill to tighten up the Clayton Act by prohibiting stock control of one corporation by another intent on restraint of competition.[41] Eicher followed Judge Healy as the commissioner who served as chief trial examiner, a role unique with the SEC.[42] Like J. D. Ross, Edward Eicher was more concerned with the effect of the Public Utility Holding Company Act on the consumer than on the investor. This

[40] O. Max Gardner to Press Secretary Marvin McIntyre, Jan. 10, 1938, Roosevelt Papers.
[41] *Business Week,* July 2, 1938, p. 17.
[42] Senate, *Administrative Procedure,* Part I, p. 397.

meant a special preoccupation with Section 11, or the death-sentence clause of that bill, which Eicher described as "the greatest single measure ever enacted in the interest of the American consumer." [43] Eicher brought to the new processes of administrative government an ideological commitment and considerable legislative experience. He also brought a definite awareness of the need to avoid unsound, injudicious, or arbitrary decisions in the exercise of the new agency's discretionary powers, lest its hard-earned reputation be damaged by loss of public confidence.[44]

Second of the New Deal trio and an even more truculent defender of the consumer at large was Leon Henderson, appointed to the SEC in May, 1939, after Chairman William O. Douglas had been named as United States Supreme Court justice. "A broker in economic ideas," as he termed himself, Henderson possessed a well-founded reputation as the New Deal's leading exponent of the consumer-purchasing power theory. A graduate of Swarthmore, Henderson had done graduate work in economics at the University of Pennsylvania from 1920 to 1922. Following a stint as assistant professor of economics at Carnegie Institute of Technology, Henderson had worked as an economist for Governor Pinchot of Pennsylvania and for the Russell Sage Foundation. In 1934 his pungency of expression and desk-slamming technique so impressed that champion practitioner of invective, General Hugh Johnson, that the latter imported him to a Washington post as economic adviser to the National Industry Recovery Board. Henderson's brash assertiveness, coupled with a quick intelligence and a profound ability to mold statistics into penetrating interpretation, brought him presidential and administration recognition. His vast energy and belligerent honesty were used in nearly a dozen New Deal agencies or committees as the occasion demanded.[45]

Although Leon Henderson was considered to have "put his

---

[43] Eicher, "Consumers and the Public Utility Holding Company Act," p. 16.
[44] Eicher, "Administrative Processes and Procedure," pp. 263–74.
[45] Leon Henderson was reputedly the only man ever to call Franklin D. Roosevelt a "son of a bitch" to his face. The occasion was an amiable dispute over the size of their respective fishing catches (Gunther, p. 83).

mark on the present Administration more firmly than anyone save Mr. Roosevelt," [46] his short tenure on the SEC was more in the nature of a temporary resting place until some defective part of the New Deal economic machinery required his energetic services. The calm detachment that accompanied Douglas' decisions, or the rarefied intellect that masked Jerome Frank's executive capacities, were lacking in Henderson. His service as a commissioner did not permit the direct dealing in slam-bang fashion that the ebullient economist characteristically employed, and his contribution to the SEC was inhibited thereby. Henderson's regrettable shortness of tenure was typical of the chief criticism that could be leveled at Commission appointments of the early years. Both personal decisions and administration moves frequently acted to diminish a continuity of service from which the SEC would have profited further.

Henderson's most notable success was in connection with the Temporary National Economic Committee, an inquiry into monopolistic practices in the American economy that he was largely credited with having initiated.[47] Commissioner Henderson energetically carried forward the exposure of the Douglas-named "termites of high finance," presenting to this body the results of SEC investigation into monopolistic tactics of investment banking.[48] In revealing evidence of collusion rather than competitive bidding on bond issues, and in pointing out great concentrations of investment banking power, Leon Henderson exhibited the hatred of monopoly and the profound belief in competition to benefit the consumer that characterized his outlook.

If Leon Henderson's appointment to the SEC aroused a storm of criticism and resentment in financial circles, Jerome Frank's simultaneous election as chairman in May, 1939, had a moderately calming effect derived from his previous year and a half as commissioner. Another of the brilliant young legal protégés of Felix Frankfurter, Jerome Frank began his New Deal career

[46] *New Republic,* May 10, 1939, p. 3.
[47] *Ibid.* See also *Current Biography, 1940,* p. 378.
[48] "The Case for Investment Banking," *Nation's Business,* pp. 55–60.

as counsel for the Agricultural Adjustment Administration. His legislative drafting ability had been put to use on both the AAA and NRA bills, and his main administrative efforts had been with the former agency. Against this background, his initial acceptance by Wall Street for a SEC post was a qualified and hesitant one. It was understood that he had received the approval of "that section of the financial community having the ear of the Administration" over several other strong candidates. Regardless of his social philosophy, one paper editorialized, it was "not on record that his competence in the field of corporate law has even been a matter of question." And twenty years of corporate law practice also was hopefully entered as evidence of a genuine conservatism at heart.[49]

A few months after Frank took over as commissioner, the publication of his book *Save America First* gave the business world a more precise insight into the new commissioner's economic and social philosophy. One of the few early efforts to arrive at a solution to the problem of relating American capitalism to the times, Frank's work proposed an abridged economic nationalism. To him, America's answer lay more with the domestic economy than in foreign trade, and he believed that subsidies of any kind should be wholly diverted to the development of domestic purchasing power. In aiming at this goal Frank insisted that the American business oligarchy must justify its existence by increasing the workers' living standard. Sharing the same distrust of concentrated economic power as Roosevelt and Douglas, Frank agreed that trust busting was scarcely the answer. Rather, the salvation of the American economy rested with persuading the enlightened corporate mind that an increased national income could be achieved only through sharing it with higher wages and lower prices.

Jerome Frank's chairmanship was asserted no less positively than that of William O. Douglas, and was frequently accompanied by acid commentaries on the laggards in the utility holding company ranks. Frank impatiently pointed out to this group that a relatively simple refunding transaction could be carried

[49] New York *Herald Tribune*, Dec. 11, 1937.

out by retiring holding company securities through the sale of new operating company securities, leaving the investor with the type of issue for which he had always shown a marked preference.[50]

Another example of Frank's pragmatic approach to the problems of the financial world emerged as a variation on the Keynesian theme. The long-term financing of major industry, Frank thought, could be handled better solely through stock issuance and by eliminating bond issues entirely. In this manner, the fixed charges of the latter would not act as a further depressant in times of recession. Bondholders suffered from financial failures equally with preferred stockholders in actual practice, Frank argued. Therefore, escaping the inevitable expense of bond interest meant less downward force exerted on dividends, wages, and public purchasing power.[51]

Favorable comment from financial circles on his suggestions and appreciation of Frank's ability by such diverse industrial leaders as Floyd B. Odlum and General Wood of Sears, Roebuck, easily offset the ridiculous charges of "Red" that his intellectual contentiousness and acidulous nonconformism sometimes aroused. Like his predecessor in the chairmanship, Frank's chief tie with the Brandeis philosophy was the same insistence on financial integrity and the same painful honesty in viewing any fiduciary relationship. Where *Save America First* was notable in displaying a comprehensive familiarity with the social sciences and the humanities, Frank's earlier work, *Law and the Modern Mind,* revealed a realist and a humanist in modern jurisprudence. In it he exposed the common fallacy that rules of law are predictable certainties. Economic and social considerations, to Frank, made any system of mechanical jurisprudence not only unwise but impossible in the modern world.

Jerome Frank's qualifications and abilities were happily focused on the successful continuation of the SEC beyond its years of consolidation. As one perceptive journalist stated, the finan-

---

[50] "The SEC Sees Integration Aiding the Utility Industry," *Electrical World*, pp. 3–5.
[51] *Time,* Oct. 3, 1938, p. 48.

cial world could expect that, despite some aura of controversy, Frank would "refrain from doing anything that might upset the SEC's big cart of liberal apples. They took too long a time to ripen." [52]

Frank's appointment was a continuation of the leadership that SEC chairmen were able to exercise, both in their individual ability to deal with the world of finance and in the reliance that President Roosevelt placed on them. During the formative years of the new agency its chairmen were relied upon heavily for their approval or disapproval of new appointments. Joseph Kennedy's influence in this respect, because of his unique contacts in the world of finance and the trust of the President, extended far beyond his own short tenure. The opinions of chairmen Landis and Douglas were consistently deferred to by Roosevelt, regardless of the political pressure that mounted when Commission vacancies occurred. Landis scrupulously insisted that it was his proper function only to comment on names submitted to him, and not to initiate any suggestions.[53] When discreet inquiries were set afoot regarding the possibility of Senator Burton K. Wheeler's son-in-law moving up from the SEC administrative ranks to a seat on the Commission, Roosevelt characteristically told Press Secretary McIntyre to "find out, very confidentially, what Landis thinks." [54]

Inquiries or suggestions addressed to the President were commonly turned over for the consideration of the chairman. When Democratic Senator Robert J. Bulkley of Ohio attempted to gain a presidential hearing regarding his candidate for the SEC, the information was merely forwarded in a confidential memorandum to Chairman Douglas. Secretary of Agriculture Wallace's suggestion that William Wasserman, an investment banker of Philadelphia, might be "a man worth talking to" concerning a Commission vacancy, was similarly passed on for Douglas' information and disposal.[55] In this case, the names of Jerome Frank

[52] "SEC," *Fortune*, p. 139.

[53] James M. Landis to Miss Marguerite A. Le Hand, May 23, 1937, Roosevelt Papers.

[54] F.D.R. memo to Press Secretary McIntyre, Jan. 29, 1937, Roosevelt Papers.

[55] F.D.R. memos to William O. Douglas, Oct. 25 and Nov. 26, 1937, Roosevelt Papers.

and John W. Hanes had already been recommended by Douglas and received Senate confirmation two weeks later. Once having decided on a Kennedy, Landis, or Douglas as the chief of a regulatory agency vitally affecting both the national economy and administration affairs, President Roosevelt placed great reliance on the chairman's judgment. His advice was solicited for administration policy toward matters of corporate finance, securities issuance, and stock exchange relations. His evaluations regarding the appointment of new colleagues on the Commission or his own successor were always sought and consistently applied.

Actually, by the time that Jerome Frank assumed Douglas' chairmanship, the position of the SEC as the "investor's advocate" and as overseer of the nation's stock exchanges was unquestioned and unshakable. In one month of 1938 this result had been made impressively evident by the SEC-directed reorganization of the New York Stock Exchange, and by the United States Supreme Court's upholding of the registration provision of the Holding Company Act, with its subsequent compliance of the once defiant utilities holding company giants. With these two great obstacles overcome, it remained for Jerome Frank and other commissioners chiefly to extend the functions and supervision of the SEC beyond the regulatory territory already consolidated.

To effect such an extension President Roosevelt had urged Congress to enact three bills sponsored by the SEC. Introduced respectively by Representative Walter Chandler of Tennessee, Representative Clarence Lea of California, and Senator Alben Barkley of Kentucky, this legislation called forth the presidential reminder that "abuse and exploitation" still marked "certain aspects of corporate reorganization practice and procedures." Congress owed to this area "legislative aid and protection comparable to that which the investor received . . . through the Securities Acts." [56]

The bill sponsored by Representative Chandler later emerged as the successful Chapter X of the Bankruptcy Act, which afforded machinery for corporate reorganization in Federal courts.

[56] *Commercial and Financial Chronicle*, May 29, 1937, p. 3597.

Under the terms of this act the SEC could function as a participant at the court's request or, with its approval, provide independent expert assistance to the courts and advisory reports on reorganization for the bondholders.[57]

The remaining legislation was enacted in later Congressional sessions as the Trust Indenture Act of 1939 and the Investment Company Act and Investment Advisers Act of 1940. The former provided for a high level of diligence and loyalty to be maintained by all indenture trustees. It required that indentures and similar securities publicly sold must be issued under terms satisfactory to the SEC, and insured independent trustees by setting up high standards of qualification. The two latter acts required the registration of all persons engaged in an investment advisory capacity, as well as all investment trusts and companies.[58] By bringing these firms and individuals within its regulatory scope, the SEC effectively eliminated another area subject to the abuse of fiduciary relationships. The agency's jurisdiction was thereby extended to cover the interests of the investor, whether affected through securities issuance or trading, through the reorganization of corporate assets, or through the deposit of his funds and the advice given him in investment trust companies.

By the end of 1940 the SEC could look back on half a dozen years of a gradual strengthening of its powers and prestige in financial circles, and the placating of many of its critics. Astute legal maneuvering and the carefully crafted phraseology of the Public Utility Holding Company Act had carried the SEC through the major crisis in the testing of its constitutionality. At the same time, other studies in an impressive series of bootstrap operations had served as the basis for additional legislative acts further extending SEC regulatory powers and functions. Aided by a fortunate succession of able and dedicated commissioners, the SEC had consolidated its position legally and administratively as the supervisor of the nation's financial standards and fiduciary ethics. The carefully formulated regulatory procedures and administrative structure that rose from the foun-

---

[57] U.S. *Statutes at Large*, LII, 883 ff.
[58] *Ibid.*, LIII, Part II, 1149 ff.; LIV, Part I, 789 ff.

dations of a pioneer agency were further evidence that the SEC had weathered its earliest storms and was performing its complex job with an ever-widening understanding and acceptance of its role.

CHAPTER EIGHT

CONCLUSIONS

IN RETROSPECT, the political and legislative basis for the establishment and expansion of the SEC had a continuity traceable to Progressive ideals and legislative attempts beginning in the twentieth century's first decade. Less clearly, they also drew upon an attitude among some southern and western Congressmen of hostility toward the financial world which was likely of Populist origin. As a legitimate offspring of Progressivism, Franklin Roosevelt led the forces that carried forward the ideas of public hydroelectric control and wide financial reform. As an executor for agrarian reformers, Roosevelt had the support both of partisan loyalties and of rural prejudice toward financial dominance. The stock market crash of 1929 and the first years of the depression drew about him further Congressional support that reflected the nation's tremendous discontent with the hegemony of business and finance.

Roosevelt's own political ancestry was most clearly visible in his regard for control by the state of its water resources and their hydroelectric potential. Opposing the grant to the Aluminum Company of America of St. Lawrence River power sites, Roosevelt's fight on the floor of the New York State Senate in 1913 carried on the Progressives' concern over the private ownership of public resources. The essentially Progressive distrust of concentrated economic power, and evidence of its abuse by utility holding companies, strengthened Roosevelt's determination to work for the utilities investor as well as the users of electric power.

While Roosevelt was governor of New York State, a committee appointed by him recommended drastic revisions in the state banking laws. Among the suggestions that received the governor's warm support was one to insure the fiduciary responsibility of a bank's directors and officers, later incorporated in the "Truth-in-Securities" Act of 1933. The prevalence of fraud in the sale of securities and the evils of excessive speculation were specifically denounced during Roosevelt's gubernatorial years. The presence in the 1932 Democratic party platform of demands for regulation of stock exchanges and further protection of the investing public was the basis for some of Roosevelt's strongest and most persuasive speeches.

Presidential support for the establishment and continued extension of regulatory powers to benefit every variety of public investor was never forgotten or neglected. Did Senators need a word of explanation on a bill under consideration? They received a "Dear George" letter earnestly stating the public need for such legislation. Were Congressional chairmen hard put to keep their committees from amending legislation to the point of emasculation? They—and the public press—received sternly polite notes that clearly threw the considerable weight of the Chief Executive on the side of their efforts.

Presidential appointments to the SEC received the most careful consideration. The influence of Joseph Kennedy, even after leaving the agency, was a notable one. In later years the recommendations of New Dealers Cohen and Corcoran were important, and the opinions of William O. Douglas were reliable sources for action. White House patronage favors played a part, as the unfortunate incident concerning Thomas Corcoran and the Quoddy project bore witness. A presidential message in 1937 urging Congress to pass SEC-sponsored bills meant some legislation passed in 1938 and some that carried on into 1939 and 1940. It was this vision of the SEC bearing the flag of New Deal reforms far in front of other administrative agencies that must have prompted Chairman Douglas' somewhat wistful remark in 1938. "It's God damn lonely in the front line trenches these days," Douglas said, as the SEC pressed doggedly ahead with its sponsorship of presidentially approved legislation.[1]

Congressionally, the Pujo Committee of 1911–13 had its worthy inheritor in the Pecora Investigation of 1932–34. Begun under Hoover as a subcommittee project of the Senate's Committee on Banking and Currency, its subsequent revelations caused it to be designated after its extremely effective special counsel, Ferdinand Pecora, who later became one of the first SEC commissioners. Here again, we are reminded, Pecora's and the committee's work was made possible "primarily by President Roosevelt's request that the inquiry proceed." [2]

The financial skulduggery so often translated to rural voters by Bryan and the Populists as "Wall Street's grip on the farmer" impelled many demands for punitive measures by Congressmen from agrarian districts. Western and southern Representatives were particularly insistent after the Pecora revelations that the transgressors be dealt with harshly. This tendency toward extremely severe treatment sometimes outran administration tactics. After the Securities Act of 1933 was passed, Senator Duncan U. Fletcher of Florida called for its increased stringency by elimination of the "good faith" provision even while the Brain Trust was counseling moderation in the bill's amendments. The holding company bill prepared by the Corcoran-Cohen-Landis group of New Dealers, while shocking enough to the utilities industry, was yet considered by most to be the mildest of several such bills to reach Congressional hoppers.

Additionally, the SEC acts were part of the growing undercurrent of resentment toward entrenched and privileged wealth that found recognition among Representatives and Senators. Smarting from their own economy moves, which resulted in salary cuts from $10,000 to $8,500, members of both houses tartly inquired of business leaders why their cries of "economy" had

[1] Rodell, p. 124.
[2] *Nation*, June 7, 1933, p. 633.

not resulted in any similar corporate action. A Midwestern Progressive, Senator Edward P. Costigan of Colorado, introduced a resolution, unanimously adopted, that Federal agencies such as the FTC, the RFC, and the Federal Reserve Board make public the corporate salaries of bank officials and of directors of companies that issued listed securities or borrowed Federal funds.[3] Such publicizing of pertinent corporate salaries was embodied in subsequent securities acts and amendments. The considerable body of regulatory legislation that derived from the authority written into early securities acts, and that resulted in continuous bootstrap extensions of the SEC's own boundaries, had to have a strong and continued Congressional mandate.

An important aspect of the Congressional scene was the legal and technical competence of a coterie of young New Dealers who worked in close cooperation with committee chairmen responsible for reporting out the legislation. An outstanding example of New Deal–Congress rapport, the legislative draftsmanship of Benjamin Cohen and James Landis was an integral part of the success of SEC bills. It was freely admitted, and with considerable awe from those accustomed to easy legal manipulation, that the securities acts were "the most effectively drawn pieces of legislation ever enacted." [4] With a legal attack from the utilities anticipated, the holding company act was drawn, largely by Benjamin Cohen, so that separate provisions of the bill might be tested rather than have the constitutionality of the act decided in its entirety. When the provision for registration was upheld by the Supreme Court, the utility holding companies finally abandoned the legal field of battle. In no instance was the constitutionality of legislation administered by the SEC ever challenged. Evidence that the SEC had built as well politically as legally was shown by the paucity of partisan election efforts. Neither the 1936 nor 1940 Republican party platforms attacked the ideals or principles of the securities acts or the SEC. In the latter year the partisan opposition limited itself to en-

[3] *Congressional Record,* 73 Cong., 1 Sess., LXXVII, Part III, 2966.
[4] *Barron's,* April 8, 1935, p. 20.

dorsing revision of the acts so as "to encourage the flow of private capital into industry." [5] In none of the political contests of the 1930's did an opposition candidate make any serious attack on the New Deal financial reforms that were a part of SEC operations.

Although the New York Stock Exchange presented the most dramatic resistance to New Deal efforts to protect the investor, this actually followed the successful passage of the basic SEC acts, and was centered in the somewhat incredible personality of its leader, Richard Whitney. The Exchange's fight against the passage of the two securities acts, in which it assumed the role of general staff for the financial and industrial world, was extravagantly pursued and lavishly financed, but was largely ineffective. Its awesome warnings of the nation's crumbling financial structure were demonstrably false, as more widespread understanding of the bills and their early administration made apparent. Crude tactics of employee coercion merely added to a sizable store of public and Congressional distrust already built up by the amazing Pecora disclosures. Stock Exchange anachronisms became ever more painfully evident, revealing themselves in Whitney's refusal to fill out the Senate investigation's simplest questionnaires, forms that Wall Street banks went out of their way to complete satisfactorily. In sharp contrast, the Exchange officials' description of their members' private-club status exposed a stubborn and alarming indifference to public responsibility. It consistently exhibited more arrogance than competence, and its ability to influence legislation was never commensurate with its undoubted resources. In the final scene, Richard Whitney's shocking fall from grace toppled the idol of the Stock Exchange reactionary forces. But this event, while it undoubtedly accelerated the process, could not have changed the final result. The attack on the Exchange's intolerable anachronism from within and the attack on its public irresponsibility from without would have made its eventual reorganization and democratization an inexorable conclusion.

The Stock Exchange played a subordinate role to the fantastic

[5] Porter and Johnson, pp. 368, 392.

propagandizing and lobbying prowess of the utilities industry during the fight over the holding company act. The public utility companies, faced with a successful concentration on a national scale of their political enemies, found that further expensive propaganda and questionable pressure tactics worked to their final disadvantage. Even the well-financed pressure of their many articulate stockholders was insufficient to offset administration pressures, old political animosities, and the exposure of their crude lobbying operations.

It served administration policy to emphasize the recovery aspects rather than the reform inherent in these early acts. It was axiomatic with Roosevelt that the same forces that had created the depression could scarcely be entrusted with the task of recovery, since they would surely ignore the needs of reform.[6] This served as a constant vehicle of reminder. Roosevelt and administration forces, in addition, never lost an opportunity to substitute "recovery" for "reform" as being more palatable to the business community. In the area of financial reforms, however, the two goals were drawn together in the idea that without an ethical foundation no economic well-being could be achieved.

The strongest expression of this approach was found, for the New Dealers, in the philosophy of Justice Louis Brandeis. More particularly, it revealed itself in the principles that Brandeis insisted must be applied in the regulation of the more predatory activities of finance, and in the financial world's fiduciary relationship with the investor. Roosevelt himself, like most of the New Dealers connected with or associated with the SEC, was strongly influenced by the Brandeisian fears of concentrated economic power.

Many New Dealers were deeply concerned, as was Brandeis, with the many abuses the financial world had to answer for in its handling of "other people's money." They did not, however, always join Brandeis in applying to national finance the solution of splitting up big business in order to encourage and protect the small businessman. The nearest approach to any such

---

[6] F.D.R., *Public Papers and Addresses*, I, xiii.

solution was the Public Utility Holding Company Act. Yet the Holding Company Act was no implementation of the Brandeisian "curse of bigness." Instead, it was the pragmatic New Deal insistence that bigness have some economic justification for its existence. The utility combinations that emerged from the act's "death sentence" clause were reborn in more compact, more integrated form. They were frequently stronger financially and certainly sounder, since they had been divested of the fraudulent superstructure that once diffused their managerial efforts and skimmed off their revenue. As Douglas related to President Roosevelt on the occasion of Electric Bond and Share's 1938 meeting of stockholders, the death sentence was evidently bullish, since utilities stocks had been rising steadily. And, Douglas noted, stockholders applauded the announcement of Electric's Chairman of the Board C. E. Groesbeck that the corporation would meet all integration and simplification provisions of the Holding Company Act.[7] Deliberate complexities were thus finally reduced to a degree manageable by regulation, and the investor as well as the consumer was relieved of the worst holding company abuses in line with Brandeisian principles of financial honesty.

The Wall Street community in 1937 saw in SEC commissioners Douglas, Frank, Healy, Mathews and Hanes not a mixture of political liberals and conservatives but only "five liberals." [8] This was a financial myopia that mistook the application of strict principles of financial integrity for a blithe willingness to scrap the old for the new. Douglas, succeeding to the chairmanship in 1937, alluded to these principles simply by saying that he was a conservative of a school perhaps too old-fashioned to be remembered.[9] In this statement lay the clue to Wall Street's confused vision. Douglas' financial conservatism was genuine, certainly, and was shared in consistent degree by his associates. It comprised those tenets and concepts traditionally and continually voiced by the world of finance but that its professional

---

[7] Memo from William O. Douglas to F.D.R., Oct. 13, 1938, Roosevelt Papers.
[8] *Business Week*, Dec. 18, 1937, p. 18.
[9] *Commercial and Financial Chronicle*, Sept. 25, 1937, p. 2005.

practitioners had long since abandoned. When the actions and deeds of financial royalism were measured with scrupulous exactitude and set against the standards insistently enunciated by financial leaders, there was visible a vast gulf in the world of finance between the concepts of integrity uttered and the concepts practiced. This discrepancy easily accounted for the view of a commission that appeared as downright radical in some of its persistent demands for the simpler honesties.

No lesser contributors to this fundamental outlook were those who followed the earliest commissioners. Whether they were partisan New Dealers, Western Progressives, New England Republicans, or representative of the more liberal elements in the New York Stock Exchange, they shared this realization that the confidence of the investor was essential to the preservation of a democratic capitalist system. It was through such continuity of effort that SEC became the outstanding demonstration that the New Deal attempted to revitalize American capitalism rather than bring about its destruction.

It was a continuity that could not, unfortunately, carry on under later administrations. In the postwar years a less sympathetic political climate prevented any exercise of SEC initiative in redressing the subsequent abuses of corporate finance that were a foreseeable outcome of decades of economic and institutional change. The later problems of mutual funds and their management, of fraudulent securities coming over international borders, and of unresolved problems in over-the-counter trading rules were forced to await the progressive climate of the 1960's and the New Frontier appointments of President John F. Kennedy, son of the SEC's first chairman.

Additional noteworthy attitudes shared by the commissioners of these first half-dozen years were the undogmatic reasonableness they demonstrated in their approach to SEC problems, and the complete dedication and high sense of purpose that aided them in their efforts. The lack of ideology and idealism noted elsewhere in the New Deal cannot be attributed to the Securities and Exchange Commission. Problems such as the precise role of the specialist in the securities exchanges and the decisions to be

made in the field of unlisted stock trading created some diver-
gences of opinion among the commissioners. However, James M.
Landis recalled, "even where there were differences of opinion,
those differences were respected. There certainly were no differences of opinion based upon petty or political beliefs." [10]

A competent and youthfully enthusiastic staff insured the
early SEC against the attitude of perfunctory bureaucracy that
was to follow when national zeal for public service had largely
disappeared. The young agency did not have the intolerance
commonly associated with such youthful bodies, nor was its aggressiveness of the evangelical type. Its youthfulness lay in its
energy, its vigor of purpose. Its aggressiveness sprang from moral
conviction, and from the challenge of solving administratively
the essential problem: to enforce, yet endure. No wildly and
militantly evangelistic approach could have accomplished this
successfully. Frequently alluded to as the agency most thoroughly
New Deal in spirit as in numbers, it yet drew the reluctant admiration of those opposed to New Deal ideology. In enumerat-
ing their qualities of honesty and technical competence a critic
stated that "where they have been at their very best, as in the
work of the SEC . . . the New Dealers have always been nearest to doing a civil servant's job." [11] From his own long association with the SEC, former Chairman William O. Douglas recalled: "We had a very, very high calibre personnel and most of
them had a sense of mission; a keen sense of the high requirements of public service; and a disdain for such corruptive influences as we have seen in recent years." [12]

The sense of mission referred to can be further defined as one
of stubborn and persistent intent to reform national financial
malpractices. It was intended firmly to impress a new mold of
financial habits on banker and broker, on securities exchange
and corporation. Such habits, adopted under the pressure of administrative law and through sheer economic usefulness to the
many, would then direct themselves to dealing with the investor

[10] James M. Landis to the author, Feb. 23, 1960.
[11] Alsop and Kintner, *Men Around the President*, p. 195.
[12] Associate Supreme Court Justice William O. Douglas to the author, March
11, 1960.

in terms of integrity, openness, and simplest honesty. The SEC outlined this pattern for righteous financial living, and dealt firmly with transgressors. Its leaders, in turn, unceasingly pointed out the benefits accruing to financial institutions from their own scrupulous self-observance of such patterns. Viewing the battleground twenty-five years later, one can see that the agency's belated and timid efforts to bring about still needed reforms in over-the-counter dealings reflect all too clearly the deterioration in Commission membership and staff, which occurs when the fervor for service in behalf of the public has departed the national scene.

Because of its early leadership the SEC must receive recognition as one of the most firmly consolidated and influential of New Deal reform agencies. Far-reaching and fundamental reforms were undertaken. Yet rarely were advances made beyond that point warranted by experience, and a willingness to confer with representatives of finance regarding the application of regulation was continually shown. The SEC tactic of suggested self-regulation rather than demands for more legislation drew from the *Wall Street Journal* the wish that "half a dozen other federal agencies could be persuaded to take a leaf from the SEC book." [13] Such demonstrations of pragmatic reasonableness and of an intent wholly lacking in animus formed a solid and workable basis of understanding with the powers of investment and finance. An agreement on the encouragement of cooperation and the subordination of police functions wherever possible formed for the Commission the essential basis of successful regulation. This agreement, in turn, prepared a bond of continuity in the knowledge of a purpose shared. No other New Deal agency saw such a concentration of intellect and administrative ability at the helm, and in such fortunate succession, as did the SEC with James Landis, William Douglas, and Jerome Frank. This is not to overlook the important contribution of its first chairman and ambassador extraordinary to Wall Street, Joseph P. Kennedy. Although a large part of his contribution was simply the symbolic significance of a former Wall Streeter leading an agency

[13] *Wall Street Journal*, March 22, 1935.

devoted to curbing finance's excesses and irresponsibilities, Kennedy was able to cajole the stock exchanges into acceptance of the two securities acts without major complaint or legal hindrance.

With the first chairman performing such necessary spadework, Landis can then be seen as the careful, patient planner, and Douglas as the architect of further structures on a firm foundation. In this succession of chairmen was displayed an increasing emphasis on the New Deal point of view, and the insistent demand for continued financial and investment reform. No more satisfactory conclusion could be offered to the Brandeis principle that if the administration of a law was to measure up to the high hopes of the reformers, "those who administered it must be equal in ingenuity and courage to those whose conduct was brought under public supervision." [14] Unfortunately in the years following, this principle could not be so satisfactorily upheld. The flush of enthusiasm for public service that brought such a wealth of administrative ability and intellectual talent to the New Deal, and particularly to the SEC, was largely to disappear in the postwar years. The considerable accomplishments of the SEC, and the chronological extension of those accomplishments beyond those of any other agency, were at a pace impossible to sustain.

As a political achievement the SEC owed no debt to expediency. Its genealogy was abundantly evident. It incorporated the Progressives' concern with moral values into the practical reform framework of the New Deal to produce an agency embodying most successfully the lasting values of both eras. In principle and in method, it had carried to a successful conclusion the efforts of those who, concerned with the dominant role of financial and corporate power, had seen their attempts of the previous three decades dismissed by an economy and a Congress dedicated to just such hegemony. A great market crash and its consequent revelations enlisted in the support of a new administration a broad public sentiment against the existence of sepa-

[14] Douglas, *Being An American,* p. 66.

rate and privileged standards of morality for the corporate and financial world.

James M. Landis, in his letter of resignation to the President, called attention to the close bond existing between Roosevelt and the SEC, adding, "and that is as it should be, for our commission and our work sprang from your mind, your utterances, your ideals." [15] In Franklin Roosevelt these economic, political, and social factors working for the reform of the investment institutions of the age found the personal force and ideals uniquely capable of guidance and consummation. Under such guidance the SEC thereby became the most important element in restoring confidence for the continued use of the tools of investment finance as a needed part of the capitalist system. Its reforms were carried on at greater length than those of other New Deal agencies, because, in a society requiring capitalist finance, an economic democracy had to extend its obligations beyond insuring honest workings of the system. The mores of American capitalism had to be drastically altered and revalued from a standpoint of mass participation and the public welfare. This new code of financial morals was legislated into practice by the SEC. It was this democratization of the institutions of finance that made possible the mass stock participation of the post-World War II era. As the administrative agency incorporating some of the most fundamental and enduring reforms of the New Deal, the SEC was the democratic solution to the problem of protecting the investing public. Even more, it was the New Deal answer to the social control of finance.

[15] *Commercial and Financial Chronicle*, Sept. 18, 1937, p. 1830.

BIBLIOGRAPHY

SECURITIES AND EXCHANGE
COMMISSION

DOCUMENTS AND PUBLICATIONS, PUBLISHED BY GOVERNMENT
PRINTING OFFICE, WASHINGTON, D.C.

Annual Report, 1935–39.
In the Matter of Richard Whitney et al. 3 vols. 1938.
Report to the Congress on the Study of Investment Trusts and Investment Companies. 1938.
Report on the Feasibility and Advisability of Complete Segregation of the Functions of Broker and Dealer. 1936.
Report on the Study and Investigation of the Work, Activities, Personnel and Functions of Protective Organization Committees. 8 vols. 1938.
Report on Trading in Unlisted Securities upon Exchanges. 1936.
Securities and Exchange Commission Decisions. Vol. I. 1938.
Securities and Exchange Commission Decisions and Reports. Vol. II. 1939.

UNPUBLISHED MATERIAL, LOCATED IN THE SECURITIES AND
EXCHANGE COMMISSION LIBRARY, WASHINGTON, D.C.

Mimeograph releases (Securities Act of 1933).
Mimeograph releases (Securities Exchange Act of 1934).
Mimeograph releases (Public Utility Holding Company Act of 1935).

"Memo Concerning Power of Congress, under the Commerce Clause, to Regulate Securities Exchanges," Noel T. Dowling. (Mimeograph, n.d.).

Untitled compilation of mimeographs and photostats of largely unsigned memoranda relating to the Securities Exchange Act of 1934 (n.d.).

Untitled compilation of photostats and memoranda relating to the legislative history of the Public Utility Holding Company Act of 1935 (n.d.).

OTHER PUBLIC DOCUMENTS, PUBLISHED BY GOVERNMENT PRINTING OFFICE, WASHINGTON, D.C.

GENERAL

U.S. Commission on Organization of the Executive Branch of the Government. *Independent Regulatory Commissions.* 1949.

U.S. Congress. *Biographical Directory of the American Congress.* House Document No. 607. 81st Congress, 2d Session, 1950.

U.S. *Congressional Record,* Vols. LXXV–LXXXIII. 72d, 73d, 74th, and 75th Congresses, all sessions, Dec., 1931, to June, 1938.

U.S. Department of Commerce. *A Study of the Economic and Legal Aspects of the Proposed Federal Securities Act.* 73d Congress, 1st Session, 1933.

U.S. Federal Trade Commission. *Annual Report 1934.* 1934.

—— *Utility Corporations.* Senate Document No. 92. 70th Congress, 1st Session, 1935.

U.S. *Statutes at Large.* Vols. XLVII–LIV.

U.S. Supreme Court Reports.

UNITED STATES HOUSE OF REPRESENTATIVES

Federal Securities Act. Hearings on H.R. 4314. 73d Congress, 1st Session, 1934. Committee on Interstate and Foreign Commerce.

Federal Supervision of the Traffic in Investment Securities in Interstate Commerce. House Report No. 85. 73d Congress, 1st Session, 1933. Committee on Interstate and Foreign Commerce.

Investigation of Lobbying on the Utility Holding Company Bills. Hearings on House Resolution 288. 74th Congress, 1st Session, 1935. Committee on Rules.

Proposed Federal "Blue-Sky" Law. 66th Congress, 1st Session, 1919. Committee on the Judiciary.

Public Utility Act of 1935. Report No. 1318. 74th Congress, 1st Session, 1935. Committee on Interstate and Foreign Commerce.

Public Utility and Holding Companies. 74th Congress, 1st Session, 1935. Committee on Interstate and Foreign Commerce.

Report of the Committee Appointed Pursuant to House Resolutions 429 and 504 to Investigate the Concentration of the Control of Money and Credit. 62d Congress, 3d Session, 1913. Committee on Banking and Currency.

Report on the Government of Securities Exchanges. Document No. 85. 74th Congress, 1st Session, 1935.

Securities Exchange Act of 1934. Report No. 1838 to accompany H.R. 9323. 73d Congress, 2d Session, 1934.

Securities Exchange Bill of 1934. Report No. 1383. 73d Congress, 1st Session, 1934.

Stock Exchange Regulation. Hearings on H.R. 7852 and H.R. 8720. 73d Congress, 2d Session, 1934. Committee on Interstate and Foreign Commerce.

UNITED STATES SENATE

Administrative Procedure. 77th Congress, 1st Session, 1941. Committee on the Judiciary.

Investigation of Lobbying Activities. Hearings pursuant to Senate Resolution 165. 74th Congress, 1st Session, 1935. Special Commission.

Public Utility Act of 1935. Report No. 621. 74th Congress, 1st Session, 1935. Committee on Interstate Commerce.

Regulation of the Sale of Securities. 67th Congress, 4th Session, 1923. Committee on Interstate Commerce.

Regulation of Securities. 73d Congress, 1st Session, 1933. Committee on Banking and Currency.

Reserve Act of 1938. Hearings on H.R. 9682. 75th Congress, 3d Session, 1938. Committee on Finance.

Securities Act. Hearings on S. 875. 73d Congress, 1st Session, 1933. Committee on Banking and Currency.

Stock Exchange Practices. Report No. 1455. 73d Congress, 2d Session, 1934. Committee on Banking and Currency.

Stock Exchange Regulation. 73d Congress, 1st Session, 1934. Committee on Banking and Currency.

LETTERS, MANUSCRIPTS, MEMOIRS, STATE PAPERS, AND OTHER DOCUMENTARY SOURCES

Commager, Henry Steele, ed. *Documents of American History*. New York, Appleton-Century-Crofts, Inc., 1958.

Hoover, Herbert. *The Memoirs of Herbert Hoover*. 3 vols. New York, The Macmillan Company, 1952.

Myers, William Starr, ed. *The State Papers and Other Public Writings of Herbert Hoover*. 2 vols. Garden City, N.Y., Doubleday, Doran and Company, Inc., 1934.

The New York Stock Exchange. *The New York Stock Exchange Yearbook, 1930–1931*. New York, New York Stock Exchange, 1931.

—— *Report of the President*. New York, New York Stock Exchange, 1932, 1935, 1937.

Porter, Kirk H., and Donald Bruce Johnson. *National Party Platforms, 1840–1956*. Urbana, Ill., University of Illinois Press, 1956.

Roosevelt, Elliott, ed. *F.D.R.: His Personal Letters*. 3 vols. New York, Duell, Sloan and Pearce, 1950.

Roosevelt, Franklin D. *The Public Papers and Addresses of Franklin D. Roosevelt, 1928–1936*. 5 vols. New York, Random House, 1938.

—— Papers (MS). Franklin Roosevelt Library, Hyde Park, New York.

—— Press Conferences (MS). Franklin Roosevelt Library, Hyde Park, New York.

ARTICLES, ADDRESSES, AND BOOKS BY SEC COMMISSIONERS

Douglas, William O. *Being an American*. New York, The John Day Company, 1940.

—— *Democracy and Finance*. New Haven, Yale University Press, 1940.

—— "Progress for Business-Government Cooperation under the Holding Company Act," *Annalist*, June 3, 1938.

—— "Trading in Unlisted Securities on Exchanges," *Investment Banking*, March 27, 1936.

Eicher, Edward C. "Administrative Processes and Procedure," *Proceedings, Twenty-Second Annual Convention*, National Association of Securities Commissioners (Skytop, Pa.), September 12–14, 1939.

—— "Consumers and the Public Utility Holding Company Act," *University of Iowa Journal of Business*, Vol. XXI, No. 4 (March, 1941).

Frank, Jerome. *Law and the Modern Mind*. New York, Coward-McCann, 1930.

—— *Save America First*. New York, Harper and Brothers, 1938.

Hanes, John W. "The Lifeblood of Our Industrial Machine," *Vital Speeches*, May 1, 1938.

Healy, Robert E. "SEC Interpretation of the Maloney Bill," *Investment Banking*, March 23, 1938.

—— "Today's Picture of What the SEC Is Doing and Planning," *Controller*, October 5, 1935.

Kennedy, Joseph Patrick. *Address to the American Arbitration Association*. SEC, Washington, D.C., 1935.

—— *Address to the Boston Chamber of Commerce*. SEC, Washington, D.C., 1934.

—— *Address to the National Press Club*. SEC, Washington, D.C., 1934.

—— *Address to the Union League Club of Chicago*. SEC, Washington, D.C., 1935.

—— "Big Business, What Now?" *Saturday Evening Post*, January 16, 1937.

—— *I'm for Roosevelt*. New York, Reynal and Hitchcock, 1936.

—— "Shielding the Sheep," *Saturday Evening Post*, January 18, 1936.

Landis, James M. *The Administrative Process*. New Haven, Yale University Press, 1938.

—— "Business Policy and the Courts," *Yale Review*, Vol. XXVII, No. 2 (December, 1937).

—— "The Direction of Recovery," *Vital Speeches*, Vol. III, No. 5 (December, 1936).

—— "The Firing Line in the Law," *Vital Speeches*, Vol. III, No. 13 (April, 1937).

—— "The Legislative History of the Securities Act of 1933," *The*

George Washington Law Review, Vol. XXVIII (October, 1959).
—— "The Mechanisms of Administration," *Vital Speeches,* Vol. III, No. 20 (August, 1937).
—— "The Regulation of Investment Banking by the Federal Government," *Investment Banking,* Vol. VII, No. 1 (December, 1936).
Mathews, George C. "Some Things Done and To Be Done," *Commercial and Financial Chronicle,* November 13, 1937.
Pecora, Ferdinand. "Are the Criminal Courts Doing Their Duty?" *Vital Speeches,* December 31, 1934.
—— "Wall Street Under the Flag," *Collier's,* March 30, 1935.
—— *Wall Street Under Oath.* New York, Simon and Schuster, 1939.
Ross, James D. "The Rationalization of the Distribution of Electric Energy," *Third World Power Conference Transactions,* Vol. VIII. Washington, D.C., Government Printing Office, 1938.

CONTEMPORARY ARTICLES,
BOOKS, AND SPECIAL STUDIES

Allen, Frederick Louis. *The Lords of Creation.* New York, Harper and Brothers, 1935.
—— *Only Yesterday.* New York, Harper and Brothers, 1931.
Alsop, Joseph, and Robert Kintner. "The Battle of the Market-Place," *Saturday Evening Post,* June 11, 1938.
—— *Men Around the President.* Doubleday, Doran and Company, 1939.
Barnett, G. E. "The Securities Act of 1933 and the British Companies Act," *Harvard Business Review,* Vol. XIII, No. 3 (October, 1934).
Beard, Charles A. "The New Deal's Rough Road," *Current History,* Vol. XLII, No. 6 (August, 1935).
Bell, Elliott V. "Wall Street's Life with SEC," *Banking,* Vol. XXXI, No. 7 (January, 1939).
Bellush, Bernard. *Franklin D. Roosevelt as Governor of New York.* New York, Columbia University Press, 1955.
Berle, Adolf A., Jr. "High Finance: Master or Servant?" *The Yale Review,* Vol. XXIII, No. 1 (September, 1933).
—— and Gardiner C. Means. *The Modern Corporation and Private Property.* New York, The Macmillan Company, 1937.

Brandeis, Louis D. *Other People's Money*. New York, Frederick A. Stokes Company, 1913.

Brayman, Harold. "FPC, FCC, and SEC," *Public Utilities*, Vol. XVIII, No. 3 (July, 1936).

Brown, Raymond F. "What the New Securities Act Means," *Magazine of Wall Street*, April 29, 1933.

Burns, J. J. "Some SEC Problems," *Investment Banking*, November 12, 1935.

Carmichael, Donald Scott, ed. *F.D.R. Columnist*. Chicago, Pellegrini and Cudahy, 1947.

"The Case for Investment Banking," *Nation's Business*, Vol. XXVIII, No. 2 (February, 1940).

Clapper, Raymond. "Is Roosevelt Changing?" *Review of Reviews*, Vol. XCII, No. 2 (August, 1935).

Clifford, J. C. "Is Federal Control of the Stock Exchange Needed?" *Magazine of Wall Street*, October 28, 1933.

Collins, E. H. "The Investor's New Deal," *Banking*, Vol. XXVII (February, 1935).

Condit, John G. "A Case History of SEC Injustice," *Northwest Mining*, November 25, 1936.

Corey, Herbert. "Kennedy, Who Guards the Investor," *Nation's Business*, Vol. XXIII, No. 3 (March, 1935).

Creel, George. "The Man from Montana," *Collier's*, August 10, 1935.

Current Biography, 1940, ed. Maxine Block. New York, H. W. Wilson Company, 1941.

Cushman, Robert E. *The Independent Regulatory Commissions*. New York, Oxford University Press, 1941.

Dean, Arthur H. "The Securities Act of 1933," *Fortune*, Vol. VIII, No. 2 (August, 1933).

Dorfman, Joseph. *The Economic Mind in American Civilization, 1918–1933*. (Vols. IV and V of *The Economic Mind in American Civilization*.) New York, The Viking Press, 1959.

Dozier, H. D. "The Securities Exchange Act of 1934," *South Atlantic Quarterly*, Vol. XXXIII, No. 4 (October, 1934).

The Editors of the *Economist* (London). *The New Deal*. New York, Alfred A. Knopf, 1937.

Estabrook, Robert H. "Last of the Brain Trusters," *Nation*, January 17, 1948.

Fletcher, Duncan U. "Our Financial Racketeers," *Liberty,* March 17, 1934.

Flexner, Bernard. "The Fight on the Securities Act," *Atlantic Monthly,* Vol. CLIII, No. 2 (February, 1934).

Flynn, John T. "The Marines Land in Wall Street," *Harper's,* Vol. CLXIX, No. 7 (July, 1934).

—— *The Roosevelt Myth.* Garden City, N.Y., Garden City Publishing Company, Inc., 1948.

—— *Security Speculation.* New York, Harcourt, Brace and Company, 1934.

—— "Washing Wall Street's Face," *Collier's,* January 29, 1938.

Frankfurter, Felix. "The Federal Securities Act," *Fortune,* Vol. VIII, No. 2 (August, 1933).

—— "Social Issues Before the Supreme Court," *The Yale Review,* Vol. XXII, No. 3 (March, 1933).

Freidel, Frank. *Franklin D. Roosevelt: The Triumph.* Boston, Little, Brown and Company, 1956.

Fusfeld, Daniel R. *The Economic Thought of Franklin D. Roosevelt and the Origins of the New Deal.* New York, Columbia University Press, 1956.

Galbraith, John Kenneth. *The Great Crash.* Boston, Houghton Mifflin Company, 1955.

Gesell, Gerhard Alden. *Protecting Your Dollars.* Washington, D.C., National Home Library Foundation, 1940.

Gordon, F. M. "Benefits of Securities Regulation," *Investment Banking,* October 7, 1933.

Gunther, John. *Roosevelt in Retrospect.* New York, Harper and Brothers, 1950.

Herring, E. Pendleton. *Federal Commissioners: A Study of Their Careers and Qualifications.* Cambridge, Harvard University Press, 1936.

Ickes, Harold L. *The Secret Diary of Harold L. Ickes: The First Thousand Days.* New York, Simon and Schuster, 1953.

"It Can't Be Done, Can't It?" *Collier's,* March 7, 1936.

"J.D.," *Scholastic,* March 21, 1936.

Jones, J. Edward. *And So—They Indicted Me!* New York, J. E. Jones Publishing Corp., 1938.

Knappen, Theodore. "The Rulers of the Stock Market," *Magazine of Wall Street,* July 21, 1934.

—— "The SEC Surprises Both Friend and Foe," *Magazine of Wall Street,* September 14, 1935.

Knauss, James I. "The Farmers Alliance in Florida," *South Atlantic Quarterly,* Vol. XXV (July, 1926).

Konefsky, Samuel J., ed. *The Constitutional World of Mr. Justice Frankfurter.* New York, The Macmillan Company, 1949.

Lefevre, E. "The Newest Era in Wall Street," *Saturday Evening Post,* September 28, 1935.

"The Legend of Landis," *Fortune,* Vol. X, No. 2 (August, 1934).

Lerner, Max. *Ideas Are Weapons.* New York, The Viking Press, 1940.

Lindley, Ernest K. *Half Way with Roosevelt.* New York, The Viking Press, 1936.

—— *The Roosevelt Revolution.* New York, The Viking Press, 1933.

Livingston, J. A. "What Is SEC Going To Do To the Utilities?" *Public Utilities Fortnightly,* January 30, 1936.

Loss, Louis. *Securities Regulation.* Boston, Little, Brown and Company, 1951.

—— and Edward M. Cowett. *Blue Sky Law.* Boston, Little, Brown and Company, 1958.

McCormick, Edward T. *Understanding the Securities Act and the SEC.* New York, American Book Company, 1948.

McCormick, Robert. "Where the Thinking Starts," *Collier's,* January 7, 1939.

McDonald, Forrest. "Samuel Insull and the Movement for State Utilities Regulatory Commissions," *Business History Review,* Vol. XXXII, No. 3 (Autumn, 1958).

Mallon, Paul. "The Ace of Clubs," *Today,* May 26, 1934.

Melville, Lewis. *The South Sea Bubble.* Boston, Small, Maynard and Company, 1923.

Merz, Charles. "Bull Market," *Harper's,* Vol. CLVIII, No. 4 (April, 1929).

Meyer, Charles H. *The Securities Exchange Act of 1934.* New York, Francis Emory Fitch, Inc., 1934.

Moley, Raymond. *After Seven Years.* New York, Harper and Brothers, 1939.

—— "Five Years of Roosevelt and After," *Saturday Evening Post,* August 19, 1939.

Moley, Raymond. *Twenty-Seven Masters of Politics.* New York, Funk and Wagnalls Company, 1949.

"Mr. Kennedy, the Chairman," *Fortune,* Vol. XVI, No. 3 (September, 1937).

Myers, William Starr, and Walter H. Newton. *The Hoover Administration: A Documented Narrative.* New York, Charles Scribner's Sons, 1936.

National Cyclopedia of American Biography, Vol. XXXV. New York, James T. White and Company, 1950.

Newman, Harry. "Redhead from Carolina," *Saturday Evening Post,* January 13, 1940.

Noyes, P. H. "Wall Street at the Wailing Wall," *Nation,* October 25, 1933.

Perkins, Frances. *The Roosevelt I Knew.* New York, The Viking Press, 1946.

Proctor, Samuel. "The National Farmers' Alliance Convention of 1890 and Its 'Ocala Demands,'" *Florida Historical Quarterly,* Vol. XXVIII, No. 3 (March, 1950).

Ramsay, M. L. *Pyramids of Power.* New York, The Bobbs-Merrill Company, 1937.

Rankin, John E. "Utilities and the Public: TVA Rates as a Yardstick," *Current History,* Vol. XLII, No. 2 (May, 1935).

Rauch, Basil. *The History of the New Deal, 1933–1938.* New York, Creative Age Press, Inc., 1944.

Raymond, William T. "Big Year for the SEC," *Barron's,* January 6, 1936.

Ripley, William Z. *Main Street and Wall Street.* Boston, Little Brown and Company, 1927.

Robbins, Lionel. *The Great Depression.* New York, The Macmillan Company, 1936.

Rodell, Fred. "Douglas Over the Stock Exchange," *Fortune,* Vol. XVII, No. 2 (February, 1938).

Roosevelt, Franklin D. "How Will New York's Progressive Proposals Affect the Investor?" *Public Utilities Fortnightly,* Vol. VII, No. 13 (June, 1931).

—— *On Our Way.* New York, The John Day Company, 1934.

—— "The Real Meaning of the Power Problem," *Forum,* Vol. LXXXII, No. 6 (December, 1929).

Rosenman, Samuel I. *Working with Roosevelt.* New York, Harper and Brothers, 1952.

Schumpeter, Joseph A. *Business Cycles.* 2 vols. New York, McGraw-Hill Book Company, 1939.

Scott, William R. *The Constitution and Finance of English, Scottish and Irish Joint-Stock Companies to 1720.* Vol. I. New York, The Macmillan Company, 1912.

"SEC," *Fortune,* XXI, No. 6 (June, 1940).

"The SEC Sees Integration Aiding the Utility Industry," *Electrical World,* April 13, 1940.

Smith, F. P. "The Future of Small Securities Exchanges," *Harvard Business Review,* Vol. XIV, No. 3 (April, 1936).

Stein, Emanuel. *Government and the Investor.* New York, Farrar and Rinehart, Inc., 1941.

Sullivan, Laurence. *The Dead Hand of Bureaucracy.* New York, The Bobbs-Merrill Company, 1940.

Tomes, L. P. "Where Stock Market Regulation Has Failed," *Magazine of Wall Street,* November 6, 1937.

Tucker, Ray. "A Master for the House," *Collier's,* January 5, 1935.

Tully, Grace. *F.D.R. My Boss.* New York, Charles Scribner's Sons, 1949.

Unofficial Observer [Jay Franklin Carter]. *The New Dealers.* New York, Simon and Schuster, 1934.

Van Arkel, Gerhard P. "James McCauley Landis '21," *Princeton Alumni Weekly,* December 6, 1935.

Weissman, Rudolph L. *The New Wall Street.* New York, Harper and Brothers, 1939.

Wheeler, Burton K. "First Senator to Back the President," *Vital Speeches,* April 15, 1937.

Who's Who in America, 1958–1959. Chicago, The A. N. Marquis Company, 1959.

Who Was Who in America, 1943–1950. Chicago, The A. N. Marquis Company, 1950.

Willkie, Wendell L. "Utilities and the Public: Campaign Against the Companies," *Current History,* Vol. XLII, No. 2 (May, 1935).

—— "Why the Wheeler-Rayburn Bill Must Be Stopped," *Forbes,* May 1, 1935.

INDEX